THE ART AND ARCHITECTURE OF THE TEXAS MISSIONS

NUMBER SIX

Jack and Doris Smothers Series in Texas History, Life, and Culture

Jacinto Quirarte

The Art and Architecture of the Texas Missions

UNIVERSITY OF TEXAS PRESS

Austin

Publication of this work was made possible in part by support from the J. E. Smothers, Sr., Memorial Foundation and the National Endowment for the Humanities.

First edition, 2002

Requests for permission to reproduce material from this work should be sent to Permissions, University of Texas Press, Box 7819, Austin, TX 78713-7819.

♾ The paper used in this book meets the minimum requirements of ANSI/NISO Z39.48-1992 (R1997) (Permanence of Paper).

LIBRARY OF CONGRESS CATALOGING-IN-PUBLICATION DATA

Quirarte, Jacinto, 1931–
    The art and architecture of the Texas missions / Jacinto Quirarte.
        p.   cm. — (Jack and Doris Smothers series in Texas history, life, and culture ; no. 6)
Includes bibliographical references and index.
    ISBN 0-292-76902-4
    1. Spanish mission buildings—Texas—History. 2. Architecture, Spanish colonial—Texas. 3. Art, Spanish colonial—Texas. 4. Missions—Texas—History.
I. Title. II. Series.
    NA5230.T4 Q57   2002
    726.5´09764´09033—dc21

2001003848

DEDICATED TO MY WIFE,

Sara Quirarte,

who never failed to provide moral support
and encouragement during the many years
that it took to complete this book,

AND

to the memory of my mother, Frutosa Quirarte,
and my brother, Frank Quirarte

Contents

Preface   IX

Introduction   I

PART İ   **HISTORICAL BACKGROUND: THE ROLE OF MISSIONS AND PRESIDIOS IN THE CONVERSION OF TEXAS**   9

CHAPTER I Missions and Presidios, 1659–1793   II

CHAPTER 2 The Conversion of Texas: Missionaries, Soldiers, and Indians, 1740–1824   27

PART İİ   **THE ART AND ARCHITECTURE OF THE TEXAS MISSIONS**   41

CHAPTER 3 San Antonio de Valero   43

CHAPTER 4 San José y San Miguel de Aguayo   65

CHAPTER 5 La Purísima Concepción   103

CHAPTER 6 San Juan Capistrano   131

CHAPTER 7 San Francisco de la Espada   149

CHAPTER 8 El Espíritu Santo   163

CHAPTER 9 Content and Meaning   177

CHAPTER 10 Summary and Conclusions   185

      Epilogue   193

APPENDIX I A Census of Missions Founded, 1680–1793   197

APPENDIX 2 The Colonial Documents, 1740–1824   207

      Glossary   215

      Selected Bibliography   221

      Index   229

PREFACE

This book grew out of an earlier research project on the decorative and applied arts at the four San Antonio missions which comprise the San Antonio Missions National Historical Park: Nuestra Señora de la Purísima Concepción de Acuña, San José y San Miguel de Aguayo, San Juan Capistrano, and San Francisco de la Espada. I directed the project, funded by the national historical park, and carried it out from September 15, 1981, to May 31, 1982, with the assistance of consultants and the staff of the Research Center for the Arts, the University of Texas at San Antonio (UTSA).

Most of the work on the research plan was done by Anne Schlosser, a research assistant with the center. The archival work on the project (research, transcriptions, and translations) was done by Donna Pierce in San Antonio and Mexico City. She prepared translations of texts relating to the decorative and applied arts of the San Antonio missions (except San Antonio de Valero) taken from the inventories by Fr. Dolores (1762), Fr. Sáenz (1772), Fr. López (1785), and Fr. Díaz (1824). The translations are now in my possession since the center was "defunded" by the university a few years ago and no longer exists. These files and other research center files will probably be deposited in the Special Collections of the University of Texas at San Antonio Library (preliminary discussions are underway). Most of the photography was done by Kathy Vargas, a research assistant with the center.

Donna Pierce and Kathy Vargas did on-site research to check out details and to determine what had to be photographed. As project director, I also did on-site research, as did the late Robert Mullen, who was a faculty associate at the research center. Harvey Smith, Jr., provided photographs and newspaper clippings from his own collection and information on the restoration work carried out by his father, himself, and others at the missions. Mardith Schuetz-Miller provided research materials on the paintings found by Carlos Castañeda in the 1930s. Their assistance and expert advice was of inestimable value. Lorene Pouncey worked on the bibliography, Félix Almaráz on the history of the missions, and Nodé MacMillan on archival materials related to the missions. Marlys Bush Thurber, our liaison with the national historical park, offered guidance during the nine months when the project was carried out.

I wrote the preliminary report and asked members of the research team for their comments. Written responses by Harvey Smith, Jr., and Donna Pierce were very valuable in the preparation of the final report, which was submitted to the San Antonio Missions National Historical Park on August 10, 1982. All drafts and the final report were typed by Margaret Rogers, Graciela Rodríguez, and María Elena González-Cid.

The excitement generated by the results of the project led me to work on the present book, which encompasses a much broader body of material. The scope of the project was enlarged to include all the missions of Texas and to focus on the historical context as well as a formal and iconographic analysis of the art and architecture of the Texas missions.

In the late 1980s and early 1990s I reviewed primary and secondary sources on the missions to gather the necessary information for the expanded project. Part of the work involved going back to the archives (aside from those reviewed by Donna Pierce) to determine exactly what they contain relative to the art and architecture of the missions. The intent was to get a sense of what the missions were like from the 1740s to the early 1820s. This included the church and sacristy furnishings, sacred items, and the religious images (sculptures and paintings) of the altarpieces as they appeared during this period.

I am indebted to a number of people who helped me gather the many photographs, drawings, and prints of the Texas missions. Photographer Sarah Pierce from the University of Texas at San Antonio made black and white prints from negatives of pictures I took of the Espíritu Santo Mission as well as other pictures taken of the San Antonio missions by Kathy Vargas during the initial project. Other photographers include César Martínez, a special consultant, who did exterior views of the San Antonio missions; Tim Summa, who did interior views of the San José mission church; Linton Tyler, who made black and white prints from the negatives of pictures taken by Kathy Vargas; and John Poindexter and Mark McClendon, who scanned images from old prints and negatives. Dennis Medina, Special Collections librarian of the University of Texas at San Antonio Library, provided nineteenth-century lithographs of the missions. Tom Palmer did the map of New Spain (based on a map I had done) and the plan of Espíritu Santo Mission, and I did the map of the Texas province (based partly on a map by Desirée McDaniel).

I am also indebted to the following people, who gave their permission to reproduce images of the missions: Eugene George for his elevations of San Antonio de Valero and San Francisco de la Espada, Jack Eaton for his plans and elevations of San Antonio de Valero, Mardith Schuetz-Miller for her drawings of the Valero facade, Rebecca Huffstuttler for the old photographs and drawings in the collection of the Witte Museum of San Antonio, and Martha Utterback for photographs in the collection of the Daughters of the Republic of Texas Library.

Finally, I am indebted to the staff of the research center and to the consultants who assisted us in carrying out the initial research project. This book would not have been possible without their assistance.

J.Q.

THE ART AND ARCHITECTURE OF THE TEXAS MISSIONS

Introduction

This is a study of the art and architecture of the missions founded in Texas by Franciscan missionaries in the seventeenth and eighteenth centuries. A formal and iconographic analysis of the extant churches and related buildings, their decorated surfaces, and the reconstructed altars with their religious images will allow us to determine their meaning and their value as art and architecture. A discussion of the sources and antecedents for the missions found in central and northern New Spain will permit us to place them within a broader historical and artistic context.

The primary focus here is on the art and architecture of the extant missions—San Antonio de Valero, San José y San Miguel de Aguayo, Nuestra Señora de la Purísima Concepción, San Juan Capistrano, and San Francisco de la Espada in San Antonio and Nuestra Señora del Espíritu Santo in Goliad. Each is discussed in a single chapter with three parts that span the periods when they were constructed, then abandoned, and finally restored or reconstructed.

The former missions suffered after they were secularized (when their mission was completed or as the result of economic and/or political changes) and then abandoned. The first major changes occurred when San Antonio de Valero (the Alamo) was secularized in 1793, followed by most of the others in 1824.[1] The most drastic change was the dismantling of the original altars with gilded architectural frames and sculptures and paintings. A few sculptures of the saints remain, but not in their original locations, as in the case of Espada.[2] The sculptures at Capistrano have been placed in a recently acquired colonial altarpiece that has nothing to do with the eighteenth-century mission. No altarpieces, sculptures, or paintings remain in the church sanctuaries of Valero and San José or in the sanctuary and transept of Concepción.

The former missions suffered extensive damage caused by vandalism and deterioration in the nineteenth century due to neglect and the elements. Some of the facade sculptures were destroyed or damaged by gunfire or stolen, and only fragments of architectural polychromy survive. A few remnants of painting and sculpture remain in situ in some of the missions: a depiction of the Crucified Christ painted above a sculptured font in the St. Michael chapel, located in one of the belfry tower base rooms of the Concepción mission, and other wall paintings in the other belfry tower base room, originally used as the baptistry, and in the sacristy of the same mission.

1. For information on the secularization of Valero, see Fr. José Francisco López, "Report on the San Antonio Missions in 1792, by Fr. José Francisco López," trans. Fr. B. Leutenegger, intro. and notes by Fr. M. A. Habig, *Southwestern Historical Quarterly* 77, no. 4 (April 1974): 487–498; for information on the secularization of the remaining missions in San Antonio, see Fr. José Antonio Díaz de León, "Inventory of the Church of Mission San José, February 29, 1824," in *The San José Papers: Edited Primary Manuscript Sources for the History of Mission San José y San Miguel de Aguayo, Part III: July 1810–February 1824,* trans. B. Leutenegger, ed. Sister C. Casso, pp. 149–159.

2. For information on the storage of the sacred items and other furnishings of Concepción at San José, see the letters written by the pastor of San Fernando and the missionaries at San José to the governor of Texas in efforts to resolve a problem regarding their use: "Rev. Refugio de la Garza to Governor Martínez, February 10, 1820"; "Fr. Miguel Muro to Governor Martínez, February 8, 1820"; "Refugio de la Garza to Governor Martínez, July 26, 1820"; and "Fr. José Antonio Díaz de León to Governor Martínez, August 5, 1822," in *The San José Papers, Part III,* trans. B. Leutenegger, pp. 84–89, 100–101, 110–112.

Other changes occurred with the restoration of the missions. Although the structural aspects of the building interiors remain intact, the images and architectural details are no longer visible. The images of saints painted on the pendentives of the Concepción church disappeared long ago. The decorative details of the San José church interior also vanished but were partially restored in the twentieth century. In the late 1920s Ernst Schuchard did colored drawings of fragments of the original paintings, which were used to restore them in the 1930s. Most of the church interiors have been whitewashed. Finally, some of the churches were altered by well-intentioned twentieth-century restorers. Wrought-iron railings and crosses were added where none had ever existed.

Regardless of the problems presented by the normal operation of the missions in the eighteenth century, the neglect of the nineteenth century, and the benevolent attention of the twentieth century, enough remains to warrant a study, analysis, and evaluation of the art and architecture of the missions.

Brief background information on the missionary enterprise is provided in the two chapters of Part One, in notes, and more fully in the appendices. A brief discussion of the many expeditions that began with the discovery of the Gulf Coast in 1519 and culminated with the initial settlement of Texas in 1690 is included in the introduction to Chapter 1, which focuses on the founding and establishment of the first missions and presidios from 1659 to 1793. Chapter 2 provides background information on the Indians and the missionaries' efforts to convert them.

Part Two consists of eight chapters focusing on the art and architecture of the Texas missions. Chapters 3 through 8 deal with the six missions that have retained the original fabric of their churches and the configuration of their facades and also have a number of extant sculptures and paintings. The order of the discussion by chapter is based on the foundation dates (from earliest to latest) of the missions within each region. Each of the chapters devoted to the extant missions is comprised of three parts. The first part, based on colonial documents, provides a reconstruction of the missions in their original state from 1740 to 1824, when they were in full operation. The primary focus is on the mission architecture and the sacred images in the church altars during the years of their optimum condition. The second part, based on texts written by American and European travelers from 1840 to 1890, provides information on the state of the former missions when they were abandoned. The discussion reviews the earliest texts to the latest within each chapter. The third part provides information on the missions from 1890 to the present, when they were restored. It is based on colonial documents, nineteenth-century texts, paintings, and photographs, twentieth-century texts on restoration, and reports on archaeological excavations. The critical analysis of the art and architecture of each mission also proceeds chronologically.

Chapter 9 deals with the content and meaning of the portal sculptures and polychromy and the reconstructed altarpieces. Chapter 10 summarizes the discussions of the original art and architecture, the former missions, and the restored art and architecture.

The appendices provide information on a census of the missions founded from 1680 to 1793 (except those included in the main body of the text) and the colonial reports and inventories, 1740–1824, which document the manner in which the missions were monitored to insure that their assigned functions were successfully carried out.

The Glossary includes definitions of art and architectural terms in English and Spanish along with other Hispanicized words used in the text derived from Náhuatl, the language spoken by the Aztecs (such as Tequitqui, *mitote,* and *xacal* or *jacal*). It also includes words used to describe church furnishings, Christian themes, and holy days.

The Original Art and Architecture, 1740–1824

CHURCHES AND ALTARPIECES

The artistic and architectural record of the Texas missions can be partially seen in the churches that were restored or completely reconstructed in the twentieth century. Their original plans and elevations are clearly evident in the San Antonio missions of San Antonio de Valero, La Purísima Concepción, and San José de Aguayo and the church of the Goliad mission of El Espíritu Santo. Some semblance of the original churches is seen in the San Antonio missions of San Juan Capistrano and San Francisco de la Espada. The sacristies of the Concepción and San José churches remain, but the other units such as the *conventos* (friars' quarters), Indian houses, granaries, and workshops have almost totally disappeared.

Nonetheless, it is still possible to get a detailed account of the art and architecture of the missions by reviewing the many documents written by the missionaries between 1740 and 1824 (see Appendix 2). They allow us to recreate a step-by-step account of the stages of construction of the buildings at each mission.

The best way to present a view of the original art and architecture of the missions is to focus on the years when they were completed and maintained before they began to deteriorate. The Concepción church was the first to be completed, in 1755. Reports from 1756 to 1824 provide information on its art and architecture. The unfinished church of Valero and the churches of the other Querétaran missions in San Antonio were at their optimum condition in 1772, the year they were transferred to Zacatecan administrative control. This is clearly seen in the inventories prepared by Fr. Juan José Sáenz de Gumiel on the holdings of Valero, Concepción, Capistrano, and Espada.[3] San José mission reached its maximum condition in the 1770s and 1780s, as evidenced by the texts written between 1778 and 1783 by Fr. Juan Agustín Morfi and in 1785 by Fr. José María Salas de Santa Gertrudis.[4]

The end of the San Antonio missions was the year when they were secularized. For Valero this was in 1793,[5] when its unfinished church and other buildings were already beginning to deteriorate. The other missions in San Antonio reached that stage twenty years later, before they were finally secularized in 1824 and the Gulf Coast missions shortly thereafter.[6] Their lowest point came in the 1840s and 1850s, when they were all abandoned.

Although the San Antonio missions have been studied extensively, little or no attention has been given to the church altarpieces which were an integral part of each mission. Even less attention has been given to the original altarpieces in the restorations and reconstructions carried out in the twentieth century. The review of the documents here includes all available references to

3. Fr. José Sáenz de Gumiel, *Inventory of the Mission San Antonio de Valero: 1772,* trans. and ed. Fr. B. Leutenegger; idem, "Inventory of Espada Mission"; idem, "Testimony and Inventory of Mission Purísima Concepción"; idem, "Inventory [of Mission San Juan Capistrano]."

4. Fr. Juan Agustín Morfi, *History of Texas, 1673–1779,* trans. C. E. Castañeda, vol. 1; "Inventory of Fr. Salas," in *The San José Papers: Edited Primary Manuscript Sources for the History of Mission San José y San Miguel de Aguayo, Part I: 1719–1791,* trans. B. Leutenegger, comp. and annotated by M. A. Habig, pp. 214–245.

5. M. A. Habig, *The Alamo Chain of Missions: A History of San Antonio's Five Old Missions,* p. 141.

6. For the secularization of the missions in 1824, see n. 1 above.

the altarpieces dating from 1740 to 1824. At that time all the remaining sacred images in the San Antonio missions were transferred to San José, where some of them are still found. The rest disappeared shortly thereafter.

A partial reconstruction of the form and content of the altarpieces presented here is based on information found in the inventories of the holdings of the five missions in San Antonio and one at Goliad. The best way to get a sense of the original altarpieces is to concentrate on the period when they were essentially completed and remained intact until they were dismantled in 1824. The midway point for the Querétaran missions in San Antonio—Valero, Concepción, Capistrano, and Espada—was 1772, the year they were turned over to the Zacatecan missionaries at San José. The inventories of these missions prepared by Fr. Sáenz provide us with a complete description of all the altarpieces.[7] The high point for San José was reached in 1785, when Fr. Salas prepared the inventory of the mission.[8]

The Former Missions, 1840–1890

The former Texas missions began to deteriorate soon after they were secularized. Valero saw the greatest changes, following its conversion to a military fortress in 1802. The other missions in San Antonio—Concepción, Capistrano, San José, and Espada—suffered primarily from neglect and vandalism in the 1840s and 1850s. Espíritu Santo was also abandoned during the same period. The abandonment of the former missions lasted until about the 1890s, when the first efforts were made to restore them.

Diaries, books, and recollections written in the nineteenth century by visitors to Texas from other parts of the United States and Europe provide a record of the deterioration of the former missions. Some of the visitors were civilians. Others were U.S. army officers who began to arrive in 1846 as preparations were made for the invasion of northern Mexico at the beginning of the Mexican American war. They all provide detailed accounts of the state of the buildings during this period.

Some of the texts were published soon after they were written in the 1840s through the 1870s. Others were published in the twentieth century. Plans, drawings, watercolors, paintings, and photographs of the missions from this period also provide a vivid account of the condition of the former missions.

The Restored Art and Architecture and the Extant Sculptures and Paintings

The original intent of the builders and artists who created the art and architecture of the Texas missions is evident in a few extraordinary examples, such as the facades of Valero, San José, and Concepción. It is also seen in the sacristy window of San José and in the few sculptures and paintings that have survived the great upheavals that caused so much damage to the missions and their furnishings in the nineteenth century.

The discussion below and the appendices demonstrate the great labors that the missionaries and others endured to establish and build missions to spread

7. Fr. Sáenz, *Inventory of the Mission San Antonio de Valero: 1772;* idem, "Inventory of Espada Mission"; idem, "Testimony and Inventory of Mission Purísima Concepción"; idem, "Inventory [of Mission San Juan Capistrano]."

8. "Inventory of Fr. Salas," in *San José Papers, Part I,* trans. B. Leutenegger, pp. 214–245.

the gospel among the Indians and to teach them all the skills believed necessary to make them good, useful, and productive subjects of the Spanish Crown. The reports and inventories provide a detailed account of the building programs and the creation of spaces for the sacred images on facades and altarpieces that were used to teach the Indians about the history, content, and meaning of the new religion. A review of these documents and the accounts of travelers during the period of their abandonment provides the background needed to analyze and assess the restored and altered art and architecture of the churches and other buildings of the former missions.

THE LITERATURE, 1824 TO THE PRESENT

Numerous documents, papers, and books on the Texas missions have been published. The earliest texts, as already noted, were written in the eighteenth and early nineteenth centuries by the inspecting teams sent by the administrative centers for the missions located at the Apostolic Colleges of the Holy Cross at Querétaro and Our Lady of Guadalupe at Zacatecas.[9] The reports, inventories, and letters written by the inspectors contain information on all of the Texas missions, as do some of the nineteenth-century accounts written by Americans and Europeans traveling through Texas. Most of the texts provide a listing of the contents and condition of the missions at the time of the reporting.

Occasionally assessments of the art and architecture are found in the writings of Fr. Morfi and Josiah Gregg, an American traveler.[10] In most cases, the early comments and observations are not of a critical nature. Almost all of the nineteenth-century travelers, among them the Englishman William Bollaert and the American John Russell Bartlett, lamented the fact that the mission buildings were in a sad state and that they were suffering daily from natural deterioration and vandalism.[11]

Although the twentieth-century literature on the Texas missions is extensive, its scope is very limited. Most of the studies—historical, anecdotal, ethnohistorical, archaeological, and others—have dealt with the art and architecture as an isolated phenomenon without reference to central New Spain, where the sources for their forms and structures are found. The same is true of the other mission fields, which have been studied in isolation. This fragmentation of the material is due to historical and political reasons as well as problems of thematic coherence, manageability, access, or the vision of historians, art historians, archaeologists, and others in the United States and Mexico who have studied the art and architecture of New Spain.

Before the work of Manuel Toussaint appeared in the 1920s, there were few studies of the art and architecture of New Spain. The state of the field reached a high point in 1948 with the publication of his book *Arte colonial de México*, later published in English.[12] This made the colonial monuments more accessible to everyone interested in their artistic and architectural qualities. The lack of major roads in the rural areas where a large number of such structures are found made it difficult to study them. It is now standard for students of colonial art to pursue their studies using the seminal works by Toussaint and others who have focused on various aspects of these materials. Examples are

9. The Apostolic College of the Holy Cross in Querétaro was founded in 1683 and the Apostolic College of Our Lady of Guadalupe in Zacatecas in 1707. For information on their founding, see M. B. McCloskey, *The Formative Years of the Missionary College of Santa Cruz of Querétaro, 1683–1733;* Fr. J. A. Alcocer, *Bosquejo de la historia del Colegio de Nuestra Señora de Guadalupe y sus missiones, año de 1788,* ed. Fr. R. Cervantes, p. 68; and *The Zacatecan Missionaries in Texas, 1716–1834,* excerpts from the *Libros de los Decretos of the Missionary College of Zacatecas, 1707–1808,* trans. Fr. B. Leutenegger.

10. Fr. Morfi, *History of Texas, 1673–1779;* Josiah Gregg, *Diary and Letters of Josiah Gregg,* vol. 1: *Southwestern Enterprises, 1840–1847,* ed. M. G. Fulton.

11. William Bollaert, *William Bollaert's Texas,* ed. W. E. Hollon and R. L. Butler; J. R. Bartlett, *Personal Narrative of Explorations and Incidents in Texas, New Mexico, California, Sonora, and Chihuahua.*

12. M. Toussaint, *Arte colonial en México;* see also his *Colonial Art in Mexico,* trans. E. Weismann.

the books by George Kubler on the sixteenth-century architecture of Mexico, by Joseph Armstrong Baird, Jr., on the colonial churches of Mexico, by Elizabeth Wilder Weismann on the sculpture of Mexico, and by John McAndrew on the open chapels of the sixteenth century.[13]

The same pattern emerged in the study of the various mission fields along the northern frontier. The distinctive character of each of the mission fields made it easy to focus on any one of them without reference to the others. The vast distances from central New Spain and the limited or nonexistent communication between the northern provinces forced the missionaries to build missions with what they had available in their respective regions. In addition, the formal characteristics of the missions differ because they reflect the styles in fashion at the time when each of the mission fields was explored, settled, and developed. Further isolation was caused by the change in national boundaries between the United States and Mexico following the war between the two countries from 1846 to 1848.

By the time the missions were considered worthy of study, they had long been within the territorial limits of the United States. This led to the study of the missions as part of the northern frontier without reference to central New Spain. This is not unique to U.S. scholars. The same is true of Mexican scholars and others who have ignored the northern and southern peripheries of New Spain, particularly the southern states of Campeche and Yucatán, in their studies of the art and architecture of colonial Mexico.

The study of the missions in Texas, New Mexico, Arizona, and California, therefore, is characterized by a focus on a particular state or a single mission and rarely on the missions of the entire area. An exception is the study of the missions of the Southwest by Cleve Hallenbeck.[14] Among the single-state studies of the mission architecture are the books on California missions by Rexford Newcomb and Kurt Baer, on Texas missions by Charles Mattoon Brooks, Jr., and on New Mexico missions by George Kubler.[15] Among the studies of single missions are those on San Xavier del Bac mission by Prentice Duell and on Acoma by Ward Alan Minge.[16]

Closer to the intent of this book is the study of the New Mexico missions by John L. Kessell to determine how they have changed over a period of two hundred years starting in 1776, when Fr. Francisco Atanasio Domínguez described them.[17] Kessell found no more than five or six missions which have retained some of their original form in plan and elevation!

The format for most studies of the art and architecture of the Texas missions was established by William Corner, who published a study of the missions and history of San Antonio in 1890.[18] A number of similar studies have been published since then, such as the book on the architecture of the San Antonio missions by C. M. Brooks, Jr.[19] Most other studies have focused on the history of the missions, including the book on the San Antonio missions by Marion A. Habig and books on all the missions of Texas by Walter F. McCaleb, James W. Burke, and Herbert M. Mason.[20]

Single missions have also been studied from a historical point of view. Among them are the articles by Willard F. Scarborough on each of the San Antonio missions and monographs on Concepción by J. W. Schmitz, on the Alamo by Frederick C. Chabot, and on San José by Ethel Wilson Harris and Marion A. Habig.[21] In recent years there have been a number of archaeological reports on the work carried out at the missions, such as those by Mardith

13. G. Kubler, *Mexican Architecture of the Sixteenth Century*; J. A. Baird, *The Churches of Mexico: 1530–1810*; E. W. Weismann, *Mexico in Sculpture: 1521–1821*; J. McAndrew, *The Open-Air Churches of Sixteenth-Century Mexico*.

14. C. Hallenbeck, *Spanish Missions of the Old Southwest*.

15. R. Newcomb, *The Old Mission Churches and Historical Houses of California: Their History, Architecture, Art, and Lore*; K. Baer, *Architecture of the California Missions*; C. M. Brooks, *Texas Missions, Their Romance and Architecture*; G. Kubler, *The Religious Architecture of New Mexico*.

16. P. Duell, *Mission Architecture as Exemplified in San Xavier del Bac*; and W. A. Minge, *Acoma: Pueblo in the Sky*.

17. J. L. Kessell, *The Missions of New Mexico since 1776*; Fr. Francisco Atanasio Domínguez, *The Missions of New Mexico, 1776*, trans. and annotated by Eleanor B. Adams and Fr. Angélico Chávez (Albuquerque: University of New Mexico Press, 1956).

18. W. Corner, *San Antonio de Béxar: A Guide and History*.

19. C. M. Brooks, *Texas Missions, Their Romance and Architecture*.

20. Habig, *The Alamo Chain of Missions*; W. F. McCaleb, *The Spanish Missions of Texas*; J. W. Burke, *Missions of Old Texas*; H. M. Mason, *Missions of Texas*.

21. W. F. Scarborough, "Old Spanish Mission in Texas II: San Francisco de la Espada," *Southwest Review* 13, no. 3 (1928): 367–397; idem, "Old Spanish Mission in Texas III: San José de [*sic*] San Miguel de Aguayo de Buena Vista," *Southwest Review* 13, no. 4 (1928): 491–504; J. W. Schmitz, *Mission Concepción*; F. C. Chabot, *The Alamo: Mission, Fortress and Shrine*; E. W. Harris, *San José, Queen of the Missions*; and M. A. Habig, *San Antonio's Mission San José*.

22. M. K. Schuetz, *Historical Background of the Mission San Antonio de Valero;* J. D. Eaton, *Excavations at the Alamo Shrine (Mission San Antonio de Valero);* M. K. Schuetz, *The History and Archaeology of Mission San Juan Capistrano, San Antonio, Texas;* D. Scurlock and D. E. Fox, *An Archaeological Investigation of Mission Concepción, San Antonio, Texas;* John W. Clark, Jr., *Mission San José y San Miguel de Aguayo: Archaeological Investigations, December 1974.*

23. K. K. Gilmore, *The San Xavier Missions: A Study in Historical Identification;* idem, *Mission Rosario: Archaeological Investigations, 1973;* idem, *Mission Rosario Archaeological Investigations, 1974;* idem, *A Documentary and Archaeological Investigation of Presidio San Luis de Las Amarillas and Mission Santa Cruz de San Sabá, Menard County, Texas: A Preliminary Report,* Office of the State Archaeologist, Archaeological Program Report 9 (Austin: State Building Commission, 1967); C. D. Tunnell and J. R. Ambler, *Archaeological Investigations at Presidio San Agustín de Ahumada.*

K. Schuetz and Jack D. Eaton on the Alamo, by Mardith K. Schuetz on Capistrano, by Dan Scurlock and Daniel E. Fox on Concepción, and by John W. Clark, Jr., on San José.[22]

Archaeological work has also been carried out at some of the other missions and presidios in Texas. Among these are the reports on the missions and presidio at San Sabá, the San Xavier missions, and the Rosario mission by Kathleen K. Gilmore and on the presidio San Agustín de Ahumada at Orcoquisac by Curtis D. Tunnell and J. Richard Ambler.[23]

Part One of this study includes historical information on all the missions founded in Texas from 1680/81 to 1793 and the conversion effort by the Franciscan missionaries up to 1830 or 1831, when the last missions were secularized. Particular attention is paid to the information that the documents provide on the geography and climate of Texas, the economy of the missions, the problems encountered by the missionaries, and the Indians, their customs, and the languages spoken by the many groups found in the province. Part Two provides historical information and an in-depth analysis of the art and architecture of the six remaining missions in Texas—San Antonio de Valero, San José de Aguayo, La Purísima Concepción, Capistrano, Espada, and Espíritu Santo. The primary focus is on the condition of the missions during the period when they were in full operation in the late eighteenth century, when they were abandoned in the nineteenth century, and when they were restored or reconstructed in the twentieth century.

PART I

Historical Background
The Role of Missions and Presidios in the Conversion of Texas

I

Missions and Presidios, 1659–1793

The missions founded in Texas are discussed chronologically by geographical area (region, settlement, or river). They are found in west Texas, east Texas, central Texas (San Antonio, San Xavier, San Sabá, and El Cañón), and the Gulf Coast (Espíritu Santo and El Orcoquisac). Each mission is identified by its full name the first time it is mentioned in the text and then by a shorter version of its name, such as La Purísima Concepción for Nuestra Señora de la Purísima Concepción de Acuña. Those with reasonably short names, such as San Antonio de Valero, remain the same.

NUEVO MÉXICO (WEST TEXAS) AND THE TEXAS PROVINCE

The oldest missions within the boundaries of the state of Texas were founded in El Paso del Norte and La Junta de los Ríos (present El Paso and Presidio, Texas). Seven missions were founded during the years 1659 through 1684, when the territory was part of the province of Nuevo México.[1] The missions in the area around Junta de los Ríos were founded in 1683 and 1684. They were refounded in 1715 and again in 1747, but eventually abandoned in 1760 due to continual Indian attacks on the Spanish settlements. The Presidio del Norte remained after the missions were abandoned.

The first missions in the Texas province were founded in 1690 in the northeastern part of the territory (east Texas) to ward off French influence in the area. The missions and the province were abandoned only three years later because the French threat had apparently disappeared and the viceregal authorities had lost interest in the enterprise. Several more attempts were made in the early eighteenth century before the settlements in the province were firmly established. The process had begun several centuries earlier with the discovery of the Texas coast in 1519 by Spaniards sailing out of Florida. Other expeditions were mounted to explore the territory during the following two centuries.

It all began with the search for the mythical strait to Cathay, the Strait of Anian, and continued with the search for Cíbola, the fabled seven cities of gold.[2]

The Texas Gulf Coast was first explored and mapped in 1519 by Alonso Alvarez de Pineda, who sailed from Florida to northern Mexico in search of the Strait of Anian. Francisco de Garay, who authorized the Pineda expedition,

1. The seven missions established in the El Paso area were Nuestra Señora de Guadalupe (1659), San Francisco de los Sumas (before 1680), San Lorenzo (1682), San Antonio del Senecú (1682), Corpus Christi de la Isleta (1680–1682), Nuestra Señora de la Concepción del Socorro (1681), and Santa Gertrudis.

2. On the mythical strait of Anian, see L. E. Huddleston, *Origins of the American Indians: European Concepts, 1492–1729*, pp. 59, 69, 125.

then sent Diego de Camargo in 1520 to establish a colony at Río de las Palmas (Río Grande). When Camargo failed to return, Garay sent another expedition to find him. Neither one returned to Jamaica. Garay led a final expedition in 1523 to continue the efforts to establish the colony. He and the men from the two earlier expeditions eventually joined Hernán Cortés in Mexico following the conquest of the Aztecs.[3]

In the following years other Spaniards explored the Gulf Coast of Texas and northern Mexico, some by accident, others by design. Explorations through the territory now known as west Texas and northern New Mexico were the result of a shipwreck off the coast of Texas in 1528. The lost ship belonged to the expedition led by Pánfilo de Narváez.[4] Alvar Núñez Cabeza de Vaca and three other survivors traveled through much of central and west Texas over a period of several years. They finally arrived in Culiacán in 1536, where they related the tales they had heard of the fabled seven cities of gold (Cíbola) located somewhere in the northern territories (Map 1.1). Explorations aimed at eventually settling the northern part of the Texas Gulf Coast were carried out by Hernando de Soto between 1539 and 1542.[5] These early efforts also failed.

The earliest entries into Texas from the west were the result of the explorations into New Mexico carried out by Fr. Marcos de Niza in 1539 and by Francisco Vázquez de Coronado from 1540 to 1542.[6] Both expeditions departed from Nueva Galicia (present state of Jalisco, Mexico). Further explorations of the northern borderlands (within the present borders of Mexico) were carried out from the northern province of Nueva Vizcaya, established in 1561.[7]

WEST TEXAS (NUEVO MÉXICO), 1680–1760

The first entries into west Texas to explore the area were made from Nuevo México in the early seventeenth century.[8] Others were made in the late seventeenth century into La Junta de los Ríos (Presidio, Texas) from the province of Nueva Vizcaya.

THE MISSIONS OF EL PASO DEL NORTE

El Paso del Norte was part of the province of Nuevo México, established by the Spaniards in the early seventeenth century. It served as a base for the Juan Domínguez Mendoza expedition of 1683–1684 into the region that is now part of west Texas and for the reconquest of the province of Nuevo México following the Indian Revolt of 1680. At least seven missions were established in the El Paso region, all on the southern side of the Río Grande. However, when the river changed course in the nineteenth century, two of them ended up on the United States side of the border. They were named after the missions abandoned in Nuevo México: Corpus Christi de la Isleta and Nuestra Señora de la Concepción del Socorro (see Appendix 1).[9]

THE MISSIONS OF LA JUNTA DE LOS RÍOS

The founding of the missions in the region of La Junta de los Ríos is related to the history of the missions in El Paso del Norte. All the initial entries into the region were made by explorers and missionaries on their way to Nuevo

3. There are a number of books on the Conquest of the Aztecs by the Spaniards that began in 1519 and culminated with the siege of Tenochtitlán in 1521. The most widely known account is by Bernal Díaz del Castillo, one of the conquerors, titled *Historia verdadera de la conquista de la Nueva España,* prologue by C. Pereyra; see also idem, *The Discovery and Conquest of Mexico, 1517–1521,* trans. A. P. Maudslay.

4. For information on the Narváez expedition, see Gonzalo Fernández Oviedo y Valdez, "The Expedition of Pánfilo de Narváez," ed. Harbert Davenport, *Southwestern Historical Quarterly* 27, no. 2 (October 1923): 120–139 (Chapter 1) and 27, no. 3 (January 1924): 217–241 (Chapter 2); see also C. E. Castañeda, *Our Catholic Heritage in Texas,* vol. 1, pp. 39–81.

5. For information on the de Soto expedition, see Castañeda, *Our Catholic Heritage,* vol. 1, pp. 116–138.

6. H. E. Bolton, *Coronado: Knight of Pueblos and Plains;* see also Castañeda, *Our Catholic Heritage,* vol. 1, pp. 93–115.

7. T. C. Barnes, T. H. Naylor, and C. W. Polzer, *Northern New Spain: A Research Guide,* pp. 61, 107.

8. For the Juan de Oñate expedition, see Castañeda, *Our Catholic Heritage,* vol. 1, pp. 186–194.

9. See note 1 above for the names of the missions founded in the El Paso area; for information on the El Paso missions, see A. E. Hughes, "The Beginnings of Spanish Settlement in the El Paso District," *University of California Publications in History* 1, no. 3: 295–392; and F. V. Scholes, "Documents for the History of the New Mexico Historical Review," *New Mexico Historical Review* 4 (Santa Fe, 1929): 45–58; for Corpus Christi y San Antonio de la Isleta (1680–1828) and Concepción del Socorro (1680–1828), see Burke, *Missions of Old Texas,* pp. 114, 116; see also G. B. Eckhart, "Spanish Missions of Texas," *Kiva* 32, no. 3 (1967): 80.

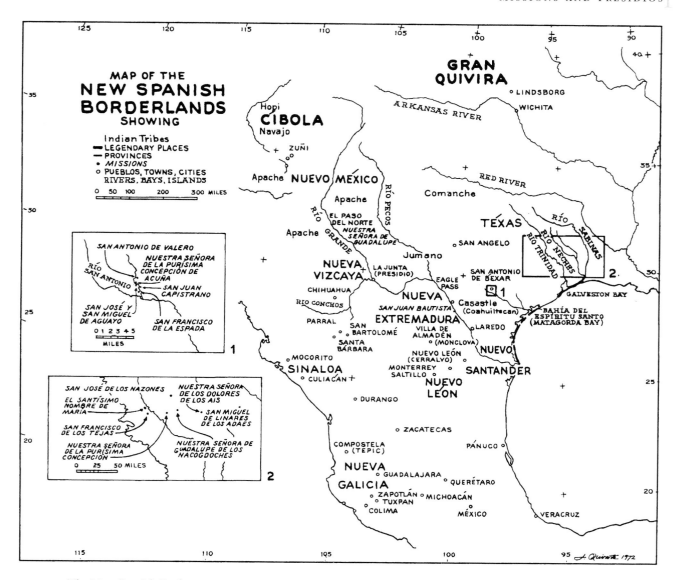

MAP 1.1. *The New Spanish Borderlands, Showing Indian Tribes, Legendary Places, Provinces, Missions, Pueblos, Towns, Cities, Rivers, Bays, and Islands. Map by Tom Palmer, based on a map by Jacinto Quirarte.*

México in the late sixteenth and early seventeenth centuries. The expeditions were mounted from settlements below the Río Grande in the Reino de Nueva Vizcaya (the modern Mexican states of Chihuahua and Durango) and later from El Paso del Norte into the province of Nuevo México.

In December 1683 Fr. Nicolás with Fr. Agustín (Antonio) Acevedo and Fr. Juan Zavaleta went on to La Junta without a military escort. Shortly thereafter, Governor Domingo Jironza Pétriz de Cruzate (1683–1686) ordered Captain Juan Domínguez de Mendoza to go to La Junta to join the missionaries and to explore the country eastward into the present state of Texas. Mendoza left El Paso del Norte in December 1683 and traveled through that area until the spring of 1684. Three missions were founded: La Navidad de las Cruces on December 29, 1683, El Apóstol Santiago two days later, and San Clemente on March 16, 1684 (Map 1.2).

A second attempt was made to establish missions and erect a presidio at La Junta de los Ríos in 1715, when the viceroy ordered a party of exploration

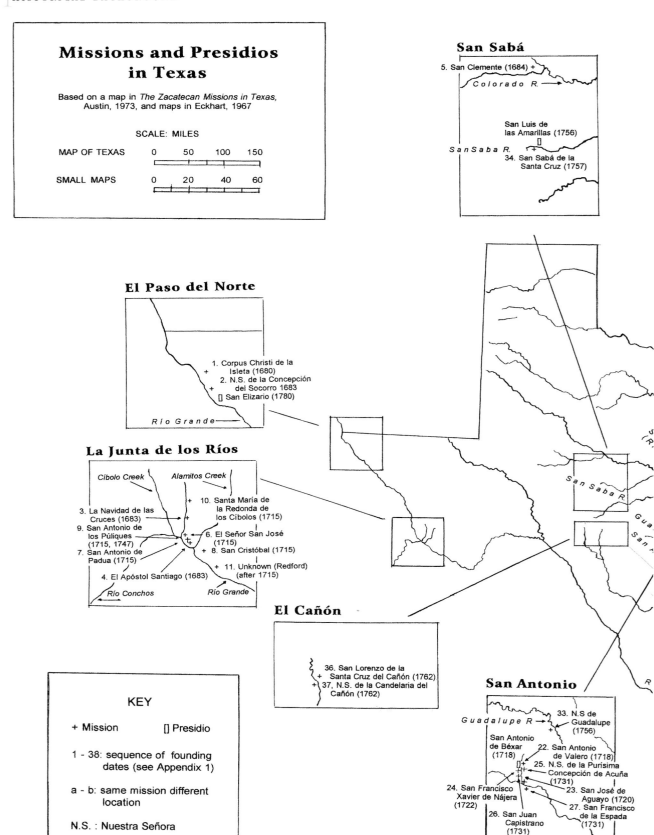

Missions and Presidios in Texas

Based on a map in *The Zacatecan Missions in Texas,*
Austin, 1973, and maps in Eckhart, 1967

SCALE: MILES

MAP OF TEXAS   0   50   100   150

SMALL MAPS   0   20   40   60

San Sabá

5. San Clemente (1684) +

Colorado R.

San Luis de
las Amarillas (1756)

San Saba R.

34. San Sabá de la
Santa Cruz (1757)

El Paso del Norte

1. Corpus Christi de la
   Isleta (1680)
2. N.S. de la Concepción
   del Socorro 1683
   [] San Elizario (1780)

Río Grande

La Junta de los Ríos

Cíbolo Creek   *Alamitos Creek*

10. Santa María de
    la Redonda de
    los Cíbolos (1715)
3. La Navidad de las
   Cruces (1683)
9. San Antonio de
   los Púliques
   (1715, 1747)
6. El Señor San José
   (1715)
7. San Antonio de
   Padua (1715)
8. San Cristóbal (1715)
4. El Apóstol Santiago (1683)
11. Unknown (Redford)
    (after 1715)

Río Conchos   *Río Grande*

El Cañón

36. San Lorenzo de la
    Santa Cruz del Cañón (1762)
37. N.S. de la Candelaria del
    Cañón (1762)

San Antonio

Guadalupe R.

33. N.S de
    Guadalupe
    (1756)

San Antonio
de Béxar
(1718)

22. San Antonio
    de Valero (1718)

25. N.S. de la Purísima
    Concepción de Acuña
    (1731)

24. San Francisco
    Xavier de Nájera
    (1722)

23. San José de
    Aguayo (1720)

27. San Francisco
    de la Espada
    (1731)

26. San Juan
    Capistrano
    (1731)

San Antonio R.

KEY

+ Mission   [] Presidio

1 - 38: sequence of founding
dates (see Appendix 1)

a - b: same mission different
location

N.S. : Nuestra Señora

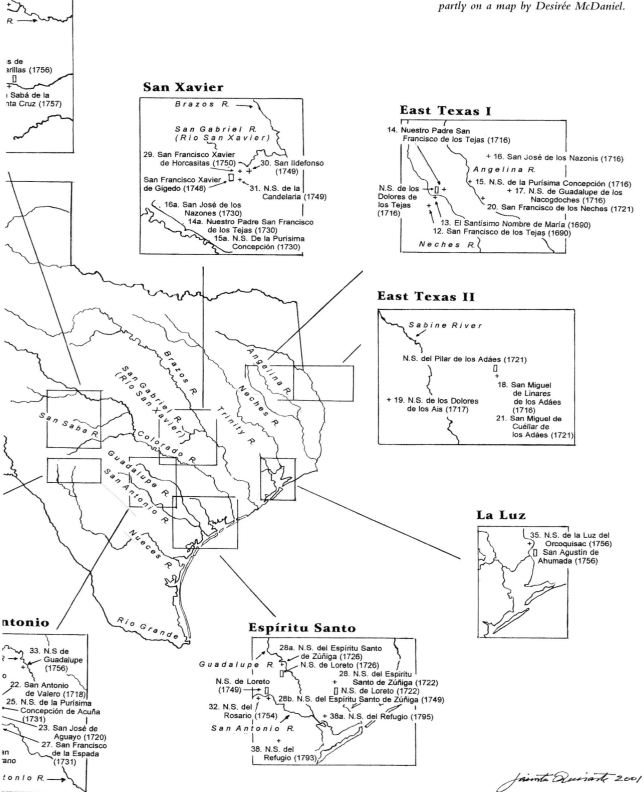

MAP 1.2. *Missions and Presidios of Texas. Map by Jacinto Quirarte, based partly on a map by Desirée McDaniel.*

San Xavier

Brazos R.

San Gabriel R. (Río San Xavier)

29. San Francisco Xavier de Horcasitas (1750)
30. San Ildefonso (1749)
San Francisco Xavier de Gigedo (1748)
31. N.S. de la Candelaria (1749)
16a. San José de los Nazones (1730)
14a. Nuestro Padre San Francisco de los Tejas (1730)
15a. N.S. De la Purisima Concepción (1730)

East Texas I

14. Nuestro Padre San Francisco de los Tejas (1716)
16. San José de los Nazonis (1716)
Angelina R.
15. N.S. de la Purísima Concepción (1716)
N.S. de los Dolores de los Tejas (1716)
17. N.S. de Guadalupe de los Nacogdoches (1716)
20. San Francisco de los Neches (1721)
13. El Santísimo Nombre de María (1690)
12. San Francisco de los Tejas (1690)
Neches R.

East Texas II

Sabine River

N.S. del Pilar de los Adáes (1721)

19. N.S. de los Dolores de los Ais (1717)
18. San Miguel de Linares de los Adáes (1716)
21. San Miguel de Cuéllar de los Adáes (1721)

La Luz

35. N.S. de la Luz del Orcoquisac (1756)
San Agustín de Ahumada (1756)

[A]ntonio

33. N.S de Guadalupe (1756)
22. San Antonio de Valero (1718)
25. N.S. de la Purísima Concepción de Acuña (1731)
23. San José de Aguayo (1720)
27. San Francisco de la Espada (1731)
[S]an [Antoni]ano
[An]tonio R.

Espíritu Santo

28a. N.S. del Espíritu Santo de Zúñiga (1726)
N.S. de Loreto (1726)
Guadalupe R.
28. N.S. del Espiritu Santo de Zúñiga (1722)
N.S. de Loreto (1722)
N.S. de Loreto (1749)
28b. N.S. del Espíritu Santo de Zúñiga (1749)
32. N.S. del Rosario (1754)
38a. N.S. del Refugio (1795)
San Antonio R.
38. N.S. del Refugio (1793)

[s de] [Cañ]arillas (1756)
[San] Sabá de la [Sa]nta Cruz (1757)

Jacinto Quirarte 2001

into the region led by Captain Don Juan Antonio de Trasviña y Retis. The expedition was the result of an earlier trip to La Junta by Fr. Andrés Ramírez in 1713 to look into the feasibility of founding missions, as requested by the Indians of the region. His report to Colonel Juan Joseph Masoni, an officer at Real de San Francisco de Cuéllar, was sent on with a *memorial* to the viceroy on May 30, 1713. This eventually led to the authorization of the Trasviña y Retis expedition.

The expedition left from Real de San Francisco de Cuéllar de Mina in the Reino de Nueva Vizcaya on May 23, 1715, and arrived at La Junta de los Ríos on June 3. Trasviña y Retis was accompanied by Fr. Andrés Ramírez, Fr. Joseph de Arránegui, adjutant general of the Custodia of the Province of Nuevo México, and two other missionaries. They founded six missions on the northern side of the Río Grande. The first four were named El Señor San José, San Antonio de Padua, San Cristóbal, and San Antonio de los Púliques. Two other missions were founded around the same time, but the exact date is not known. One was Los Cíbolos; the other, whose name is unknown, was located near present Redford, Texas.[10]

The missions at La Junta de los Ríos were abandoned in 1726 because of constant Indian attacks on the Spanish settlements. There were no resident missionaries at the missions when Captain Joseph Idoyaga's expedition visited the area in 1747 to find the best site for a presidio. Two other expeditions, led by Captain Fermín de Vidaurre and Pedro Rábago y Terán, governor of Coahuila, were mounted in 1747 for the same purpose.[11] The presidio was built in 1760.

EAST TEXAS, 1690–1693

Conquests of the north-central region as far as Saltillo and possibly Monterrey had been made by 1565. The province of Nuevo León was created in 1582 from the eastern limits of Nueva Vizcaya to the Gulf of Mexico as far south as Pánuco (Tampico, México). (It eventually extended two hundred leagues, or almost five hundred and twenty miles, from Pánuco to near the mouth of the Colorado River.)

The impetus for the settlement of east Texas came from the ever-present worry that other European powers would move into the region claimed by Spain. The fear of European encroachment appeared as early as 1613, when Captains José Treviño and Bernabé Casas, two citizens of Nuevo León, made an offer to the viceroy to conquer the region to the north in order to expel the English from "La Florida" (this appears to be a reference to the 1606 English settlement at Jamestown). They offered to undertake the conquest of the interior provinces of Nuevo León. There is no record that the proposal was accepted.[12]

Throughout the seventeenth century, soldiers and missionaries continued to use the fear of European intrusion into Spanish territory to gain official support for their proposals to conquer or Christianize the Indians. They also emphasized the practical aspects of their projects by pointing out the possibility of finding vast riches in these territories and establishing closer links between the provinces of New Spain.

The settlements were intended to reinforce Spanish claims to the territory.

10. See "Itinerary of Juan Domínguez de Mendoza, 1684," in *Spanish Exploration in the Southwest, 1542–1706,* ed. H. E. Bolton, pp. 320–343; ibid., pp. 325–326, 338, for the founding of La Navidad de las Cruces, El Apóstol Santiago, and San Clemente as well as a description of the bastion built there; for information on the Trasviña y Retis expedition, see R. C. Reindorp, "The Founding of Missions at La Junta de los Rios," *Mid-America* 20 (April 1938): 107–131; the text includes statements by Fr. Gregorio Osorio and Fr. Juan Antonio García and Joseph de Arránegui as well as daily entries by Trasviña y Retis; ibid., p. 118, for the order given by Trasviña y Retis to repair the churches and build quarters for the missionaries, and p. 120, for information on the founding of El Señor San José de los Púliques, San Antonio de Padua de los Conchos, and San Cristóbal de los Poxalmes; for the founding of Los Cíbolos and the mission at Redford, see G. B. Eckhart, "Some Little-Known Missions in Texas," *Masterkey* 37, no. 1 (1963): 13.

11. For information on the Idoyaga, Vidaurre, and Rábago y Terán expeditions to La Junta de los Ríos, see Castañeda, *Our Catholic Heritage,* vol. 3, pp. 214–228.

12. Ibid., pp. 61, 106, for the establishment of the Provincia de Nuevo León in 1582; see also Castañeda, *Our Catholic Heritage,* vol. 1, pp. 207–208; Viceroy Diego Fernández de Córdoba (1612–1621) received the offer from Casas and Treviño to conquer the region to the north.

But the settlement of Texas could not be accomplished until the provinces of Nuevo León and Coahuila south of the Río Grande were settled. (The northern limits of Nuevo León became the territory of Nueva Extremadura in 1674 and then the province of Coahuila in 1687.) The expeditions to explore and settle Texas were organized and carried out from the settlements just south of the Río Grande. Coahuila served as the base of operations for the founding of missions in east Texas in 1690, the year Texas was designated a province.

The first event to arouse the Spaniards to action in east Texas involved Diego de Peñalosa, the former governor of Nuevo México (1661–1664), who tried to interest a number of foreign powers in his schemes to take over the silver mines in Nueva Vizcaya. The second—a French settlement on the Gulf Coast founded by Robert Cavelier, Sieur de la Salle, in 1684—so alarmed the Spanish authorities that in 1690 they sent the first settlers to east Texas, where they established the first missions.[13]

THE EAST TEXAS MISSIONS

The venture in east Texas and western Louisiana was intended to solidify Spain's claim to the Texas territory and keep the French out of the area. Such efforts had been aimed at the French incursions for some time.

General Alonso de León, governor of the province of Coahuila and captain of the presidio, led the fifth expedition to find the French, who were reported to be in the Bay of Espíritu Santo and the Texas Province. The previous four expeditions had failed to find the French in Texas. De León was accompanied by Fr. Damián Massanet, a member of the College of the Holy Cross of Querétaro. The expedition left Villa de Santiago de la Monclova on March 26, 1690, and arrived in east Texas in late May. Construction of the first mission began soon thereafter. It was named San Francisco de los Tejas. A second mission, named El Santísimo Nombre de María, was founded in June 1690. The two missions were located near the Neches River among the Nabedache Indians, the westernmost division of the Tejas or Asinai (Hasinai) Confederacy.[14]

The Tejas country was abandoned in October 1693 after the French threat appeared to subside, because of the vast distances from other Spanish settlements and the lack of support from the viceroy, Gaspár de la Cerda Sandoval Silva y Mendoza (1688–1696).

EAST AND CENTRAL TEXAS AND THE GULF COAST, 1715–1731

The settlement of the Texas province (east and central Texas and the Gulf Coast) continued over a period of thirty years from 1690 to 1721, a century after comparable efforts had been made by Juan de Oñate in Nuevo México. Although east Texas was initially settled in 1690 and then again in 1715, the province was not brought under Spanish control until 1721, when it was resettled for the third time and the settlements established in 1715 in central Texas and the Gulf Coast were reinforced.

Two important events in the early years of the eighteenth century led to the support needed to reestablish and maintain the missions in Texas. The first

13. For information on the establishment of the Provincia de Coahuila (Nueva Extremadura) in 1674, see H. E. Bolton, "The Spanish Occupation of Texas, 1519–1690," *Southwestern Historical Quarterly* 16, no. 1 (July 1912): 15–16; see also Barnes, Naylor, and Polzer, *Northern New Spain,* pp. 61, 102; for a summary of the Peñalosa schemes, see M. B. McCloskey, *The Formative Years of the Missionary College of Santa Cruz of Querétaro, 1683–1733,* pp. 62–63.

14. For information on the De León and Fr. Massanet fourth and fifth expeditions of 1689 and 1690, on the missionaries who accompanied Fr. Massanet on the fifth De León expedition, and on the abandonment of the missions, see Fr. Isidro Félix de Espinosa, *Crónica de los colegios de Propaganda Fide de la Nueva España,* pp. 671–682; for information on the 1689 and 1690 expeditions, see "Letter of Fray Damián Massanet," "Itinerary of the De León Expedition of 1689," and "Itinerary of the De León Expedition of 1690," in *Spanish Exploration in the Southwest, 1542–1706,* ed. Bolton, pp. 357–364, 388–423; see also Castañeda, *Our Catholic Heritage,* vol. 1, pp. 341–356; for the founding of San Francisco de los Tejas, see Bolton, *Spanish Exploration in the Southwest,* pp. 379–380, 417; for the founding of Santo Nombre de María, see Burke, *Missions of Old Texas,* pp. 67–68.

occurred in 1702, when Mission San Juan Bautista was established on the southern side of the Río Grande. The mission subsequently served as the base of operations for the reoccupation and continued support of the Texas settlements in the eighteenth century. The second event occurred in 1706, when the College of Nuestra Señora de Guadalupe was established in Zacatecas. The college served as the northernmost training center for the missionaries working in Texas.

One final event led to the reoccupation of Texas in 1715. Fr. Francisco Hidalgo, who had accompanied Fr. Damián Massanet to east Texas in 1690, had not forgotten the Indians formerly under his care. He had repeatedly tried but failed to get the attention of the Spanish authorities in his efforts to return to the east Texas missions. He then wrote to the French governor of Louisiana, hoping to get assistance for the east Texas Indians. The Spanish authorities finally took notice when they learned of Hidalgo's letter to the French authorities.

When the French governor received the first Hidalgo letter in May 1713, he immediately summoned Louis Juchereau de St. Denis and ordered him to establish a French presence in that region. St. Denis built the fort of Natchitoches on the Red River in late 1713 and spent the winter trading with the Indians. Not finding Hidalgo in east Texas, St. Denis set out for the Río Grande with three other Frenchmen and twenty-five Indians on June 1, 1714. They reached their destination on July 18, 1714, and found that Hidalgo had gone on to Querétaro. The presence of the Frenchmen at San Juan Bautista aroused the Spanish authorities, and the move to reoccupy Texas began shortly thereafter in Mexico City and its northern frontier outposts. St. Denis was sent to Mexico City, where he was imprisoned and later released when he convinced the authorities that he could accompany an expedition to east Texas to reoccupy the province.[15]

THE EAST TEXAS MISSIONS

Captain Domingo Ramón, accompanied by Fr. Isidro Félix de Espinosa of the College of Querétaro, went into east Texas in 1716 to reclaim the region for Spain following the appearance of St. Denis with other Frenchmen at San Juan Bautista. They founded six missions and erected a presidio in east Texas. The original plan was to build a presidio and four missions—three for the Querétaran missionaries and one for the Zacatecan missionaries. When the Spaniards saw the French settlements in the area they decided to build two more missions to strengthen their presence in the region. The presidio was named Nuestra Señora de los Dolores de los Tejas. The Querétaran missionaries refounded and relocated San Francisco de los Tejas on July 10, 1716, renaming it Nuestro Padre San Francisco de los Tejas. The other two missions were San José de los Nazonis, founded on the same day, and Nuestra Señora de la Purísima Concepción, founded on July 17, 1716. The Zacatecan missionaries founded the planned Nuestra Señora de Guadalupe de los Nacogdoches on July 9, 1716, and two other missions in 1717: Nuestra Señora de los Dolores de los Ais and San Miguel de Linares de los Adáes.

The war between France and Spain in 1719 led to the second abandonment of the missions and the presidio in east Texas. When French forces in Louisiana attacked the missions, the Spaniards fled to San Antonio.[16]

15. For the founding of San Juan Bautista, see R. S. Weddle, "San Juan Bautista: Mother of Texas Missions," *Southwestern Historical Quarterly* 71 (April 1968): 542–563; idem, *San Juan Bautista: Gateway to Spanish Texas;* and *Inventory of the Rio Grande Missions: 1772, San Juan Bautista and San Bernardo,* trans. and ed. F. D. Almaráz; Morfi, *History of Texas,* pp. 93–94; see Introduction, note 9, for information on the Apostolic College in Zacatecas; for information on the Hidalgo letter, see R. C. Clark, "Louis Juchereau de Saint-Denis and the Re-establishment of the Texas Missions," *Quarterly of the Texas State Historical Association* 6, no. 1 (July 1902): 8.

16. For information on the Ramón expedition to reoccupy the Texas province, see Fr. Isidro Félix de Espinosa, "Ramón Expedition: Espinosa's Diary of 1716," trans. G. Tous, *Mid-America* 12 (April 1930): 339–361; see ibid., p. 360, for the first Zacatecan mission founded on July 9, 1716, and the other two founded in 1717; the founding date for the last two is also given by Espinosa, *Crónica de los colegios de Propaganda Fide,* p. 724; for information on the war between Spain and France in 1719, see ibid., p. 739, n. 8; and also W. N. Hargreaves-Mawdsley, *Eighteenth-Century Spain, 1700–1788,* pp. 37–51.

Following the abandonment of the east Texas missions in 1719, efforts were made to reclaim the east Texas territory by refounding the missions and erecting presidios in the same region and to strengthen those settlements by occupying the Bay of Espíritu Santo (La Bahía). The Marqués de San Miguel de Aguayo, the governor of Texas, led an expedition to reoccupy the province in 1721. Fr. Antonio Margil de Jesús and Fr. Félix Isidro Espinosa accompanied Aguayo into east Texas, where they had served as missionaries in 1716. They reestablished the missions and erected new presidios. Some of the mission buildings were repaired and used for the new missions. Other missions were moved from their original locations, and some were given new names. San Francisco de los Tejas was renamed San Francisco de los Neches and founded at a new location on August 5, 1721. Refounded with the same names were Nuestra Señora de la Concepción on August 6, 1721, and San José de los Nazonis on August 13, 1721. The expedition led by Aguayo rebuilt the presidio of Nuestra Señora de los Dolores de los Tejas and erected a new one named Nuestra Señora del Pilar after August 23, 1721.[17]

The three Zacatecan missions in east Texas were refounded: Nuestra Señora de Guadalupe de los Nacogdoches on August 18, 1721; Nuestra Señora de los Dolores de los Ais, at a new site, on August 23, 1721; and San Miguel de los Adáes, renamed San Miguel de Cuéllar de los Adáes and relocated on August 29, 1721.

Within a few years the Querétaran missionaries petitioned Viceroy Juan de Acuña Marqués de Casa Fuerte (1722–1734) for permission to move their three east Texas missions, and viceregal sanction was received in October 1729. San Francisco de los Neches, Nuestra Señora de la Purísima Concepción, and San José de los Nazonis were temporarily refounded on the banks of the Colorado near present Austin. They were moved to the San Antonio River in 1731.

THE SAN ANTONIO MISSIONS

Following the reoccupation of east Texas by the Domingo Ramón expedition, plans were made to strengthen Spain's claim on the Texas province by founding a mission and erecting a presidio in San Antonio, occupying the Bay of Espíritu Santo, and erecting a presidio on the bay. Don Martín de Alarcón, interim governor of Coahuila, was given the authority to lead the new expedition to establish settlements in San Antonio and Espíritu Santo. He was accompanied by Fr. Antonio de San Buenaventura Olivares. Alarcón was also given the new position of governor of the Texas province on December 7, 1716.

The Alarcón expedition arrived in San Antonio on April 25, 1718, and founded the Mission of San Antonio de Valero and the Presidio of San Antonio de Béxar on May 1.

San José y San Miguel de Aguayo, the second mission founded in San Antonio, was the first founded by the Zacatecan missionaries at that site, in 1720. San José de Aguayo was moved twice to sites along the river before it was established at its present location. The Querétaran missionaries founded four other missions in San Antonio. San Francisco Xavier de Náxera was founded in 1722 but was soon abandoned. The missionaries had petitioned the viceroy on June 27, 1730, for permission to move three other missions from the Colorado River to the San Antonio River. The petition was granted, and the final

17. For information on the Aguayo expedition, see Eleanor Claire Buckley, "The Aguayo Expedition, 1719–1722," *Quarterly of the Texas State Historical Association* 15 (July 1911): 1–65.

move was made in 1731. "De Acuña" was added to the name of Nuestra Señora de la Purísima Concepción de Acuña to honor the viceroy, Don Juan de Acuña. San José de los Nazonis was renamed San Juan Capistrano on March 5, 1731, because there was already a San José mission in San Antonio. San Francisco de los Neches was renamed San Francisco de la Espada. When the San Francisco Xavier de Náxera mission was abandoned, the Indians were moved to the Valero mission, and the lands were added to Nuestra Señora de la Purísima Concepción.[18]

THE ESPÍRITU SANTO MISSION

The first Gulf Coast mission, named Nuestra Señora del Espíritu Santo de Zúñiga, was founded in 1722 by the Marqués de Aguayo and the Querétaran missionaries.

Captain Domingo Ramón, who had led the expedition to east Texas in 1716, was placed in charge of the Presidio Nuestra Señora de Loreto de La Bahía in 1722.[19] In the fall of 1723 a quarrel between the soldiers and the Indians caused his death and the flight of the Indians from the mission. The unjust treatment of the Indians in this incident led them to attack the Spanish settlement continually for the next twenty-five years.

The mission and the presidio were moved northwest to the Guadalupe River in 1726 because of the continuing problems with the Indians and the soldiers at the presidio. The presidio and the mission were moved one more time in 1749 to the San Antonio River near present Goliad.

CENTRAL TEXAS AND THE GULF COAST, 1747–1762

Continual raids by the Indians on Spanish settlements in central and west Texas throughout the decades starting in the 1730s led to the founding and erection of new missions and presidios to maintain and consolidate the frontier. The pacification of the Indians was coupled with the desire to Christianize them and ultimately to make them loyal and productive subjects of the Spanish Crown.

As the missions in San Antonio and the Gulf Coast region became firmly established, efforts were made starting in 1747 to establish new missions north of San Antonio in central Texas. The missionaries of the College of the Holy Cross of Querétaro sought to establish missions by the San Xavier (San Gabriel) River to save souls and to build a defense against the Apaches and against the French, in case of war.

THE SAN XAVIER MISSIONS

The viceroy authorized the founding of the San Xavier missions on December 23, 1747. Shortly after the authorization was received, Lieutenant Juan Galván was sent to the San Xavier area with thirty soldiers borrowed from the presidios of La Bahía and Los Adáes to assist in founding the missions. Fr. Mariano Francisco de los Dolores y Viana founded the three missions along the San Xavier River (near Rockdale, Texas): San Xavier de Horcasitas on May 7, 1748; San Ildefonso on February 25, 1749; and Nuestra Señora de la Candelaria on April 1749.

18. For a full discussion of the founding and history of San José de Aguayo, La Purísima Concepción, San Juan Capistrano, and San Francisco de la Espada, see Habig, *The Alamo Chain of Missions,* pp. 83–117, 119–154, 156–233; see also Don Martín de Alarcón, *Diary of the Alarcón Expedition into Texas, 1718–1719,* trans. F. Celiz and ed. F. L. Hoffman, p. 49.

19. For the Ramón-Espinosa expedition to reoccupy the Texas province, see Fr. Espinosa, "Ramón Expedition: Espinosa's Diary of 1716."

A presidio named San Francisco Xavier de Gigedo was erected in 1748 to protect the three San Xavier missions. It was located four and one-half miles north of the junction of Brushy Creek and the San Xavier River.

The intense rivalry between the missionaries and the military proved to be disastrous for the missionary effort in this region. Following the murder of Fr. Juan José Ganzábal and a settler in 1752, the Indians abandoned the San Xavier missions. (Felipe Rábago y Terán, captain of the presidio, was implicated in the murder.) Although the Indians were brought back to the missions in the winter of 1752–1753, the missions were finally abandoned on August 23, 1755, and moved shortly thereafter to the San Marcos River. The mission ornaments and sacred vessels were set aside for the planned mission on the San Saba River, and a formal decree issued on May 18, 1756, ordered the transfer of the presidio to that area.[20]

The properties of the San Xavier missions were delivered to Fr. Dolores on January 14, 1757, and turned over to Fr. Giraldo de Terreros for the San Sabá de la Santa Cruz mission.

THE GUADALUPE MISSION

Following the failure of the San Xavier missions and their move to the San Marcos before their final abandonment, Fr. Dolores y Viana proposed on January 25, 1756, to Fr. Francisco Xavier Ortiz that a mission be established on the Guadalupe River for the San Xavier Indians. The plan was approved on July 5, 1756. Nuestra Señora de Guadalupe was established shortly thereafter on the Guadalupe River (near present New Braunfels). By January 25, 1757, Fr. Francisco Aparicio and Fr. Miguel de Aranda were working with forty-one persons at the mission. They were ordered to abandon the mission for their own safety, shortly after the massacre and destruction of the mission on the San Saba River on March 16, 1758, less than a year after it was established.[21]

THE ROSARIO MISSION

A new mission, authorized by the viceroy in April 1755, was established on the lower San Antonio River, near Espíritu Santo, in November 1754. The mission, named Nuestra Señora del Rosario, was established as a result of a number of conflicts over a period of years between the soldiers and the Indians, between the missionaries of the two colleges of Querétaro (in San Antonio) and Zacatecas (in Espíritu Santo), and between Indian tribes in the region.[22]

The new mission was placed under the care of Fr. Juan Diós María Camberos. Shortly after the mission was founded, the region became part of the new territory called Colonia del Nuevo Santander (the state of Tamaulipas, Mexico), which stretched from Pánuco (Tampico) to the lower San Antonio River. Although the mission was within the northern limits of Nuevo Santander, it was administered as part of the Texas province. The Indians deserted the mission in 1781. By the end of the century it was abandoned because there were too few Indians to keep it in operation.

THE SAN SABÁ MISSION

Spanish experience with the Apache region began when the Spaniards sought to stop Apache raids on San Antonio by mounting punitive expeditions

20. Viceroy Juan Francisco de Güemes y Horcasitas (1746–1755) authorized the founding of the San Xavier missions; see H. E. Bolton, "The Founding of the Missions on the San Gabriel River, 1745–1749," *Southwestern Historical Quarterly* 17, no. 4 (April 1914): 365, 373, 375; for information on the San Xavier missions, see Morfi, *History of Texas,* pp. 300–346; for information on the martyrdom of Fr. Ganzábal, see H. E. Bolton, *Texas in the Middle Eighteenth Century,* pp. 260–262; see also Castañeda, *Our Catholic Heritage,* vol. 3, pp. 329–333.

21. Bolton, *Texas in the Middle Eighteenth Century,* pp. 273–278.

22. Viceroy Güemes y Horcasitas (1746–1755) authorized the founding of Nuestra Señora del Rosario. In 1750 missionaries from San Antonio attempted to take Karankawa Indians from the Gulf Coast region to their missions in San Antonio. The ensuing conflict with the missionaries from the Gulf Coast region caused concern in Mexico City. By the end of 1753 the conflicts between the Karankawas and the inland tribes of the Tamique and Xaraname Indians led the Espíritu Santo missionaries to propose that one of the east Texas missions be transferred to the Gulf Coast to solve the problem. When this failed, they proposed that a new mission be established for the Cojane Indians (Bolton, *Texas in the Middle Eighteenth Century,* pp. 301–315).

against them in the 1730s. Continued Apache raids on San Antonio in the following years led Fr. Benito Fernández de Santa Ana, president of the San Antonio missions, to suggest the founding of missions rather than punitive expeditions as a solution to the problem. He presented his case in a petition to the viceroy in 1743 calling for the founding and erection of missions and a presidio on the San Saba River. In his view, a presidio in Apache country would relieve the one in San Antonio from continual threats by the Apaches, the mineral deposits in the region could also be mined, and souls could be saved.

By 1749 relations between the Spaniards and the Apaches had greatly improved, and serious thought was given to the San Sabá proposal for a Spanish settlement in Apache country. In 1753 and again in 1754 expeditions were undertaken to look for a suitable site. On May 18, 1756, the viceroy issued a decree authorizing the establishment of a presidio at San Sabá. Funding for the presidio would be provided by the royal treasury. Colonel Diego Ortiz Parrilla, commander of the San Xavier Presidio, was to serve as the commander of the new presidio. He was ordered to move the garrison to the San Saba River region.

The mission project was funded in July 1756 by Don Pedro Romero de Terreros, a wealthy mine owner from Pachuca (central New Spain). He was convinced of the need for the missions by his cousin, Fr. Alonso Giraldo de Terreros. Romero de Terreros committed himself and his heirs to the founding of the missions for the Apaches for a period of three years and further stipulated that Fr. Terreros be placed in charge of the mission enterprise at San Sabá. Formal approval of the Terreros and San Sabá plans was given by the viceroy on August 20, 1756.

San Sabá de la Santa Cruz was founded in 1757 by Fr. Giraldo de Terreros. The Presidio of San Luis de las Amarillas was erected to protect the missionaries. The second mission, planned for Fr. José Santiesteban and Fr. Juan Andrés from the College of San Fernando de México, was not built, because Indians failed to congregate at the site.

The entire enterprise was doomed when the Comanches, the Tejas, and their allies saw the San Sabá mission and the presidio as evidence of an alliance between the Spaniards and their old enemies, the Apaches. After some problems that began on February 25, 1758, the stockade was attacked by two thousand Indians on March 16. They included Comanches, Tejas, Bedias, and Tonkawas, all enemies of the Apaches. By the morning of March 17 the presidio and the mission had been destroyed.

A punitive campaign against the Comanches and their allies was authorized by the viceroy on June 27, 1758, and finally organized and carried out the following year. The Spanish forces moved north and on October 6, 1759, fought a four-hour battle with Indians from some Toavaya villages on the Red River. They suffered casualties and retreated back to San Sabá. This proved to be the end of the northward movement by the Spaniards.

The San Sabá presidio continued to operate until June 1768, when its commander, Felipe Rábago y Terán (who had replaced Parrilla in 1761), abandoned it without authorization.[23]

THE ORCOQUISAC MISSION

Before the final pullback from the San Sabá region, the Spaniards had continually moved beyond their frontiers to ward off threats by outside forces. The San

23. For information on the expeditions related to the founding of the San Sabá mission and presidio, see R. S. Weddle, *The San Sabá Mission: Spanish Pivot in Texas,* pp. 40–65; see also Morfi, *History of Texas,* pp. 353–406; ibid., pp. 371–372, for the authorization of the presidio at San Sabá by Viceroy Agustín de Ahumada y Villalón (1755–1758); for information on the punitive campaign authorized by Viceroy Francisco Cajigal de la Vega (1758–1760), see Weddle, *The San Sabá Mission,* pp. 102–133.

Sabá enterprise was designed to resolve the Apache problem. The missions established in east Texas, first in 1690 and later in 1716, were intended to counter French incursions into territories claimed by the Spaniards. Fear of French encroachment along the Gulf Coast reappeared when Joseph Blancpain, a French trader, was arrested by Spanish soldiers near the mouth of the Trinity River on October 10, 1754. The soldiers were under the command of Lieutenant Marcos Ruiz from La Bahía Presidio.

To ward off French influence in the area, Governor Jacinto Barrios y Jáuregui (1751–1759) recommended that a presidio, a mission, and a civil settlement be established for the Orcoquiza and Bidai Indians on the Gulf Coast near the mouth of the Trinity River. The Spanish settlement was authorized on February 12, 1756. The mission and presidio were intended to affirm Spanish authority in that section of the country known as El Orcoquisac.

The presidio, named in honor of the viceroy, was erected in midsummer 1756, with soldiers recruited mainly at Los Adáes. Domingo del Río was made lieutenant in command. Governor Barrios y Jáuregui, aided by Fr. Anastasio de Jesús Romero of Mission Los Ais, founded the mission of Nuestra Señora de la Luz del Orcoquisac in 1756 or 1757.[24]

THE MISSIONS OF EL CAÑÓN

The missions and presidios built along the San Saba, San Xavier, and Trinity Rivers were intended to ward off internal and external threats to the safety of the Spanish settlers, extend the northern borders of New Spain, find and exploit new sources of wealth, and civilize and Christianize the Indians. These goals were often thwarted by the intractability of the Indians, the failure of the friars and soldiers to work together, and the problems caused by the vast distances between settlements. These problems were made even more difficult, if not impossible, to resolve when the people involved were irresponsible in carrying out their assigned duties.

The wrong person at the wrong place seems like a fitting description of Felipe Rábago y Terán, who served as commander of the San Xavier and San Sabá presidios. The failure of the San Xavier missions can be partly attributed to him, since he was implicated in the murder of Fr. Ganzábal and a settler in 1752. The Indians abandoned the missions shortly thereafter. He was later exonerated of the charge of murder and sent as a replacement for Parrilla as commander of the San Sabá presidio in 1761. He proved to be the wrong choice. Instead of maintaining his position at San Sabá, he repeatedly tried to abandon the presidio because of the continuing problems with the Indians. Although he was ordered to extend his presence northward from his post, he chose instead to found missions for the Apaches south of the presidio near the Río Grande. He moved south toward El Cañón, southwest of San Antonio, to establish missions without the authorization of the viceroy.

Two missions were established in early 1762 by Rábago y Terán and Fr. Diego Jiménez, president of the missions of the Río Grande: San Lorenzo de la Santa Cruz del Cañón and Nuestra Señora de la Purísima Concepción Candelaria del Cañón. The missions were too far from San Sabá to be protected by the presidio, and the lack of viceregal support led to their abandonment within a few years. La Candelaria was abandoned in 1766 and San Lorenzo in 1769.[25]

24. Bolton, *Texas in the Eighteenth Century*, pp. 337–339; the presidio was named in honor of Viceroy Agustín de Ahumada y Villalón.

25. Weddle, *The San Sabá Mission*, pp. 147–180.

EAST TEXAS AND THE GULF COAST, 1762–1794

As the missions and presidios in San Antonio and Espíritu Santo became firmly established and their settlements grew and prospered, the international situation in Europe and the Americas again intervened to bring one more change to the Texas province. The Seven Years' War (1756–1763) between England and France had its repercussions in Texas. Spain, as an ally of France against England, received title to the western part of the Louisiana territory on November 3, 1762, because France feared losing it to England. Even though the transfer of Louisiana was not scheduled to be implemented for another seven years, it had the effect of making Texas an internal province. This put an end to the strategic importance of the east Texas missions and presidios, which had been designed to counter the French presence in the area.

The entire mission enterprise in Texas was curtailed further when the Spanish Crown sought to cut back on expenditures that were not providing a sufficient return for the investment. A final inspection tour of the northeastern frontier missions and presidios was authorized to see how they could be made more efficient. The expedition led by Cayetano María Pignatelli Rubí Clement, Marqués de Rubí, left Mexico in March 1766 and arrived in Texas in August 1767. He submitted his report following his inspection of the missions and presidios.

Rubí's recommendations and plan of reorganization were adopted by a decree issued by the king on September 1772 known as the "New Regulation of Presidios" pertaining to the frontiers of New Spain. It called for the removal of the San Sabá presidio to the Río Grande to be in line with the other presidios protecting the province, Arroyo del Cíbolo to be garrisoned as an outpost between La Bahía and San Antonio, the San Antonio presidio to be increased from twenty-three to eighty men, and the presidios of Los Adáes and Orcoquisac with their missions to be suppressed and the settlers in the region moved to San Antonio. The capital of the Texas province was to be moved from Los Adáes to San Antonio.

Juan María de Ripperdá, the governor of Texas (1770–1778), received the instructions to implement the "New Regulation of Presidios" in May 1773, but by that time many of the instructions were obsolete because the settlements at San Sabá, El Cañón, and El Orcoquisac had been abandoned. The San Sabá garrison was moved in 1768 to El Cañón and then in 1771 to San Fernando de Austria, a settlement south of the Río Grande. Governor Ripperdá erected the Santa Cruz fort at Arroyo del Cíbolo in 1771 to protect the settlers in the region. The Presidio San Agustín de Ahumada was abandoned in 1771. La Luz del Orcoquisac was abandoned in 1771 because of the unhealthy conditions at the site. That left only the settlements at Nacogdoches, Los Ais, and Los Adáes in east Texas. Nuestra Señora de Guadalupe de los Nacogdoches was suppressed in 1772 and Nuestra Señora de los Dolores de los Ais in 1773. San Miguel de Cuéllar de los Adáes was abandoned in 1773. The settlers left Los Adáes and reached San Antonio two months later on September 26, 1774. Two presidios and four missions were abandoned, and the settlers moved to San Antonio, the new capital of Texas.[26]

26. For the turnover of the Louisiana territory to Spain by France, see Bolton, *Texas in the Eighteenth Century,* p. 102; for information on the Rubí expedition, see L. Kinnaird, *The Frontiers of New Spain: Nicolas de Lafora's Description, 1766–1768,* pp. 7, 29–32; see also Morfi, *History of Texas,* pp. 415–440.

THE MISSIONS AFTER 1772

Following the expulsion of the Jesuits from the Americas by the king, the missions in Pimería Alta (the Mexican state of Sonora and southern Arizona) were turned over to the Franciscans from the College of the Holy Cross in Querétaro. This forced the Querétarans to pull back from the mission field in Texas in order to fulfill their new responsibilities. They therefore requested and were granted permission to leave their missions in Texas. In 1772 the missions were turned over to the Zacatecan missionaries, who administered them for the remainder of their stay in Texas.[27]

THE REFUGIO MISSION AND THE MISSIONS AFTER 1793

A final mission, named Nuestra Señora del Refugio, was founded in 1793 by Fr. José Francisco Mariano de la Garza and Fr. Manuel Julio de Silva for the Indians who had wandered away from the other missions in the Gulf Area. It was located near the junction of the Guadalupe and San Antonio Rivers, on present Gulf Bayou in Calhoun County, and was moved in 1794 to a healthier location (near present Refugio, Texas).

The final changes for the missions came after San Antonio de Valero was secularized in 1793. The remaining missions were ordered secularized on July 14, 1794. The missionaries in Texas were to be replaced by secular clergy. La Espada and Espíritu Santo were secularized in 1794. San José de Aguayo, Concepción, and Capistrano were partially secularized. Some of the lands of Concepción were parceled out to the remaining Indians. Capistrano became a *visita* or submission of La Espada, even though La Espada was secularized in 1794; the mission property was divided among the Indians, and each family was given a land grant. The Indians still at the mission continued to receive some attention from missionaries in the following years. The remaining missions were totally secularized in 1824 (following Mexican independence in 1821). El Refugio was secularized in 1828 or 1829, El Rosario in 1831.[28]

27. The Jesuits were expelled during the reign of King Charles III (1759–1788). For information on the events leading up to the expulsion, see Hargreaves-Mawdsley, *Eighteenth-Century Spain,* pp. 116–117; for the impact in Texas, see Bolton, *Texas in the Eighteenth Century,* pp. 108–109; for the transfer of the Querétaran missions to the Zacatecan missionaries in San Antonio, see Castañeda, *Our Catholic Heritage,* vol. 4, pp. 259–272.

28. For the founding of El Refugio Mission, see Bolton, *Texas in the Middle Eighteenth Century,* p. 73; see also W. E. Dunn, "The Founding of Nuestra Señora del Refugio, the Last Spanish Mission in Texas," *Southwestern Historical Quarterly* 25 (1921–1922): 178–182; for information on the secularization of the missions, see Introduction, n. 1.

2

The Conversion of Texas

Missionaries, Soldiers, and Indians, 1740–1824

The missions established by the Franciscan missionaries on the northern frontiers of New Spain were intended to bring the gospel to the Indians and to make them useful subjects of the Spanish Crown. But they were also part of the Crown's multilevel policy of exploring, settling, and consolidating the ever-expanding frontiers of the Spanish holdings in the Americas (see Appendix 1 for a census of the missions).

The missionaries were primarily interested in saving souls as well as teaching the Indians useful trades with the ultimate aim of making them spiritually and economically self-sufficient. The soldiers were charged with making the mission areas safe militarily. Unfortunately, the two goals were often in conflict. The soldiers charged the missionaries with reckless behavior when they went into uncharted areas without adequate protection to seek out converts. They seemed to court disaster by this behavior. The missionaries charged the soldiers with abusing the missionary Indians. These internal conflicts led to the abandonment of some of the missions (such as the San Xavier missions) and to the ultimate failure of others (such as San Sabá).

THE COLONIAL DOCUMENTS, 1740–1824

The documents—memorials, letters, diaries, reports (*informes*), and inventories—written by the missionaries between 1740 and 1824 provide information on the art and architecture of the missions.[1] They also include facts about the location and geographical area surrounding the missions, the Indians for whom they were established, and, most importantly, the many aspects of the missions that relate to their religious, economic, social, and political functions (see Appendix 2).

Reports, memorials, and inventories served to ensure that the functions of the missions were being carried out successfully on a given schedule. They were part of the monitoring function carried out by the administrative centers at the Apostolic Colleges of the Holy Cross in Querétaro and Our Lady of Guadalupe in Zacatecas. Memorials and some reports provide assessments of the conversion effort and recommendations aimed at making those efforts more effective. Other reports and inventories include information on all the holdings needed to carry out the many functions of the missions. These docu-

1. According to Barnes, Naylor, and Polzer, *Northern New Spain,* a *memorial* is an "[a]dvisement, usually written, of some event or events which have already taken place"; an *informe* is a "[g]eneral title for a variety of documents, most of which carried information as opposed to orders or laws" (pp. 136, 135).

ments were part of the administrative process that made the entire missionary enterprise possible.

The information contained in the documents can be broken down into three main categories. First, the letters and reports relate to the Indians and the missionaries' efforts to convert them to Christianity. They usually contain information on the names of the Indian groups (inside and outside the missions), the languages they spoke, the lands they inhabited, their nature as evidenced by their behavior, and in some cases their social, economic, and political organization prior to their experience at the missions. The other two categories, contained primarily in inventories, revolve around the physical plant and the religious, economic, and other functions of the mission.

The material in this chapter is based on reports written between 1740 and 1824. The missions are discussed in chronological order according to the apostolic colleges under which the missions were administered. Each chronological unit includes the prefatory portions of the reports, which contain background information focusing on the history and geography of the Texas province followed by information on the Indians and missionaries and the status of the conversion effort.

THE QUERÉTARAN MISSIONS, 1740–1762

The Querétaran missionaries founded and abandoned missions in east Texas several times, first from 1690 to 1693 and again from 1716 to 1719. The missions were moved from east Texas in 1729 to the area around present Austin and in 1731 to San Antonio, where they were refounded (some with different names). The missions refounded in San Antonio are Nuestra Señora de la Purísima Concepción de Acuña, San Juan Capistrano, and San Francisco de la Espada. The first Querétaran mission in San Antonio, San Antonio de Valero, was founded in 1718.

The other Querétaran missions were founded near the Gulf Coast and along the San Xavier, Guadalupe, and San Saba Rivers. Nuestra Señora del Espíritu Santo de la Bahía, founded in 1722, was moved in 1726 and again in 1749, to its final location near present Goliad. The San Xavier missions—San Xavier de Horcasitas, founded in 1748, and San Ildefonso and Nuestra Señora de la Candelaria, founded in 1749—were abandoned in 1757. Nuestra Señora de Guadalupe, founded in 1756, and San Sabá de la Santa Cruz, founded in 1757, were abandoned in 1758 following the disaster at San Sabá.

THE REPORTS

The letter/report prepared by Fr. Benito Fernández de Santa Ana (1740) contains information on the presidio, the five missions along the San Antonio River, the Indians, the lands and rivers of Texas, and the regions beyond the province.[2]

The Fr. Dolores y Viana Report (1762) provides information on the four Querétaran missions in San Antonio, the Indians, and the status of the conversion effort (the conditions of each mission in relation to its religious and economic functions).[3] It begins with San Antonio de Valero and continues with La Purísima Concepción, San Francisco de la Espada, and San Juan Capistrano. Fr. Dolores y Viana referred briefly in the first part of the report to the

2. Fr. Benito Fernández de Santa Ana, "Descripción de las misiones del colegio de la Santa Cruz en el río de San Antonio," in *The San José Papers, Part I,* trans. B. Leutenegger, pp. 51–73.

3. "Report of Fr. Dolores," in Fr. Mariano de los Dolores y Viana, *Letters and Memorials of Fray Mariano de los Dolores y Viana, 1737–1762,* trans. Fr. B. Leutenegger, intro. and notes by Fr. M. A. Habig, pp. 327–363.

unsuccessful missions on the San Xavier, San Marcos, Guadalupe, and San Saba Rivers as well as the four Zacatecan missions in east Texas and the two near La Bahía.

MISSIONS, LANDS, AND RIVERS

Fr. Fernández (1740) included the five San Antonio missions in his report even though one of them, San José de Aguayo, was under the jurisdiction of the Zacatecan missionaries. He gave the location of the presidio, the Villa de San Fernando, and each mission in relation to the San Antonio River and the distances between them in leagues (equal to 2.597 statute miles). He also identified the territories beyond San Antonio and the direction in which they were found: Nuevo León (south and southwest), Nuevo México (northwest), Quivira (north), Louisiana (northeast), the Asinais or Texas Indians (northeast and east), New Orleans, Pansacola (Pensacola), Apalache, and Florida (east), and La Bahía del Espíritu Santo and the Gulf of Mexico (southeast). Fr. Fernández noted that the French blocked access to "Panzacola" (Pensacola) and Florida. In another part of the report he referred to the French near the northern limits of the province near the presidio of the Adáys (Adáes). He described the rivers of Texas from the Río Grande del Norte to the Trinity and noted the geographical limits of the province from southwest to northeast.

Fr. Dolores y Viana (1762) also provided information on the location and distances between the San Antonio missions and identified the provinces near Texas—Coahuila (southwest and west), Sonora (northwest and west), and the "savage" Indian nations (north).

INDIANS AND MISSIONARIES

Fr. Fernández discussed the nature of the San Antonio mission Indians and the difficulties encountered in converting them to Christianity. He considered those problems minor when he saw "how steadfast and firm the Indians [were] in the Faith once the vacillations of the initial years [were] over." In more temporal matters the Indians could learn anything, given their great potential, once they reached the "use of reason." Fr. Fernández noted that the Joyuanes (Yohuanes) and Tancames (Tancagues or Tonkawans), who resided near the Texas and the Asinai Indians in east Texas, could not be brought to the missions.

Although the Indians spoke many languages, Fr. Fernández found four common ones, which he distinguished according to their pronunciation. The first was "prolific and lovely," the second very clear, and the last two difficult to pronounce. In spite of these difficulties, they could all be written if care was taken "to pronounce the alphabet the way the Italians do." All the Indians used a universal sign language.

Fr. Fernández finished his report by discussing a recent campaign against the Indians, which he considered ill-timed and a failure because the citizens who joined the soldiers did so only for profit: "Just as the goal is so base, so is the outcome." (This was the unsuccessful military campaign led by Captain Joseph de Urrutia of the Presidio San Antonio de Béxar against the Apaches in 1739.)[4]

4. Fr. Fernández, "Descripción de las misiones," pp. 51–73 (quotation on p. 57); Castañeda, *Our Catholic Heritage in Texas,* vol. 3, p. 47.

THE CONVERSION EFFORT

Fr. Fernández referred to the flat lands north, southeast, and west of the Texas province where there were many Indians hostile to the Spaniards, "because many were among the insurrectionists in New Mexico, and this [was] a great obstacle to their conversion." In his view, this would change once a mission was established for them using their own language. (These turned out to be the ill-fated missions along the San Xavier River, authorized in 1748.)[5]

Fr. Dolores y Viana reiterated what so many of his predecessors had said in urging the conversion of the Indians. Aside from saving souls, it would also keep the English and French from coming into the region. He warned that if the other European colonies in the Americas were not checked they would expand further. A more immediate problem was posed by the French in east Texas, whose only interest was in trading with the Indians; in so doing they were making it difficult for the missionaries to carry out their work.

The last part of the report prepared by Fr. Dolores y Viana includes a discussion of the conversion efforts and the reasons for the setbacks and failures, including the diversity of languages spoken by the Indians and the lack of "words of knowledge and even about things and almost no terms to express spiritual and eternal realities."[6] The missionaries therefore made every effort to teach the Indians the Spanish language. Another problem was the decline of the Indian populations at the missions due to the fatal illnesses they contracted because they failed to take proper precautions against disease and the elements. They did not take medications or follow a proper diet. Another problem was caused by the different aims of the military, soldiers, and civilians and the missionaries. Finally, there were not enough soldiers at the missions to protect the missionaries and the Indians.

THE ZACATECAN MISSIONS, 1749–1768

The Zacatecan missionaries founded Guadalupe de los Nacogdoches, San Miguel de los Adáes, and Dolores de los Ais (Ainais) in east Texas in 1717, San José de Aguayo in San Antonio in 1720, and Espíritu Santo on the Gulf Coast in 1722. The east Texas missions were refounded in 1721–1722 after their abandonment in 1719, some with new names and new sites. San Miguel de los Adáes became San Miguel de Cuéllar de los Adáes. Dolores de los Ais was refounded on a new site. San José de Aguayo was moved several times to sites along the San Antonio River, and Espíritu Santo was moved from its original location on the bay to a site further inland in 1726 and to a third site along the lower San Antonio River in 1749. El Rosario was founded in 1754 and La Luz del Orcoquisac in 1756. Other missions such as Guadalupe de los Nacogdoches remained the same. El Refugio, founded in 1793, is discussed in the final part of this chapter.

THE REPORTS

The main focus of the Fr. Ignacio Antonio Ciprián report (1749) is on the progress made by the Zacatecan missionaries in propagating the faith among the Indians. He provided information on the history of each mission, the Indians for whom the missions were founded, the buildings and other hold-

5. Fr. Fernández, "Descripción de las misiones," pp. 51–73 (quotation on p. 63); H. E. Bolton, "The Founding of the Missions on the San Gabriel River, 1745–1749."

6. "Report of Fr. Dolores," p. 343.

ings needed for their religious and economic functions, and the status of the missionary effort. The missions included in the report are San José de Aguayo, Espíritu Santo, and the east Texas missions of Guadalupe, Dolores de los Ays (Ais), and San Miguel de los Adáys (Adáes).

For example, Fr. Ciprián listed the number of Indians at San José de Aguayo, described the church, the Indian houses, and the *convento,* and included the size of the herds of cattle, the number of sheep, and the corn yield. He considered the mission "the most outstanding in temporal and spiritual gains." Fr. Ciprián also provided a census of the Indians at Espíritu Santo, discussed the success of their religious training, and noted the construction of "the needed living quarters and the granaries."[7]

The Fr. Simón Hierro Report (1762) provides information on the seven Zacatecan missions (in San Antonio, Espíritu Santo, and east Texas), the Indians, and the status of the conversion effort. The missions included are San José de Aguayo, Espíritu Santo, El Rosario, La Luz del Orcoquisac, Guadalupe de los Nacogdoches, Dolores de los Ais, and San Miguel de los Adáes.

Fr. Hierro's original text has been lost. Only a summary of the report is available in H. E. Bolton's *Texas in the Middle Eighteenth Century.* For San José de Aguayo, Fr. Hierro discussed the number of Indians at the mission, the church, the cemetery chapel, the *convento,* the Indian houses, the number of cattle, the corn crop, the cotton yield, and the textile workshop. He listed the number of Indians at Espíritu Santo and described the church, the *convento,* the cultivated fields, and the pasture lands, but said nothing about the workshops. He commented briefly on the other five Zacatecan missions.[8]

The Fr. Gaspar José de Solís Diary (1767–1768) provides information on the seven Zacatecan missions in Texas and the different Indian tribes in the province.[9] Fr. Solís left Zacatecas on November 20, 1767, and arrived on the banks of the Río Grande on February 13, 1768. He inspected the missions of La Bahía (El Rosario and Espíritu Santo), San Antonio (San José de Aguayo), and east Texas (San Miguel de los Adáes, Dolores de los Ais, and Guadalupe de los Nacogdoches) from February 29 to June 6, 1768, and was back in Zacatecas by October 13, 1768.

HISTORICAL BACKGROUND AND GEOGRAPHY

Fr. Ciprián included a brief historical background of the missionary effort in his report. His narrative begins with the founding of the college in Zacatecas and continues with the early missionary efforts in east Texas in 1715, the founding of missions in 1716 and 1717, their abandonment in 1719, their reestablishment in 1721, the founding of San José de Aguayo on the San Antonio River in 1720, and the founding of Espíritu Santo on the lower San Antonio River in the same year (actually founded in 1722).

Fr. Solís discussed the land and the rivers he traveled along (the Río Grande, Nueces, San Antonio, Salado, Guadalupe, Colorado, Brazos, Navasoto/a, Trinity, Angelina, and Neches) on his long inspection tour of the Zacatecan missions, describing the flora and fauna in great detail. He noted that the weather was "extremely cold in the winter" in east Texas and that in "the summertime the heat is intense and rains are abundant." A noteworthy passage from his diary for April 10, 1768, provides a vivid description of the land east of San Antonio on the way to Espíritu Santo:

7. "Report of Fr. Ignacio Ciprián," in *The Texas Missions of the College of Zacatecas in 1749–1759,* trans. Fr. B. Leutenegger, intro. and notes by Fr. M. A. Habig, p. 21.

8. "The Fr. Guardian Simón Hierro Report," in Bolton, *Texas in the Middle Eighteenth Century,* pp. 99–101.

9. Fr. Gaspar José de Solís, "Diary of a Visit of Inspection of the Texas Missions Made by Fray Gaspar José de Solís in the Year 1767–68," trans. M. Kenney Kress, intro. M. Austin Hatcher, *Southwestern Historical Quarterly* 35 (July 1931): 30–76.

The road was through plains very pleasant and flowery, dotted with many and varied flowers, yellow, red, purple, blue, white, yellow, tinted, in short the fields and plains seem to be carpeted with flowers and throughout the hills and plains are found simarron, hemp and wild marjoram, and through some parts *cejas de monte,* pin oaks, post oaks, walnut trees, ash trees and many others.[10]

INDIANS AND MISSIONARIES

According to Fr. Ciprián, the Indians of Espíritu Santo "were unbearable in their ways and most troublesome." Difficulties continued with the Indians at the second location of the mission, further inland. For ten years, their sustenance was provided by the lone missionary from his own allowance.

Fr. Ciprián listed the number of Indians at Nuestra Señora de Guadalupe and discussed their social customs: "more than a third have two or three wives. Many unmarried women live as spouses. There are many children because of their laxity." In his view, the east Texas Indians were "difficult to manage because they [were] tricky and would resort to violence should they feel pressure, which they could not escape or overcome." If that happened, they would join the French, who were located nearby.

Fr. Solís discussed the shortcomings of the Indians of El Rosario at some length. "They are all barbarians, given to idleness, lazy, and indolent." He considered the Indians of Espíritu Santo more civilized and cleaner. "But they have the same customs, inclinations and vices as those of the Mission of Rosario and of the rest of the Province of Texas."

Fr. Solís was even more critical of the east Texas Indians. He described the Tejas Indians as "great thieves and drunkards because whiskey and wine are furnished to them by the French of Nachitos with whom they have commerce." He considered the Indians of Dolores de los Ays (Ainais)

the worst of this Province: drunkards, thieves, given to *mitotes* and dances, and to all kinds of vice principally that of licentiousness. They are idle, overly audacious, shameless.[11]

THE CONVERSION EFFORT

Fr. Ciprián described the Indians of San José de Aguayo as "well trained and . . . good Christians." He noted that Espíritu Santo was abandoned in 1726 when the Indians fled the mission. The missionaries had difficulties with the Indians ("unbearable in their ways") and problems in getting supplies from the Río Grande and San Antonio missions. Efforts were made to draw water from the river for the crops, but the plan to construct an irrigation system was finally abandoned in 1736; planting was thereafter done during the rainy season. Beginning in 1747, plentiful crops made Espíritu Santo a successful mission. The mission was moved one more time in 1749 by order of Viceroy Juan Francisco de Güemes y Horcasitas (1746–1755).

Fr. Ciprián discussed the east Texas missions and the reasons for the failure of the conversion effort. "The effort of 28 years without results would have been intolerable and could have discouraged the most ardent zeal." Nonetheless, the missionaries continued their efforts to bring "the light of the Gospel" to the Indians.

10. Ibid., p. 53.
11. "Report of Fr. Ciprián," p. 25; Fr. Solís, "Diary," p. 67.

Nuestra Señora de Guadalupe had only one missionary (this may have been Fr. José de Calahorra y Sáenz, who served at the mission from before 1746 to 1768). His assistant was transferred to La Bahía (Espíritu Santo) because there was a need for a friar at that mission. Matters were made worse when the three Querétaran missions in east Texas were abandoned in 1730. The missionary at the Guadalupe mission had to minister to the needs of the Indians of Concepción, San Francisco de los Tejas, and San José de los Nazonis.

According to Fr. Ciprián, the Indians abandoned the Guadalupe mission when their crops were damaged by the Vidays (Bidai) Indians. The missionary continued to visit their settlement but found that the Indians feared baptism because they believed that "the water of baptism [killed] them." He encountered similar problems at Nuestra Señora de los Dolores de los Ais and San Miguel de los Adáys (Adáes). The situation at San Miguel differed to the extent that it was close to the presidio (Nuestra Señora del Pilar de los Adáes).

Finally, Fr. Ciprián considered the failure to convert the Indians at San Miguel de los Adáys (Adáes) and the other two east Texas missions the result of several factors. The Indians were not dependent on the friars because they planted their own "crops and [reaped] abundantly"; they did not feel the restraint of military force because they were "ten times more numerous" than the Spaniards; and it was hard to manage them because they were "tricky" and sometimes resorted to violence.

Fr. Hierro noted the "little progress" made at El Rosario and La Luz del Orcoquisac and the failure of the east Texas missions (Guadalupe, Dolores, and San Miguel).

Fr. Solís listed four primary reasons the friars found it difficult, if not impossible, to Christianize the Indians of El Rosario. "One reason [had to do with] their natural inconstancy and tendency to escape from subjection and from work." A second reason was their "repugnance and aversion to everything connected with Our Holy Faith," and a third was their "cowardly fear and wickedness which is natural to them." The final reason was "the neglect of the military chiefs in congregating them and gathering them together and not punishing those who [ran] away or following them or searching for them in order to bring them back."

Fr. Solís found many things to commend at San José Mission. In referring to the work carried out at the mission (in the workshops, including carpentry, iron, and tailoring, and in the quarry), he noted that the Indians were "industrious workers and very skillful in everything." Among other things, they served as "mule-drivers, stone-masons, cow-herders, shepherds and in short [did] everything" at the mission. They were also "very well trained in civilized customs and christianity." He was impressed with their Spanish-language ability, "except those who came from the forest when grown and who have remained untamed and wild." They played musical instruments and sang well.[12]

Fr. Solís found that there was no Indian congregation at Nacogdoches because the Indians did "not wish to congregate, and [went] to the presidio rather than to the mission." He noted that there were no Indians at San Miguel, and those remaining at Dolores de los Ays (Ainais) were "the worst of this province." He had "no hope, not even a remote one, of [the] reduction and congregation" of the Dolores Indians. He was also deeply concerned

12. "Report of Fr. Ciprián," pp. 22, 24, 25, 27; "The Fr. Guardian Simón Hierro Report," p. 100; Fr. Solís, "Diary," pp. 44, 51–52, 65, 67–69.

"that there [was] imminent and almost certain danger to the life of the ministers among these pagans." However, he considered the Indians of Guadalupe "gentle, jovial, except now and then some [were] bad and perverse."

THE TRANSFER OF MISSIONS, 1778–1785

The expulsion of the Jesuits in 1767 from all the colonies of Spain led to the change in administration of the Texas missions.[13] When the Franciscans were asked to take over the missions founded by the Jesuits in Sonora and Arizona, the Querétaran missionaries requested permission to leave Texas so they could serve at the newly assigned missions. They were not ready to have the missions turned over to the secular authorities. Their request to have the Querétaran missions in Texas turned over to the Zacatecan missionaries was granted by the viceroy on July 28, 1772.

The transfer was carried out with the assistance of Juan María Barón de Ripperdá, governor and general commander of Texas, Fr. Pedro Ramírez de Arellano, president of the Zacatecan missions, and Fr. Juan José Sáenz de Gumiel, president of the Querétaran missions. The inventories were turned over to Governor Ripperdá and Fr. Ramírez in December 1772. Fr. Buenaventura Antonio Ruiz de Esparza, guardian of the College of Zacatecas, accepted them in March 1773.

THE REPORTS

According to Fr. Morfi's diary, the expedition left Mexico City on August 4, 1777, arrived at the Presidio del Río Grande on December 21, and reached the Medina River and La Espada on December 31, 1777.[14] He stayed two weeks in San Antonio then left the area on January 14, 1778, arriving at the Nueces River on January 18 and the Río Grande on January 21, 1778.

In his book *History of Texas,* Fr. Morfi discussed the art and architecture of the San Antonio missions, their furnishings, the workshops, farms, pasturelands, and animals, and the Indian groups for whom they were founded. The text begins with the Villa of San Fernando and continues with the missions of San Antonio de Valero, La Purísima Concepción, San José de Aguayo, San Juan Capistrano, and La Espada. The text on El Rosario, Espíritu Santo, and the Presidio de la Bahía, on the lower San Antonio River, is based on the Solís report, which Fr. Morfi had available for study and reference.[15]

Fr. Morfi devoted an entire chapter to the Indians of Texas and paid particular attention to the temporal and spiritual progress at each of the missions discussed in his book. He provided information on the Indian population, the status of the conversion effort, the economic state of the missions, and the names of the tribes for whom they were founded. Fr. Morfi had high praise for Fr. Pedro Ramírez de Arellano, who was in charge of San José de Aguayo, for his "dedication, zeal, and religious spirit."[16]

The Fr. Joseph Mariano Cárdenas Inventory/Report (1783) provides information on Espíritu Santo, the status of the conversion effort, and the Indians.[17] Fr. Cárdenas also discussed matters relating to the religious training and government among the Indians and the state of all the missions. The inventory of Espíritu Santo includes the sacred items and ornaments of the church and the altarpieces with sacred images, furnishings in the church and living

13. For information on the expulsion of the Jesuits, see Chapter 1, n. 27.

14. Fr. Juan Agustín Morfi, *Diario y derrotero, 1777–1778,* ed. E. Del Hoyo and M. D. McLean, pp. 99–103.

15. Fr. Morfi, *History of Texas,* pp. 17–18; "Report of Fr. Solís," in *San José Papers, Part I,* trans. B. Leutenegger, pp. 138–160.

16. Fr. Morfi, *History of Texas,* p. 98.

17. Fr. Joseph Mariano Cárdenas, "Inventory—1783, Mission of Espíritu Santo de la Bahía" (November 17, 1783), in W. H. Oberste, "Texas Missions of the Coastal Bend, Espíritu Santo, Rosario, Refugio," Appendix.

quarters of the missionaries, the books in the library, the workshops (tallow, weaving), kitchen, refectory, forge, horses, oxen, cattle and sheep, and a census of the Indian population.

The Fr. José Francisco López Report (1785) includes information on the conversion status at the seven remaining missions: San Antonio de Valero, La Purísima Concepción, San José de Aguayo, San Juan Capistrano, Espada, Espíritu Santo, and El Rosario.[18] He discusses the reasons for the temporal and spiritual decline of these missions.

INDIANS AND MISSIONARIES

According to Fr. Morfi, the Indians at San José de Aguayo spoke Spanish "perfectly, with the exception of those who [were] daily brought in from the woods by the zeal of the missionaries."

Fr. López (1785) found that all the Indians of San Antonio de Valero were considered Samas and Payas, whose languages were in general use, even though the mission was founded for many different groups. In spite of the diversity, Spanish was commonly used by the Indians of the mission. He also noted that nearly all the Indians of La Purísima Concepción spoke Spanish with "notable imperfection." The Indians of San Juan Capistrano spoke their own languages. Fr. López identified the Indians of La Espada but did not comment on their language ability.[19]

THE CONVERSION EFFORT

The number of Indians of San Antonio de Valero had been reduced by 1778, when Fr. Morfi visited the mission. There were few Indians to cultivate the fields, and the looms were abandoned because there were no workers available. The Indian population of La Purísima Concepción and La Espada had also been greatly reduced. The Indian population of San Juan Capistrano, like the other missions, had declined each year.

In Fr. Morfi's view, the Indians of San José de Aguayo were "well instructed and civilized and [knew] how to work very well at their mechanical trades and [were] proficient in some of the arts."

Fr. Cárdenas (1783) was primarily concerned about the Indians fleeing from Espíritu Santo when too much pressure was applied, particularly in religious instruction. They all attended Mass on Sundays, important feast days, and Fridays but were not required to attend all the church services, such as High Mass on Saturdays. It was difficult to maintain discipline among the Indians because the new converts had a bad influence on those who resided at the mission. Fr. Cárdenas also discussed the distribution of supplies and food rations to the Indians and the annual produce of the missions aside from supplies received from outside.

According to Fr. Cárdenas, most of the missions had deteriorated in the number of Indians and in material wealth. The decline in numbers was due to the missionaries' inability to bring in Indians as they used to because they were surrounded by hostile Indians and had no military escorts. The decline in wealth was the result of having only one missionary at each mission instead of two as in the past. There were also not enough resources to clothe and feed the Indians. Some of the missions had gone into debt to those who provided them with supplies.

18. Fr. José Francisco López, "Documents: The Texas Missions in 1785," trans. J. A. Dabbs, *Mid-America* 22 (January 1940): 38–58.

19. Fr. Morfi, *History of Texas*, p. 98; Fr. López, "Documents," p. 41.

Fr. Cárdenas believed that the best way to resolve these problems would be to have two missionaries assigned to each mission and to have protection provided by the authorities. If the situation did not change, it would be impossible for them to spread the "faith in this province."

According to Fr. López, the population of the Indians at La Purísima Concepción had declined by 1785. It was clear to him that most of the Indians fled El Espíritu Santo because of the diminishing wealth of the mission. He added a note to the report to explain the loss of that wealth, which was derived from the herds of cattle. The decline of Espíritu Santo and the other missions was due to the decree issued in 1778 by Teodoro de la Croix, the commander general, making all wild and unbranded cattle royal property. This had the immediate effect of diminishing the herds of cattle, because they could be killed without fear of reprisal by the government. Fr. López suggested that the people responsible for killing the cattle were the Apaches, the Spanish hunters, the purveyors for the presidio, the soldiers in charge of the horses, the troops of the presidio, and others who took entire herds.

In the summary of his report Fr. López stated that the fee of four reales (half a peso) imposed for each head of cattle slaughtered made the economic situation of the missions even worse. The missionaries were immediately impoverished, because the cattle, the main source of their wealth, were killed by the Indians and the soldiers with impunity. This made it impossible to feed the Indians under their care and had the effect of reducing the number of Indians at the missions. The decline in population was also due to the constant flight of the Indians from the missions as well as the sickness and plagues of smallpox and buboes that further reduced the numbers of those who stayed.

According to Fr. López, the cattle and horses of El Rosario were totally decimated by the Apaches, Lipans, and coastal tribes. He further attributed the many problems of this mission (beyond those caused by the new decree making the cattle royal property) to one particular Indian of the mission who spoke Spanish very well and led all the others astray. This man "committed execrable evils, and [was] the reason that many fugitives from other missions . . . never returned."[20]

THE SECULARIZATION OF THE MISSIONS, 1792–1824

San Antonio de Valero was secularized on January 9, 1793, by order of the viceroy at the request of the superiors of the College of Zacatecas.[21] Upon receiving the viceregal order, Manuel Muñoz, the governor of Texas (1790–1798), issued a proclamation to that effect on February 23. Fr. López delivered the inventory to Governor Muñoz on April 23 in the presence of Fr. José Mariano de la Garza, the representative of the College of Zacatecas, who was asked to supervise the delivery and the secularization of the mission.

THE REPORTS

Fr. López listed his recommendations for the secularization of the seven missions discussed by Fr. Cárdenas and of Guadalupe de los Nacogdoches.[22] Given the declining state of the missions, he recommended the secularization of several and consolidation of others for greater efficiency in carrying out the work of the missionaries. He was primarily concerned with finding ways to

20. Fr. Morfi, *History of Texas,* p. 98; Fr. Cárdenas, "Inventory—1783," p. 25; Fr. López, "Documents," p. 49.

21. Fr. José Francisco López, "Inventory of San Antonio de Valero, April 23, 1793."

22. Fr. López, "Report on the San Antonio Missions in 1792," 488–498.

use the missionaries where they were most needed to carry on with their apostolic mission.

Fr. Bernardino Vallejo (1815) prepared a report on the state of the Zacatecan missions of San José de Aguayo, La Purísima Concepción, Espada, San Juan Capistrano, Espíritu Santo, and Refugio to the end of 1814, the number of missionaries serving at the missions, their allowances, and a census of the Indians, Spaniards, and others at the missions.[23] He was unable to compare the present report to the one he had sent the governor in 1809 because it had been destroyed along with others at San José during the "last destructive revolution." He was also unable to provide information on Guadalupe de los Nacogdoches and El Espíritu Santo. All the Indians had fled the first, and most had fled the second; the missionaries assigned to the two missions had returned to the College of Zacatecas.

Fr. Vallejo included seven additional notes on the state of the mission buildings, their finances (from the royal treasury), the teaching of Christian doctrine, financial resources of the missions, the daily labor (farming), the Indians, and the dangers suffered by Indian attacks from the "North."

The Juan Antonio Padilla Report (1820) includes information on the Indians, divided into friendly and hostile nations.[24] The four remaining missions in San Antonio are included in the last part of the report: La Purísima Concepción, San José de Aguayo, San Juan Capistrano, and La Espada.

THE SECULARIZATION OF THE MISSIONS

Fr. López (1792) recommended the secularization of San Antonio de Valero and Guadalupe de los Nacogdoches because there was no longer a need for them. First, there were no Indians remaining to be converted at San Antonio de Valero within a radius of 150 miles of the mission. Indians beyond that radius to the east, north, and south could not be brought to the mission because of the distances involved. Fr. López believed the missionaries in San Antonio had essentially completed their work "by instructing the Indians in the Catholic religion, by teaching them to live as Christians, as obedient sons of the holy Church, and true subjects of the [Spanish] Sovereign." Second, there were no Indians left at Guadalupe de los Nacogdoches. If secularized, the missions could both be administered by a local pastor. At San Antonio de Valero the pastor of the Spaniards could take care of the Indians remaining at the mission, given its close proximity to the presidio and the Villa of San Fernando. At Guadalupe de los Nacogdoches the local Spanish residents could support a pastor.

Fr. López did not suggest any changes for El Espíritu Santo or El Rosario but recommended reducing the four missions in San Antonio to two, because few Indians lived there. San José de Aguayo and La Espada could be joined, given their location on one side of the river and the overlapping boundaries of their lands; likewise La Purísima Concepción and San Juan Capistrano, because of their location on the other side of the river. He further recommended having the residences of the two remaining missionaries at San José de Aguayo and La Purísima Concepción because the churches and *conventos* (friaries) at those missions were "larger and better" than those at the other two. La Espada and San Juan Capistrano could then be designated *visitas* or mission stations. Finally, he recommended placing the remaining missions

23. Fr. Bernardino Vallejo, "Report on the Texas Missions, February 11, 1815," in *The San José Papers, Part III,* trans. B. Leutenegger, p. 22.

24. Juan Antonio Padilla, "Report on the Barbarous Indians of the Province of Texas," trans. M. A. Hatcher as "Texas in 1820," *Southwestern Historical Quarterly* 23 (1919–1920): 47–60.

under a secular administrator. In his view, the changes would release five missionaries from duty at those missions (Nacogdoches and San Antonio) to work elsewhere, such as the "coast of San Bernardo [La Bahía], in Refugio, Brazos de Dios, and Orcoquiza," where there was a greater need for them.[25]

Fr. López's recommendations were carried out, but with a few changes. San Antonio de Valero was completely secularized in 1793, and the remaining four missions in San Antonio were merged into two and placed under the administration of Spanish justices or alcaldes. However, the consolidation of the missions was not carried out according to his recommendations. La Purísima Concepción became a submission of San José de Aguayo and San Juan Capistrano of La Espada. Although technically they were no longer missions, they were so considered because some of the Indians continued to reside there. They were therefore partially secularized. Guadalupe de los Nacogdoches remained under the care of a missionary until 1811.

LANDS AND RIVERS

Fr. López (1792) and Fr. Vallejo (1815) did not describe the lands and rivers of Texas because their main concern was the status of the missionary effort. Padilla (1820), who was not a missionary but a military man, described the many rivers and the possibility of building ports along the coast. In his view, the land from the Colorado River to the coast was "extremely fertile," with immense forests and a great abundance of cultivated and wild plants. There were large quantities of fish in all the rivers, minerals on the Colorado River, and other "commodities and advantages for the establishment of *haciendas* and *pueblos* of great importance." The climate north of San Antonio was "very healthful because of the altitude of the country and the purity of the air." This was not the case with the country along the coast, because it "is so low, so covered with vegetation [and] rainy at all times and especially during the rainy season."[26]

INDIANS, MISSIONARIES, AND THE CONVERSION EFFORT

According to Fr. López (1792), the Indians of Valero, which he administered, could not be considered "neophytes, or even Indians, since most of them, [were] children of marriages between Indians and white women." He concluded that the mission could "not be called a mission of Indians but a gathering of white people."

Fr. Vallejo (1815) reported that most of the Indians at the remaining Texas missions spoke Spanish because they had been under the care of the missionaries for many years. He also noted the conditions of the missions. The Guadalupe de los Nacogdoches church was abandoned because the Indians had fled, and the religious images (sculptures), vestments, and other items had been taken at that time. The church of Espíritu Santo and the materials used to repair it were badly deteriorated. The other Texas missions, however, were in good condition and were provided with the necessary vestments and furnishings for the sacristy.

According to the report prepared by Padilla (1820), there were still numerous Indian tribes living as they had before the arrival of the missionaries. He focused on the "customs, habits, and modes of life, . . . of the best known tribes," which he divided "into friendly and hostile groups." He included

25. Fr. López, "Report," pp. 493, 495.
26. Padilla, "Texas in 1820," pp. 58–59.

sixteen friendly tribes found in east Texas and six hostile tribes found in the plains area in west Texas, New Mexico, and Mexico. He noted that the language of the Cadó (Caddo), one of the friendly tribes, "like that of all barbarians, [consisted] of a small number of words. They [used] signs and gestures with the spoken word." Because of trade with the French, some of them "learned the French language, and a few spoke Spanish, poorly pronounced." In his view, the Comanches, one of the hostile tribes, were "treacherous, revengeful, sly, untrustworthy, ferocious, and cruel, when victorious; and cowardly and low, when conquered."

Padilla believed the missions could be repaired at small cost. If this were done, the lands, water, and the buildings could be divided among a new settlement of Spaniards. This would increase the population of the province, preserve the missions, and serve in the defense of the province.[27]

27. Fr. López, "Report," p. 490; Fr. Vallejo, "Report," pp. 21–26; Padilla, "Texas in 1820," pp. 47, 48, 49, 53, 60.

PART ii

THE ART AND ARCHITECTURE OF THE TEXAS MISSIONS

3

SAN ANTONIO DE VALERO

The Mission of San Antonio de Valero was founded by Fr. Antonio de San Buenaventura Olivares on the west bank of the San Antonio River on May 1, 1718.[1] It was intended for the Xaranames, Payayes, Zanas, Ypanis, Cocos, Tops (Tovs), and Karankawas. The mission was later moved to the east side of the river, where the church was begun in 1744. An adobe hall was used as a church during the period of construction. The new church collapsed due to faulty construction in 1756. The present stone and mortar structure was still under construction in early 1778 when Fr. Juan Agustín Morfi visited the San Antonio missions.

THE ORIGINAL ART AND ARCHITECTURE, 1740–1824

THE THIRD CHURCH

According to Fr. Sáenz (1772), the church, still under construction, had a transept and a cross-vaulted roof (Fig. 3.1). The completed portions were the cross vault of the sanctuary (main altar area), the arches of the cross vaults of the choir loft and two of the three bays of the nave, and the four pendentives over the crossing for the support of the dome. The construction of the church appears to have stopped shortly thereafter.

Fr. Morfi (1778) referred to the unfinished Valero church in his diary and again in his *History of Texas* a few years later. In his view, the old church collapsed because of "the ignorance of the builder, but a new one, simple, roomy, and well planned, [was] being erected on the same place, though it [was] not finished."

The third and last church of Valero remained unchanged between 1772 and 1793, the year Fr. López prepared the last inventory of the mission. He described the condition of the unfinished church in almost the same terms used by Fr. Sáenz in 1772. The only additional details were the lunettes of the cross-vaulted roof of the nave and several other rooms with vaulted roofs—the finished lavatory with a carved font and "a great deal of light," the baptistry, and other rooms (at the front of the church) with carved doors and windows. The other rooms had the springers for the two towers that were planned for the facade.[2]

1. For the early history of San Antonio de Valero, see Morfi, *History of Texas,* p. 93; see also Habig, *The Alamo Chain of Missions,* pp. 29, 38, 50, 64.

2. Fr. Juan José Sáenz de Gumiel, *Inventory of the Mission San Antonio de Valero: 1772,* trans. and ed. B. Leutenegger, p. 7; Fr. Morfi, *Diario y derrotero,* p. 103 (all translations from this work are mine); idem, *History of Texas,* vol. 1, p. 93 (quotation); Fr. López, "Inventory of San Antonio de Valero, April 23, 1793," pp. 1–2. For the first and second Valero churches, see Fr. Francisco Xavier Ortiz, *Visita de las missiones;* idem, *Razón de la visita a las misiones de la provincia de Texas, 1756,* vol. 3, p. 11 (all translations from this work are mine); Fr. Mariano Francisco de los Dolores y Viana, "Inventories of the San Antonio Missions, 1759," p. 12; idem, "A Report about the Status of the Texas Missions in 1762," in *Letters and Memorials,* trans. Fr. Leutenegger, p. 331.

FIGURE 3.1. *Interior view of the Alamo. Drawing by Edward Everett. Lithograph by C. A. Graham, published in George W. Hughes, Memoir (1850), follows p. 32.*

THE FACADE

According to Fr. Sáenz, there were "very devotional" sculptures of St. Francis and St. Dominic in the two niches framed by double columns on each side of the entrance of the "very beautiful" portal (Fig. 3.2). The two niches on the second stage lacked the columns and the images of St. Clare and St. Margaret. One of the images was almost finished. A sculpture of Our Lady of the Immaculate Conception was intended for a niche in the planned third stage of the portal. Portions intended for this stage were already available.

The facade of the church remained essentially the same in 1785 when Fr. López prepared his report. He noted that the "beautiful facade of carved [sculptured] stone" was completed to the cornice level of the church walls. He also referred to the sculptures of St. Francis and St. Dominic in the two niches flanking the main doorway (first stage), which he considered a "beautiful" portal of Tuscan style, and the two unfinished niches of the second stage, which still lacked the architraves and the stone cornices of the columns.[3]

THE MAIN ALTARPIECE IN 1772 AND 1793

The altar table of the main altarpiece was undoubtedly made of wood, as indicated in the reports and inventories of 1756, 1759, and 1762. According to Fr. Ortiz (1756), the altarpiece was on a table made of "some good" boards with some wooden risers placed on it. Fr. Dolores (1759 and 1762) described the altarpiece as a wooden table and risers made of the same wood, with several wooden ledges above it and a baldachin as backdrop (Fig. 3.3).

Fr. Sáenz (1772) listed the sacred images and described them in great detail but did not give their location in the altarpiece. This can be determined,

3. Fr. Sáenz, *Inventory: 1772*, pp. 7–8; Fr. López, "Documents," pp. 39–40.

FIGURE 3.2. *Mission San Antonio de Valero (the Alamo). Elevation of the facade. Courtesy of Walter Eugene George.*

FIGURE 3.3. *The main altar of San Antonio de Valero, 1772. Drawn to the scale of the sanctuary wall. The sacred images are no longer extant, with the possible exception of image D. Diagram by Jacinto Quirarte.*

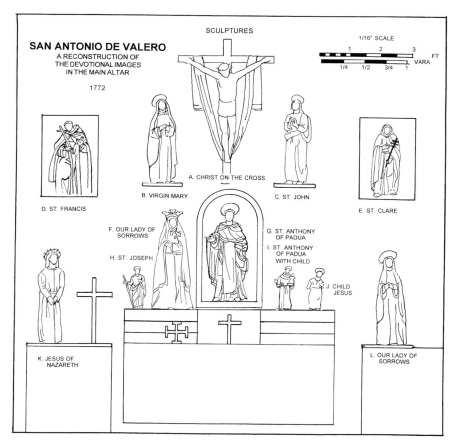

however, by consulting the earlier documents (1745, 1756, 1759, and 1762), in which many of the same images appear repeatedly, with their location noted (Table 3.1). The list of images in the 1772 inventory begins with the titular saint of the mission.

The sculptures of St. Anthony of Padua and the Crucified Christ with a crown and covering (used for the services of the Descent from the Cross) were located in the center of the altarpiece. The sculptures of the Sorrowful Mother and St. John the Evangelist, dressed in ribbed silk garments, cinctures, and mantles, were placed on each side of the Crucified Christ. There was a sculpture of Our Lady of Sorrows "with 2 garments, one of cloth with trimmings, and the other of velvet . . . [and] a silver dagger and crown." A slightly

TABLE 3.1. THE ALTARPIECES OF SAN ANTONIO DE VALERO

SACRED IMAGES	1745	1756	1759	1762	1772	1793
Christ Crucified	2+ v	large	1.75 v	1.3 v	1.75 v	——
Virgin Mary		no dim.	no dim.	no dim.	1 v	——
John Evangelist		no dim.	no dim.	no dim.	1 v	——
Anthony of Padua	1± v	1± v	1± v	1 v	1 v	.75 v
Crucifix					.33 v	——
Crucifix					.75 v	——
Jerusalem Cross					.25 v	——
Francis (P)					no dim.	——
Clare (P)					no dim.	——
OL of Sorrows					1 v	——
Anthony of Padua w/ Child					.5 v	.66 v
Child Jesus			no dim.	——	.5 v	
Joseph w/ Child						.75 v
Jesus Christ			.75 v	——	——	——
Tecali Cross						1.3 v
		choir	other	choir	main	main
Jesus of Nazareth		1 v	1 v	no dim.	1 v	1 v
Virgin Mary (P)	"pinturas"	no dim.	——	——	——	——
			no dim.	no dim.	——	——
	sacristy	sacristy	sacristy	port.		
Immaculate Conception	1 v	——	——	——	——	——
Joseph		.5 v	——	——	.5 v	——
Francis Xavier (P)		2 v	3 v	——	——	——
OL of Sorrows				1 v	1+ v	no dim.
	convento					
1 (P) on stairs	2 v	——	——	——	——	——
10 (P) in cell	no dim.	——	——	——	——	——

Note: (P) = painting/s; "pinturas" = paintings; OL = Our Lady; v = vara (32.909 inches); dim. = dimensions; main = main altarpiece; port. = portable altar.

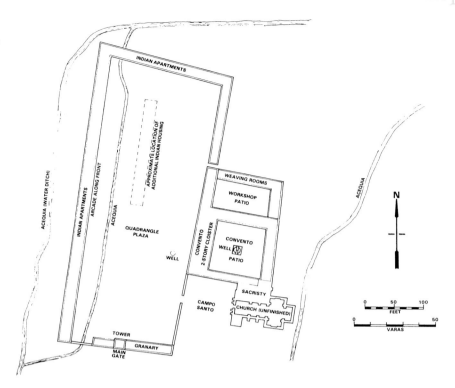

smaller, "very beautiful" Our Lady of Sorrows was dressed in taffeta garments, one black and the other blue. The other sacred images included a Child Jesus with two tunics, one red and one blue, and two framed canvas paintings of St. Francis and St. Clare.

A sculpture listed for the first time was a St. Anthony holding the Child Jesus in his hands. The other sculptures, of varying sizes, were two crucifixes made of carved wood and a Jerusalem cross. A sculpture of Jesus of Nazareth in another altarpiece was dressed in a garment and a crown and had a silk cord.

The final inventory, prepared by Fr. López in 1793, includes a reference to the gilded altarpiece and a number of sacred images as well as the wooden table used as an altar. There was a carved and gilded sculpture of an unidentified saint with a diadem, silver feather, and rays, holding a child in its arms and placed in a glass-covered niche. (This was undoubtedly the St. Anthony listed in the 1772 inventory prepared by Fr. Sáenz.) The others were a *tecali* (alabaster) cross, a Jesus of Nazareth with a ribbed silk tunic and a cross on his shoulders, a St. Joseph with a diadem and silver staff, holding the Child Jesus in his hands, and Our Lady of Sorrows.[4]

The sculptures of the crucified Christ and the flanking figures of the Sorrowful Mother and St. John the Evangelist were not listed in 1793.

THE SACRISTY AS TEMPORARY CHURCH

According to Fr. Sáenz (1772), the actual "well-plastered" and whitewashed sacristy (of the third church under construction) served as a temporary church (Fig. 3.4). It had a cross-vaulted roof, two carved stone door-frames, and two "beautiful" windows with glass panes and iron gratings. One of the doors was an entrance, and the other led to the transept of the new church. There was also

4. Fr. Ortiz, *Razón,* vol. 3, p. 11; Fr. Dolores, "Inventories, 1759," p. 12; idem, "A Report," p. 331; Fr. Sáenz, *Inventory: 1772,* pp. 8, 9; Fr. López, "Inventory, 1793," pp. 8, 9.

Table 3.2. The Architecture of San Antonio de Valero, 1745–1762

STRUCTURES	1745	1756	1759	1762
New Church	under construction	fell down	almost finished	fell down
New Sacristy				
Temporary Church	no dim.	no dim.*	no dim.	no dim.**
Temporary Sacristy		no dim.	no dim.	no dim.
Convento	2-story	2-story	2-story	2-story
Bldgs.	unspecified	unspecified	west bldg.	unspecified
Patio			2 patios	50 × 50 v
West Bldg.	unspecified	unspecified	main	2-story
Cells (rms)	3	4 upper	16	1 upper
Guest	unspecified	1	others	2 lower
Portería				
Obraje	no dim.	——	no dim.	
East Bldg.				
Cells (rms)				
South Bldg.				2-story
Cells/Offices				
North Bldg.	unspecified	unspecified	other	unspecified
Cells (rms)	unspecified	——	offices	
Kitchen	no dim.	——	——	no dim.
Refectory	no dim.	——	——	no dim.
Carpentry	no dim.	——	no dim.	tools
Forge	no dim.	——	no dim.	tools
Masonry/Kiln	tools/	——	tools/	——
Indian Houses		30	unspecified	unspecified
Rows/Arcades		1/no dim.	plaza	7/arcade
New Granary				no dim.
Old Granary	no dim.	——	——	no dim.
Sugar Mill			no dim.	——
Outer Wall				no dim.
Gate/S Wall				no loc.

Note: v = vara (32.909 inches); dim. = dimension; *portería* = main entrance to the *convento* (friary); *obraje* = spinning room.
*Old church used as a temporary church in 1756.
**Old granary used as a temporary church in 1762.

a larger window with shutters and an iron grating. The room temporarily used as a sacristy was "properly adorned from floor to ceiling and [had] ample room."

The actual sacristy of the third church was still being used as a temporary church when Fr. Morfi visited the mission in 1778. He considered it small, "but very tidy and neat." Seven years later it was still being used as the temporary church when Fr. López prepared his report of 1785 (Tables 3.2 and 3.3). Another room served as the sacristy. Both structures with vaulted ceilings were built with stone and mortar. According to Fr. López (1793), the sacristy was still being used for the same purpose. It was in "good condition," as were the plastered and whitewashed cross-vaults of the roof.[5]

5. Fr. Sáenz, *Inventory: 1772,* pp. 7–8; Fr. Morfi, *History of Texas,* p. 93; Fr. López, "Documents," p. 39; idem, "Inventory, 1793," p. 2.

One of the two doors of the temporary church with carved door-frames led to another room which served as a sacristy. The roof made of cedar was supported by a basket handle arch in the center. The room with walls supported by wooden props was in very poor condition. It had doors on the east and north sides and windows facing south and west. The doors had locks and bolts, and the east window had an iron grating. The entire structure was in need of repair.

TABLE 3.3. THE ARCHITECTURE OF SAN ANTONIO DE VALERO, 1772–1793

STRUCTURES	1772	1793
New Church	35 × 9 v unfinished	34 × 9 v unfinished
Transept	no dim.	no dim.
New Sacristy	12 × 5.5 v	12 × 5 × 5 v
Temporary Church	new sacristy	——
Temporary Sacristy	no dim.	8.3 × 7.3 × 5.5 v
Convento (friary)	2-story	2-story (west and south bldgs.)
Bldgs./Patio	4/30 × 30 v	
West Bldg.	2-story	2-story
Arcaded Cloister		23 v long
Portería (West Building)	9 × 5 v	——
Rooms (1st floor)	2 rooms	5 rooms (5 × 4 v each)*
Obraje	9 × 5 v	——
Office	9 × 5 v	——
Cells (2nd floor)	3 rooms	3 rooms
Guest Room	9 × 5 v	——
Living Quarters	2: 9 × 5 v each	——
South Bldg.	2-story	2-story
Arcaded Cloister		22 v long
Rooms		4 rooms (5 × 4 v)
East Bldg.	1-story	1-story
Arcaded Cloister		23 v long
Rooms		4 rooms
North Bldg.	1-story	1-story
Arcaded Cloister		22 v long
Rooms		5 rooms
Kitchen	no dim.	5 × 4 v
Refectory	unspecified	——
Forge	7–8 × 7–8 × 7–8 v	——
Masonry/Kiln		19 v circumf. × 52 v ht.
Indian Houses	15 total, 8 v each	unspecified
Rows/Arcades	5 rows (3 houses in each)	12 habitable
New Granary	no dim.	no dim.
Outer Wall		175 v n–s × 58 v e–w
Gate: S wall		5 × 4 v high

Note: v = vara (32.909 inches); dim. = dimensions.
*Four of the five rooms measured 5 × 4 v each. Room 5 was a "small" room.

SACRED ITEMS AND CHURCH FURNISHINGS

The liturgical vestments and sacred vessels were stored in a variety of containers located in the sacristy. According to Fr. Sáenz, they were stored in a leather-lined wooden framework, with eight drawers in the center and two cabinets on each side. The church furnishings included three confessionals, a gilded missal stand, a bench, and two chairs, one of them upholstered, a carved stone holy water font, and a baptismal font.[6]

THE *Convento* (FRIARY) AND OTHER BUILDINGS

According to Fr. Sáenz, there was a well in the center of the patio of the *convento* defined by an arcaded cloister on all four sides. The well had a "curb-stone and arch surmounted by an artistically carved stone cross." The first floor of the cloister was completed and roofed over on three sides, with the east side partially completed. The second-story walls and the roofs on the west and south sides were completed. The main entrance to the cloister (*portería*) on the west side had two rooms of the same size on the first floor. One was used as a workshop and the other as an office. There were three rooms of the same size on the second story. Two were used as the living quarters for the missionaries and the third as a guest room. The latter was "almost uninhabitable because part of the roof [was] propped up." It was nonetheless furnished, as were the other two rooms.

Fr. Morfi (1778) noted that the two-story building of the *convento* with an "arched gallery" around the court had all the necessary rooms for the missionaries, a refectory, offices, and a kitchen.

Fr. López (1785) stated that the *convento,* made of stone and lime (mortar), had "good roofs, doors, windows, and locks." He included far more information on the four-unit *convento* in the inventory he prepared in 1793. The stone and lime *convento* of 1785 inexplicably became the *convento* made of stone and mud. Although the unit on the east side had four arches with "good walls, all evenly finished," it still had no roof, floor, or plastered walls. The unit on the north side also had four arches, although three of them were without roofs. The five rooms of the unit had roofs with good cedar supports, but the roofs were in bad condition because the boards were damaged. The first room, used as a kitchen, had a door with lock and key, a chimney, a window facing south, and a closet with a wooden door, with its lock, latch, and key. The other four rooms had the same kind of locks.

The west and south units were two-story buildings with porches. Each had four offices on the first floor; the one on the west side had a small office on the landing of the stairs. Both had brick floors on the second story. The boards of the roofs of the three rooms on the second floor of the west-side building were rotten. The flat roofs of the four offices of the south building were in need of repair because they leaked and the boards were damaged. Fr. López referred to the well with a stone arch and a pulley in the center of a patio mentioned in 1772.

Finally, the *convento* had several storerooms attached to it (on the west side where the Indian houses were located). One had an adobe floor and a roof with only the "good" beams in place and a door with lock and key. The other one, made of plastered stone and mud, had a flagstone floor.[7]

6. Fr. Sáenz, *Inventory: 1772,* pp. 8–14.

7. Ibid., p. 30; and Fr. Morfi, *History of Texas,* p. 93; Fr. López, "Documents," p. 39; idem, "Inventory of San Antonio de Valero, 1793," p. 11.

According to Fr. Sáenz (1772), there were five rows of houses for the Indians. Each row had three houses with a door on the east side and a window on the west. The houses had "corridors with stone arches for lighting and the comfort of those who [lived there]." Separate from those already mentioned were two other houses without corridors but "well built for protection against the wind and rain."

Fr. López (1785) reported that the fifteen or sixteen Indian houses built against the wall were covered with wood and mortar and had carved wooden doors with locks and iron keys. By 1793 only twelve of the Indian houses built against the arcaded square on the west side were habitable.

According to Fr. Morfi (1778), there was a textile shop with two adjoining rooms used for storing the raw materials and tools in the "second" patio (the first one being the main patio of the *convento*). Fr. López (1793) noted that there was a kiln made of stone and mud for burning lime on the eastern side of the mission, beyond the *convento* (over 330 feet away).

Fr. Ortiz (1745) mentioned a granary, and Fr. Dolores (1762) referred to a granary being used as a temporary church. In 1785 Fr. López reported a "large" granary made of stone and lime (mortar). In 1793 he indicated that a hut of reeds and mud (*xacal de palizada y tule*) served as a granary because the granary (listed in his 1785 report) was damaged.[8]

THE MISSION WALL

Although Fr. Morfi (1778) does not specifically mention the mission wall, it clearly existed, given the defensive measures taken at the mission: the well (to be used in case of attack) and the fortifications including a watchtower, three swivel guns, and other weapons.

Fr. López (1785) was the first to refer to the mission wall, noting that the enclosed square of the mission was defined by a stone and mud wall. He estimated the distance from the center of the square to the wall to be three hundred paces. His 1793 inventory added more details. The wall around the mission was made of stone, adobe, and mud. Half of the north-south wall (on the west?) was in ruins. The main entrance to the plaza was on the south wall.[9]

RANCH BUILDINGS

According to Fr. Sáenz (1772), the ranch known as La Mora, located south of the mission, had three stone houses with "good wooden roofs for every comfort." They were not used, however, because of the dangers caused by the Indians in the area.[10]

THE FORMER MISSION, 1840–1890

The former mission has been known as the Alamo since 1802, when troops from Mexico were quartered there.[11] They belonged to the Second Flying Company of San Carlos de Parras del Alamo. The name of the former mission actually became the Pueblo San José y Santiago del Alamo. The Alamo served

8. Fr. Sáenz, *Inventory: 1772*, p. 25; Fr. López, "Documents," p. 39; idem, "Inventory, 1793," pp. 11–12; Fr. Morfi, *History of Texas*, p. 93; Fr. Dolores, "Inventories, 1759," pp. 34–35; Fr. López, "Inventory, 1793," p. 12; Ortiz, *Visita de las missiones;* Fr. Dolores, "Report," p. 333.

9. Fr. Morfi, *History of Texas*, pp. 93–94; Fr. López, "Documents," p. 39; idem, "Inventory, 1793," p. 11.

10. Fr. Sáenz, *Inventory: 1772*, p. 35.

11. For the history of the Alamo in the nineteenth century, see W. Corner, *San Antonio*, pp. 8–12. For a more recent review of the history, see B. A. Meissner, *The Alamo Restoration and Conservation Project: Excavations at the South Transept*, pp. 9–24.

as a military fortress from 1802 to 1836, when the last of the sieges between the Mexican army and Anglo-American settlers took place. This was preceded by the earlier political unrest that began in 1811 during the war of independence between Mexico and Spain from 1810 to 1821. The Alamo remained abandoned and unclaimed from 1836 until January 13, 1841, when it was declared the property of the Catholic church by the Congress of the Republic of Texas.

In 1849, following disputes over who owned the property, the Alamo was chosen as the headquarters of the Eighth Military District of the United States Army. Major E. Babbitt, who was made the acting quartermaster of the district, began the clearing of the debris in and around the former church. He also had some of the buildings repaired at that time so they could be used for storage and offices.

At the beginning of the Civil War, the Alamo became the quartermaster depot of the Confederate Army in Texas. The United States Army returned at the end of the war and remained at the Alamo until the Quartermaster's Depot was moved to Government Hill, on January 31, 1878.

Negotiations to buy the property were begun in early 1883 by the state of Texas, and on May 16, 1883, the Alamo became the property of the state. Efforts to restore Alamo Plaza to its configuration before 1836 began in 1893.

THE FORMER MISSION AND CHURCH (THE ALAMO)

All early travelers commented on the ruined state of the Alamo, including George Wilkins Kendall, William Bollaert, Charles Kingsbury, and William A. McClintock, who wrote about their visits to the site in the 1840s. Edward Everett, an artist, drew up a plan showing the remnants of the structures along the west and south walls, the friary, sacristy, and the church (Fig. 3.5).

According to Kendall, Bollaert, and Kingsbury, the Alamo was "in ruins," a "sacred pile of ruins," and "a shapeless mass of ruins" respectively. Kingsbury, however, described it in more detail in his notes:

The walls on the north-eastern side are level with the ground, and there are broad openings on the other fronts, which preserve only detached portions of their original dimensions.

McClintock noted that the wall had

the appearance of having been in a state of utter ruin for a long time past and is only discernable from the heap of rubbish elevated a few feet above the surrounding plain.[12]

One of the earliest depictions of the Alamo is a sketch of the church facade which was reproduced on the cover of a book published in London in 1841 (Fig. 3.6). Other artists depicted the ruins of the former church (the Alamo), among them Edward Everett and Seth Eastman. Everett did drawings of the exterior and interior of the Alamo in 1846 (Figs. 3.1 and 3.7). He also did drawings of San José mission. Eastman did a number of drawings of the Alamo and some of the other missions.

12. G. W. Kendall, *Narrative of the Texan Santa Fé Expedition,* vol. 1, p. 49; Bollaert, *William Bollaert's Texas,* p. 222; C. P. Kingsbury, "Notes from My Knapsack," *Putnam's Monthly* 3, no. 14 (1854): 177; W. A. McClintock, "Journal of a Trip through Texas and Northern Mexico in 1846–1847, II," *Southwestern Historical Quarterly* 34, no. 2 (October 1930): 144–145; see also A. F. Muir, ed., *Texas in 1837: An Anonymous Contemporary Narrative* (Austin: University of Texas Press, 1958), pp. 97–98.

FIGURE 3.5. *Plan of the Alamo drawn by Edward Everett, 1846. Published in George W. Hughes,* **Memoir** *(1850), follows p. 32.*

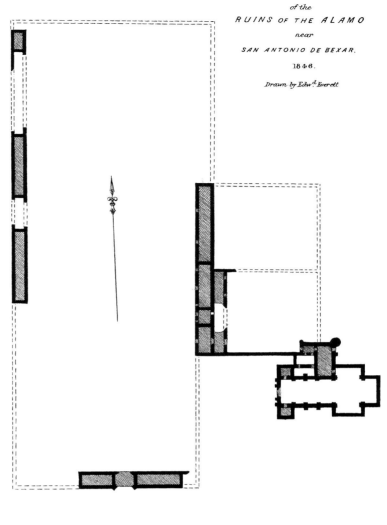

PLAN
of the
RUINS OF THE ALAMO
near
SAN ANTONIO DE BEXAR.
1846.

Drawn by Edw.ᵈ Everett

Scale of 100 feet to an Inch

FIGURE 3.6. *The Alamo. Published (cover) in Arthur Iken,* **Texas, Its History, Topography, Agriculture, Commerce, and General Statistics** *(London: Wood, Gilbert & Piper, Paternoster Row, 1841), cover.*

FIGURE 3.7. *Ruins of the church of the Alamo, San Antonio de Béxar. Drawing by Edward Everett. Published in George W. Hughes, Memoir (1850), follows p. 32.*

Joseph Addison Hatch (1850) remembered long afterward that the "old adobe wall" on the eastern side of the Alamo extending to the area where the Menger Hotel was later built and the "old wall" on the northern side were "broken and crumbled in parts."

Frederick Law Olmsted (before 1856) noted that it "is now within the town, and in extent, probably, a mere wreck of its former grandeur" and that a few stuccoed buildings of different sizes were clustered around the church in a large court enclosed by "a rude wall."

The first full description of the Alamo during this period was provided by William Corner (1890), who wrote: "Hardly a vestige of these enclosing walls of the Mission Square could be found today." He discussed in some detail the state of the church, the *convento,* and other buildings of the Alamo (Fig. 3.8).[13]

Josiah Gregg noted that the walls were still standing "nearly entire"; the roof rested "upon an arch, but [had] fallen in." According to Corner, the former church was restored in the 1850s under the direction of Major Babbitt:

the [church] walls were raised to an equal height [first stage of the facade], a roof was added, and to assist in bearing up this roof, two stone pillars were built inside . . . the wings of the cross in line with the arch pillars.

Some of the upper windows and the flooring were also restored. Corner was the first to compare the general design of the Alamo church with the plan and elevation of the Concepción church:

Both churches were built in the form of the cross and had similar arches and

13. Hatch quoted in A. A. Fox, F. A. Bass, and T. R. Hester, *The Archaeology and History of Alamo Plaza,* p. 15; F. L. Olmsted, *A Journey through Texas or a Saddle-Trip on the Southwestern Frontier,* p. 155; Corner, *San Antonio,* p. 9.

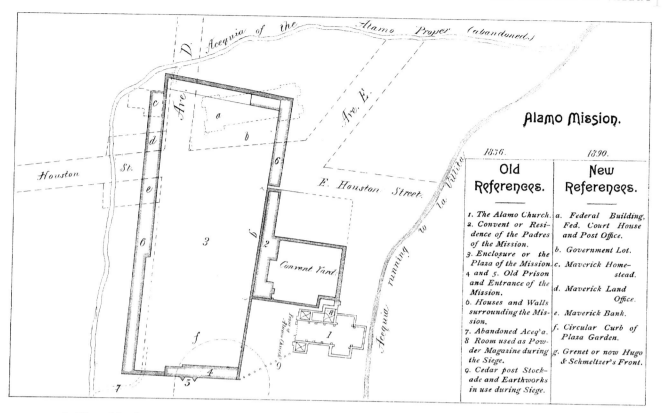

FIGURE 3.8. *Plan of the former mission. Published in W. Corner, San Antonio (1890), between pp. 16 and 17.*

arched stone roofs. The Alamo Church, probably like the Mission Concepción Church, had a dome at the intersection of the cross arches.[14]

THE FACADE

According to an anonymous traveler (1837), the sculptures in the niches flanking the doorway of the main portal were still in place a year after the famous battle at the Alamo. They disappeared sometime after that, because Kendall and Bollaert referred to the niches as "empty." They described the remaining architectural features of the church in positive terms. Kendall stated that the "much ornamented gateway . . . still remains, though deprived of the figures which once occupied its niches." Bollaert suggested that the four empty niches must have originally held "images of saints." The "fine scroll work on the front" indicated to him that "[t]he church . . . must have been a very fine building." He saw the date of 1758 inscribed on a shield over the doorway as a reference to the year "the church was finished."[15]

To Kingsbury, the "elaborately cut stone which formed the facade . . . [showed] no ordinary degree of taste and skill." He added that the arched doorway was "supported by two lofty columns." Gregg noted that the portal "show[ed] some architectural remains." Like Bollaert before him, he saw the date 1758 over the doorway of the church as the date of construction. Olmsted was not overly impressed with the "church-door," which he thought was "meagerly decorated by stucco mouldings, all hacked and battered in the battles it has seen."

According to Corner, the facade was repaired in the 1850s; it was impractical to restore the upper part of the church to its original form, so "the top was

14. Gregg, *Diary and Letters,* pp. 232–233; Corner, *San Antonio,* p. 10.

15. Muir, *Texas in 1837,* pp. 97–98; Kendall, *Narrative,* vol. 1, pp. 49–50; Bollaert, *William Bollaert's Texas,* pp. 222–224.

FIGURE 3.9. *The Alamo, 1868. Used as a U.S. Commissary store (1850–1878). Photograph by E. Raba. Courtesy of the Witte Museum, San Antonio, Texas.*

FIGURE 3.10. *General view of the Alamo facade. Stereoscopic photograph by John Copeland, nineteenth century. Courtesy of the Witte Museum, San Antonio, Texas.*

finished off in its present modest shape." The characteristic gable is seen in a number of nineteenth-century photographs (Figs. 3.9 and 3.10).[16]

THE *Convento*

Kingsbury described the *convento* as a wing that extended from the western side of the church. Its construction was the same as that of the church. He reported the different views regarding its former function: "as a convent, according to some, and by others, supposed to have been a barrack for soldiers." Finally, he doubted that there had ever been an *acequia* (irrigation ditch): "since all signs have so completely disappeared, . . . one may be pardoned for doubting whether it ever had an existence."

Corner gave the dimensions of the *convento* building and its location as "running to the south line of East Houston Street, so no doubt on the north side of the Convent yard was another enclosure probably fenced by a wall." He described the patio of the *convento*:

> a rectangular enclosure, about 100 feet square, surrounded by strong walls, it touched and joined with its southeast corner the wall of the near corner of the north wing of the cross formed by the walls of the mission church.

Kingsbury called Indian houses "hovels":

> There is a rank growth of weeds within the outline of the walls, and a few Mexican hovels on one side, which seem to have been erected from its fallen materials. Every thing around it is stamped with gloom and desolation.

Gregg referred to them as "inferior":

> Scattered along below it [the Alamo] on the east bank of the river, are several inferior houses and huts with perhaps between one and two hundred population, known as the village of the Alamo.

Corner indicated the locations of the former Indian houses and *convento* within the Alamo. On the west side there were "dwellings and barracks for the use of those connected with or dependents of the old missions." He also identified the location of the two irrigation ditches or *acequias* abandoned many years earlier. In addition, "[s]imilar dwellings and buildings to those mentioned formed the northeastern corner of the square." The convent buildings were included with the eastern wall or boundary.[17]

THE RESTORED ARCHITECTURE, 1890 TO THE PRESENT

Interest in restoring the Alamo began in 1893.[18] Following a number of controversies over who should control the Alamo, the Daughters of the Republic of Texas assumed its care in 1904. In 1915 the restoration of the buildings now seen by visitors to the Alamo began. The area in front of the church was widened and landscaped in 1934. All historical focus during this period was on

16. Kingsbury, "Notes from My Knapsack," p. 177; Gregg, *Diary and Letters,* pp. 232–233; Olmsted, *A Journey through Texas,* p. 155; Corner, *San Antonio,* p. 11.

17. Kingsbury, "Notes from My Knapsack," p. 177; Gregg, *Diary and Letters,* p. 232; Corner, *San Antonio,* pp. 9–10.

18. For a history of the Alamo in the twentieth century, see A. A. Fox, *Archaeological Investigations in Alamo Plaza, 1988 and 1989,* pp. 9–10; for other archaeological excavations, see A. A. Fox, F. A. Bass, and T. R. Hester, *The Archaeology and History of Alamo Plaza;* Eaton, *Excavations at the Alamo Shrine;* A. A. Fox, *Testing for the Location of the Alamo Acequia at Hemisfair Plaza;* and Meissner, *The Alamo Restoration and Conservation Project.*

the church and the *convento* buildings. Starting in 1975 with the plans to redesign the park area to emphasize the historical importance of the plaza, the outline of the low barracks building was constructed above ground, and the area beyond the west side of the plaza was opened up to provide a more direct access to the river.

Extensive archaeological excavations have been carried out at the Alamo (1996), the Alamo plaza (1976, 1988, and 1989), the Alamo shrine (1980), and the Alamo *acequia* (1985 and 1990).

THE MISSION WALL, THE CHURCH, AND OTHER BUILDINGS

The original wall of the Valero mission had a north-south orientation. It was narrower at the southern end, where the main entrance was located. The church facade faces almost directly west (Fig. 3.8). The orientation of the church is slightly to the northwest. The Latin cross plan of the church also called for belfry towers and a dome on pendentives over the crossing. All architectural members up to the cornice level of the first story including the pendentives were built by 1772. The church remained unfinished in 1793, when it was secularized.

The church and its sacristy were appended to the southeastern corner of the large patio of the *convento*. The west walls of the *convento* and the workshops formed part of the east wall, so that they remained outside the enclosure of the mission. The *camposanto* (cemetery) in front of the church was located in the space created by the southern part of the east wall and the southern wall of the *convento*.

The granary was located inside the south wall to the right of the main entrance. The Indian houses were built along the west and north walls.

THE CHURCH FACADE

The unfinished facade of Valero (1793) presents a problem to anyone who attempts to analyze and evaluate it in formal and iconographic terms. The sculptures that were in the niches flanking the main doorway disappeared sometime after 1837. The gable added in the 1850s has so obscured the original form of the facade that few people realize that something else was planned (Figs. 3.9 and 3.10). In spite of these problems, the original portions of the facade can be compared to the original plans in order to get a better sense of its intended form and meaning.

STYLE

The three bays of the unfinished Valero portal on the first stage are divided by paired columns flanking niches on either side of the main doorway, which has a Roman arch and spandrels (Fig. 3.11). The capstone of the archivolt extends upward and echoes the capitals of the four columns which support the entablature. The shafts of the columns, placed on high bases, are divided into two sections, each with its own decorative motif. The lower half of each shaft has the traditional fluting, and the upper has a spiral motif. The deep niches with shell-shaped arches have shallow-relief sculptures on the jambs and archivolts.

FIGURE 3.11. *Main portal of the Alamo. Postcard photograph, 1908. Courtesy of the Witte Museum, San Antonio, Texas.*

The same style of carving is seen in the archivolt and spandrels of the main doorway. The second stage has niches in line with those on the first stage and a rectangular choir window in line with the main doorway.

The style of the portal is consistent with traditional arrangements of such retable facades found in New Spain. Although it was planned by the 1760s, its configuration harks back to earlier centuries, when such arrangements were commonplace. There is no breakup of the horizontals or verticals of the various parts that would place it within the style then current in New Spain—the Ultra-Baroque.[19]

Essentially, the form of the portal is related to the Renaissance style, given the Roman arch of the main doorway, surmounted by a typical spandrel, and the framing of the niches in the side bays with two columns each. The only elements that separate it from sixteenth-century portals are the shafts of the columns divided into two units and the scalloped shell arches of the niches. The division of the shafts is typical of late-seventeenth- and early-eighteenth-century designs. The prototypal shafts, however, are divided into three units instead of the two found at Valero. The shell arches of each of the four extant niches are also typical of this unit found throughout New Spain during this period.

Mardith Schuetz provided a conjectural drawing of the Valero facade as it might have looked like had it been completed as planned (Fig. 3.12). She based her projection on the 1772 description by Fr. Sáenz and a geometric analysis of the church plan. In her view, the third stage would have included a single space defined by a broken pediment for the sculpture of Our Lady of

19. For the "Ultra-Baroque," see Toussaint, *Arte colonial en México;* see M. Schuetz, "Professional Artisans in the Hispanic Southwest: The Churches of San Antonio," *Americas* 40 (July 1983): 23, for the published version of the reconstructed facade.

PLATE

CONJECTURAL DRAWING OF SAN ANTONIO D⸌E⸍ VALERO

FIGURE 3.12. *Conjectural drawing of San Antonio de Valero by Mardith Schuetz-Miller. Courtesy of Mardith Schuetz-Miller.*

FIGURE 4.2. *Interior view of the San José church dome and pendentives. Architectural polychromy: vaulted ceiling. Courtesy of Tim Summa.*

crowded with unnecessary ornaments." Nonetheless, given "its size, good taste, and beauty, [the church] would grace a large city as a parish church."

Fr. Salas (1785) referred to the vaulted ceiling of the church nave, the lack of a transept, the dome with glass windows, and the choir window with screens. In addition, the room to the left of the church entrance (the baptistry) had a window with glass and screen; a similar room on the opposite side had two windows facing south, with glass panes but no screens. He noted that the vaulted ceiling was painted.

Fr. López (1785) considered the church and sacristy "the most beautiful structures to be seen anywhere this side of Saltillo." According to Padilla (1820), the "hewn-stone" church was "damaged by time through lack of repair." In spite of the neglect, he thought the "rich ornaments, sacred vases, and much silver set with jewels and ornaments [showed] its former splendor and riches."

Fr. Díaz (1824) described the church in great detail, noting the vaulted roof of the church and the lack of a transept. He also listed some of the exterior and interior architectural features and details of the church.

The doorway of the main portal had a double door with a large latch (or handle) and two small doors with latches. The spiral staircase of the one-stage bell tower was made of dark oak. The tower platform had three balconies of turned wood, and the bell tower, with an iron cross and weathervane on the small lantern, contained four medium-sized bells and one small one, two of them with cracked clappers. The dome, without a lantern, had an iron cross and wire grilles on the four windows with glass panes, which were in poor condition, as were the two windows of the church on the south side.

The "very ample" vaulted choir loft had a railing of turned wood and a lectern. The oval-shaped choir window had double doors (shutters) and a wire screen, "mostly in good condition." The two rooms with vaulted roofs, on the left and right sides of the choir loft, each had a door, one of them with a key. The room below the choir loft (the baptistry to the left of the church entrance) contained a glass window with its wire screen and an iron grate and a double door with the upper half made of carved wood. The room of the same size on the opposite side (a store room) had a door and no lock.

The sanctuary of the church had two steps of smooth stone and a small iron railing. There was a raised wooden stand with a carved railing and a door with a latch that led to the patio of a room on the second floor of the *convento* that was used for guests and as a retreat.[3]

THE ALTARPIECES IN 1785

The altarpieces of the old and new churches are described in the many reports and inventories prepared during that period. It is not surprising to learn that the early altarpieces were not as elaborate as the later ones. Nonetheless, many of the sacred images were used in both sets of altarpieces.

According to Fr. Salas (1785), the new church had a main altarpiece, "another altarpiece," and others on litters or portable altars (Fig. 4.3). The main altar had a throne or backdrop of blue-painted boards adorned with twelve medium-sized screens and one small one, all made of mirror, with gilded edges or frames, and eighteen other screens of gilded wood with their wall lamps. Two of the wall lamps were broken. "Another altarpiece [had] five

3. Solís, "Diary," pp. 48 (quotation), 50; Fr. Morfi, *Diario y derrotero,* pp. 99, 103; idem, *History of Texas,* pp. 95–96 (quotations); "Inventory of Fr. Salas," in *The San José Papers, Part I,* trans. B. Leutenegger, p. 217; Fr. López, "Documents," p. 42; Padilla, "Texas in 1820," p. 59; Fr. Díaz de León, "Inventory of the Church of Mission San José," p. 151.

other small screens of mirror, one broken and another disjointed." A wooden table on a platform was used for the main altarpiece.

The main altarpiece of the new church had a sculpture of St. Joseph in an "old niche" above a carved and gilded tabernacle. Its diadem and staff were both made of silver. The niche in which the St. Joseph was placed had a small taffeta valance and another of printed cotton with a fringe. Both were trimmed with lace where they were tacked onto the niche. Listed for the first time were a small baldachin used to crown the altar and inside it a sculpture of the Crucified Christ with a base inlaid with bone. The baldachin was made of gilded wood with a mirror as a background. There was another sculpture of St. Joseph, similar to the one above the tabernacle, and a St. Francis, "said to be from Mission Espada." A sculpture of Our Lady of the Rosary, first listed in the 1753 inventory, was dressed in an "old garment of lustring, . . . [a] silver crown, and a rosary with silver chain and cross" (Table 4.3).

There was "another altarpiece with a wooden platform and a table that [had] little cotton curtains." In the altarpiece was a small metal figure of Christ on the cross as well as a "large sculpture of Jesus," dressed in an old

FIGURE 4.3. *The main altar of San José de Aguayo, 1785. Drawn to the scale of the sanctuary wall. The sacred images listed as A, E, F, and G are no longer extant. Images B, C, and D are in the sacristy of the church. Diagram by Jacinto Quirarte.*

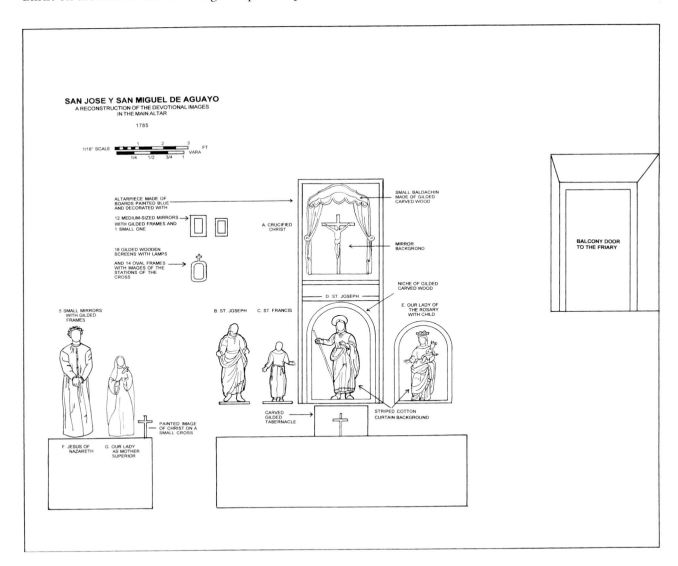

TABLE 4.3. THE ALTARPIECES OF SAN JOSÉ DE AGUAYO

SACRED IMAGES	1753	1755	1785	1824 IN STORAGE
OL of Guadalupe	large	——	——	——
4 (P) (? Subj.)	smaller	——	——	——
Joseph	1.25 v	no dim.	1+ v	1.5 v
Joseph, Michael, Roch, and Anthony	all listed as smaller	——	——	——
Christ Crucified			.5+ v	1+ v
Francis			no dim.	no dim.
Bronze Crucifix			small	small
	altar two			
OL of the Rosary w/Child Jesus	1 v	——	1- v	1- v
Joseph	small	——	.5? v	——
Jesus of Nazareth	1 v	no dim.	large	no dim.
OL as Mother Superior			no dim.	——
Crucifix (P)			small	——
	altar four			
OL of Sorrows	1.5 v	no dim.	——	——
7 (P) of Christ's Passion	small	——	——	——
(P) Stations of the Cross	.5 v (unspecified)	——	no dim. (14 P)	——
		sacristy		
Ildefonso		no dim.	——	——
			portable altar	
OL of the Rosary w/Child Jesus			.5+ v	——
Joseph w/Child			.5+ v	——

Note: OL = Our Lady; (P) = painting/s; v = vara (32.909 inches); dim. = dimensions.

4. "Inventory of Fr. Salas," pp. 218–219, 224; for the images not found in the 1785 altarpieces, see "Inventory of San José by Fr. Núñez de Haro, December 1753," in *The San José Papers, Part I,* trans. B. Leutenegger, pp. 108–110; "Inventory and Report of San José by Fr. Ildefonso Marmolejo, October 4, 1755," in *The San José Papers, Part I,* trans. B. Leutenegger, pp. 110–111.

purple garment of Chinese silk. Other sacred images in the altarpiece, not previously listed, were a sculpture of Our Lady as Mother Superior "in very poor condition (in fact peeling)" and a small cross with Christ painted on it. The altar also had a brass lamp, a bench for the officials, and niches for sculptures of St. Joseph and Our Lady of the Rosary. The latter had a striped cotton curtain in the background.

Sculptures of Our Lady of the Rosary with Child and St. Joseph with Child were placed on two litters or portable stands, which in turn rested on two small tables with satin coverings. One of the two small tables, "with lathed bars, [was] somewhat broken." According to Fr. Salas, the carved sculpture of Our Lady of the Rosary and the Child had silver crowns. The St. Joseph had a silver diadem, and the Child "nine silver rays extending from his crown." (The St. Joseph was smaller than the other two listed in the earlier reports and inventories, as was the Lady of the Rosary. They were probably the two sculptures on order from the College of Querétaro, listed by Fr. Ildefonso Marmolejo in his progress report of 1755.)[4]

THE MAIN ALTARPIECE IN 1824

According to Fr. Díaz (1824), the main altarpiece, made of wood and painted blue, had a large table on a platform and a simulated side altar with two niches in the center. There were three small chairs for the ministers at the altar and a bench for the magistrate in front of the steps. The sculptures originally placed in the altars were stored in the sacristy. The saints are identified in the inventory by name, size, clothing (if any), and condition.

The sculpture of St. Joseph had a garment made of carved, gilded, and painted wood (*estofado*) and a silver diadem and a silver lily staff. The Christ Child had a garment of fine linen, a silk mantle, and a halo of silver rays. The silver baldachin for this sculpture, listed separately, had a silver pedestal and a mirrored background. The second sculpture of St. Joseph, wearing clothes and a silver diadem, was "disfigured." The Jesus of Nazareth was still dressed in a garment of Chinese silk.

There were also two images of the crucified Christ. Both were the same size. The one originally located inside the baldachin had three silver rays, a wooden cross, and a pedestal, inlaid in bone with silver corner-brackets. The other one was made of bronze. The sculpture of Our Lady of the Rosary was still dressed in an "old garment . . . made of lustring." Its crown and rosary were made of silver, and the cross was set in silver. The St. Francis, originally from Espada, was also included in the 1824 inventory along with a St. Michael "with an arm broken off," first listed by Fr. Núñez de Haro in 1753.[5]

THE FACADE

All those who referred to the facade of the new church in their reports and inventories admired its artistic qualities (Fig. 4.4). Fr. Morfi noted in his diary entry for January 9, 1778, that the balcony over the door "beautified" the facade. He added that the rough sandstone (limestone), used with mortar to make one solid piece, was taken from a quarry near La Purísima Concepción.

Fr. Morfi referred in his *History of Texas* to the facade as "very costly because of the sculptures and ornaments with which it was heavily decorated detracting somewhat from its natural beauty." However, he still thought the

FIGURE 4.4. *Reconstruction of the facade. Paintings by Ernst Schuchard, 1927 (a) and 1932 (b). Schuchard Collection. Courtesy of the Daughters of the Republic of Texas Library.*

5. Fr. Díaz de León, "Inventory of the Church of Mission San José," pp. 152, 154; "Inventory of San José by Fr. Núñez de Haro, December 1753."

balcony gave "much majesty to the building," although it could have been improved "if the hexagonal window that illuminates the choir . . . had been made to simulate a door." (The choir window is oval, not hexagonal as Morfi described it.) All in all, he admired the church, adding that "no one could have imagined that there were such good artists in so desolate a place."

Toward the end of his discussion of the mission, Fr. Morfi referred again to the qualities of the limestone, noting that the figures on the facade, the balustrade of the stairway of the *convento,* and an image of St. Joseph on a pedestal "all were made more beautiful by the ease with which the stone [was] worked."

Fr. Salas (1785) simply referred to the "very good" sculptured portal of the facade. Almost forty years later, Fr. Díaz (1824) expressed the view that the facade was made of "very ornately carved stone with 5 stone statues."[6]

THE SACRISTY

Fr. Morfi wrote in his diary on January 1, 1778, that the chapel where three missionaries received them (the sacristy?) was "very beautiful and adorned." In his *History of Texas* he specifically referred to the sacristy and identified it as the temporary church which provided access to the *convento.* In his view, the sacristy was "a handsome and cheerful room, large and well decorated, with vaulted roof, good light, and everything in good taste."

Fr. Salas (1785) referred to the architectural features of the sacristy: the painted vaulted ceiling, divided into three bays, the two doorways with sculptured frames and carved doors, and the sculptured window with an iron grating, glass, and a screen.

Fr. Díaz (1824) described the architectural features of the sacristy in more detail: the sacristy, with a vaulted roof, had a brick floor and two windows, a large one with a broken wire screen and two shutters and a smaller one with an iron grate. Its three cedar doors were "carved with curious forms." The first door listed was in the doorway that leads to the church, the second in a partition wall, and the third (a double door) in the main entrance, with an exterior doorway made of carved stone. The area outside the main doorway had a roof of beams and three walls joined to the sacristy. The roof was in poor condition.[7]

CHURCH FURNISHINGS AND SACRED ITEMS

Fr. Salas (1785) was the first one to refer to the "very well-carved font" in the room to the left of the new church entrance (baptistry). The copper font, used for holy water, had a lid. Fr. Díaz (1824) referred to a small copper tray and vessel for holy water on a stone font (in the baptistry room) "carved with curious designs." He also reported seeing a "beautifully carved stone for holy water" on one side of the church.

Fr. Salas saw a confessional inside the new church "in very poor condition," a brass lamp on the altar, dedicated to Jesus of Nazareth, a bench for the officials, and a communion railing (with an iron grating). Fr. Díaz listed two confessionals (only one with a good grating was in use) and a pulpit made of cedar with a ladder and sounding board (fastened to the wall with a small iron rod).

According to Fr. Marmolejo (1755), there was a new cabinet for vestments found in the sacristy. The items stored in a vestment case were also listed by

6. Fr. Morfi, *Diario y derrotero,* p. 103; idem, *History of Texas,* pp. 96–97; "Inventory of Fr. Salas," p. 217; Fr. Díaz de León, "Inventory of the Church of Mission San José," p. 150.

7. Fr. Morfi, *Diario y derrotero,* p. 99; idem, *History of Texas,* pp. 96–97; "Inventory of Fr. Salas," pp. 219–220; Fr. Díaz de León, "Inventory of the Church of Mission San José," p. 153.

Fr. Salas (1785). He included descriptions of the vestment trimmings ("fine gold edging") and colors and their condition. Some were new; others were somewhat or "extremely worn-out, that is, unusable."[8]

THE *Convento* AND OTHER BUILDINGS

Fr. Morfi (1778) wrote that the two-story building of the *convento* had "spacious galleries," enough rooms for the missionaries and guests, offices, "a large well-ordered kitchen, a comfortable refectory, and a pantry." The gallery of the second story opened out on the flat roofs of the Indian houses, where two sundials, made of limestone, were set up.

Fr. López (1785) reported that the two-story building of the *convento* had a flat roof and was constructed with stone and lime (mortar). It had offices and a kitchen on the first floor and private quarters for the missionaries on the second. A door on the second floor of the *convento* led to a pulpit on the east wall of the church sanctuary. In his view, every part of the *convento* was "in good taste." Padilla (1820) wrote that part of the *convento* was in danger of falling.

Fr. Solís (1767–1768) reported that the Indian houses were built against the wall. According to Fr. Salas (1785), there were fifty-four Indian houses with roofs, windows, and doors, many of them with keys. Fr. López (1785) indicated that there was a street in the area between the church and the *convento* and the Indian houses along the north wall. He noted that all the houses had hand-carved wooden doors, some with good locks.

Fr. Solís referred to the workshops for carpentry, ironwork, and textiles and a furnace to burn lime and brick. Fr. Salas provided more details on the workshops and the granary, which had a vaulted roof, two doors, and a window. Two rooms adjacent to it were used for carpentry work, living quarters for the carpenters, and a storeroom for tools, lumber, and other building materials. Another room with a door and key on the other side of the granary was used for the blacksmith shop, which had all the necessary tools and equipment. There was also a workshop for looms and spinning wheels and next to it a room where cotton and wool were stored. On the opposite side, another room with a door and key was used to store the manufactured goods. It had ten windows, five with iron gratings and five with wooden ones.[9]

THE MISSION WALL, THE RANCHES, AND OTHER CHAPELS

Fr. Solís (1767–1768) noted that the stone masonry wall built around the mission had one door and towers at opposite corners. Fr. Morfi referred to the four doors of the enclosed square and a tower or rampart over each one of them in his diary entry for January 1, 1778. In his *History of Texas* he added that the walled-in enclosure had a gate, with "good strong locks," at each of the cardinal points. Smaller gates were built to accommodate the increase in the Indian population.

The only reference to construction of the ranches is found in the Fr. Marmolejo report (1755). He indicated that a corral was built for the larger herds of cattle. According to Fr. Hierro (1762), there was a chapel of the Sacra Via (Stations of the Cross) at the cemetery of San José de Aguayo.[10]

8. "Inventory of Fr. Salas," pp. 217–220; Fr. Díaz de León, "Inventory of the Church of Mission San José," pp. 151–152; "Inventory and Report of San José by Fr. Ildefonso Marmolejo, October 4, 1755," p. 110.

9. Fr. Morfi, *Diario y derrotero,* p. 97; Fr. López, "Documents," p. 42; Padilla, "Texas in 1820," p. 59; Fr. Solís, "Diary," p. 50; "Inventory of Fr. Salas," p. 215.

10. Fr. Solís, "Diary," p. 50; Fr. Morfi, *Diario y derrotero,* p. 99; idem, *History of Texas,* p. 95; "Inventory and Report of San José by Fr. Ildefonso Marmolejo, October 4, 1755," pp. 124–125; "The Fr. Guardian Simón Hierro Report," in Bolton, *Texas in the Middle Eighteenth Century,* p. 100.

FIGURE 4.5. *Side view of the San José church with collapsed roof. Photograph by Latourette, ca. 1880. Courtesy of the Witte Museum, San Antonio, Texas.*

The Former Mission, 1840–1890

According to eyewitness accounts, some of the soldiers quartered at the mission from 1841 to 1850 used the church facade sculptures for target practice.[11] As a result many of the figures and decorative details were severely damaged. Most of the visitors to the missions during this period were distressed by the vandalism. Later visitors also wrote about the mission and the condition of the buildings.

Most visitors noted that services were occasionally held for the Mexican families that continued to live in some of the mission buildings and in the vicinity and that a few Anglo-Americans began to use the buildings during this period as well.

From 1859 to 1868 the Benedictine Fathers had a priory at the former mission. They did some repairs on the former *convento,* but the work was not completed. The results of their work are seen in the Gothic arches of the portico.

The church sustained great damage during the remainder of the nineteenth century. Part of the north wall collapsed in 1868, and in 1874 the greater part of the north wall and the dome fell (Fig. 4.5).

THE MISSION

11. For the nineteenth-century history of the former mission, see Habig, *San Antonio's Mission San José,* pp. 135–153.

The mission was described as a "large square" by Kendall and "still in good preservation" by Bollaert. Gregg called it "the best piece of ancient architecture in this country." Bartlett thought the buildings "were constructed with a

FIGURE 4.6. *Mission of San José near San Antonio de Béxar. Drawing by Edward Everett. Published by George W. Hughes, Memoir (1850), follows p. 32.*

greater display of art, and still remain in better preservation" than those of the other San Antonio missions.

Sidney Lanier (1873) considered the mission "more elaborate and on a larger scale than the buildings of . . . [Concepción] Mission." In his view, it was "still very beautiful." An unidentified visitor (1876) indicated without specificity that the ruins were "very extensive; more than half of the walls have fallen."[12]

THE CHURCH

The church had been repaired by the time Kendall visited the mission in 1844. But two years later, when Bollaert was there, the church was "full of bats' nests." He thought the date 1781 on the church tower probably referred to the year it was finished. Everett's drawing of the church gives no indication, however, of its condition (Fig. 4.6).

Kingsbury was concerned with "a broad fissure in one of the arches, which must be constantly widening, and unless speedily arrested will not long hence bring the old edifice to the ground." He provided a more detailed description of its architecture than others during this period: "The roof [of the church] is formed by three cloistered arches, resting upon massive pillars, and dome, of perhaps thirty or forty feet in diameter." He also mentioned the steps of the tower used to ascend to the roof of the church.

The date of 1781 mentioned by Bollaert was also seen by Gregg. He added that it was put on with paint but doubted its authenticity. More alarming was his reference to the lack of any furnishings in the church and its use as a granary!

12. Kendall, *Narrative,* vol. 1, p. 50; Bollaert, *William Bollaert's Texas,* p. 232; Gregg, *Diary and Letters,* p. 235; Bartlett, *Personal Narrative,* vol. 1, p. 42; Sidney Lanier, "San Antonio de Bexar," in Corner, *San Antonio,* p. 93; an unidentified visitor (1876), in R. Sturmberg, *History of San Antonio and the Early Days in Texas,* p. 126.

According to Eastman, the "very finely constructed" church and the mission had been deserted for years. Bartlett indicated that two towers had been planned for the church, but only one was completed (Figs. 4.7 and 4.8). He also noted the spiral staircase mentioned by Kingsbury but added that a "rude ladder" was used to ascend the tower, where "[a] fine view of the surrounding country may be had"; the ladder consisted of "a stick of timber with notches cut into its sides."

FIGURE 4.7. *Mission of San José, Texas. Print published by J. R. Bartlett,* **Personal Narrative of Explorations and Incidents in Texas** *(1854), vol. 1, p. 42.*

FIGURE 4.8. *General view of San José mission. Reproduction of a lithograph, ca. 1850. Courtesy of the Witte Museum, San Antonio, Texas.*

FIGURE 4.9. *San José church portal. Reproduction of a lithograph, nineteenth century. Courtesy of the Witte Museum, San Antonio, Texas.*

FIGURE 4.10. *Mission San José church portal. Photograph by Sommerville, before 1879, possibly 1860. Courtesy of the Estate of Harvey P. Smith, Jr.*

According to Corner, the gateway on the western wall mentioned by Kendall was gone. However, the road still entered "the Mission Square just at the right of the granary, where the old entrance was." Although the "ramparts of the Mission Square" were in ruins, Corner believed that in a few years "these now hardly to be defined foundations" would disappear.[13]

THE SCULPTURE OF THE FACADE

Visitors to the mission in the 1840s and 1850s described the portal with its carved architectural details and its figural sculptures in glowing terms (Figs. 4.9 and 4.10). Bollaert wrote that the portal contained "much exquisite work and labor." According to Kingsbury, the portal had an "elaborate finish, six figures in alto relievo, and richly sculptured ornaments." Gregg described the portal and the tower in equally positive terms. "The frontis piece, as well as steeples show some elegance—six full sized images of saints and two angels handsomely carved in frontis piece." Eastman simply described the church as "very finely constructed with much sculptur [sic] . . . around and over the door." Bartlett noted the "elaborate carving" of the architectural details of the portal and identified some of the figural sculptures as "San José, the patron of the church, and the Virgin and Child."

13. Kendall, *Narrative,* vol. 1, p. 51; Bollaert, *William Bollaert's Texas,* p. 232; Seth Eastman, *A Seth Eastman Sketchbook, 1848–1849,* p. xxii; Kingsbury, "Notes from My Knapsack," p. 177; Gregg, *Diary and Letters,* p. 235; Bartlett, *Personal Narrative,* p. 43; Corner, *San Antonio,* p. 17.

FIGURE 4.11. *A Carving, San José Mission (1882). Theodore Gentilz (1820–1906). Gray wash drawing, 8¼ × 5⅜ inches. Courtesy of the Witte Museum, San Antonio, Texas.*

14. Bollaert, *William Bollaert's Texas*, p. 232; Kingsbury, "Notes from My Knapsack," p. 176; Gregg, *Diary and Letters*, p. 235; Eastman, *A Seth Eastman Sketchbook*, p. xxii; Bartlett, *Personal Narrative*, p. 43; unidentified visitor (1876), in Sturmberg, *History of San Antonio*, p. 125; Corner, *San Antonio*, p. 17.

15. Kendall, *Narrative*, vol. 1, pp. 50–51; Bollaert, *William Bollaert's Texas*, p. 232; Gregg, *Diary and Letters*, p. 235; Bartlett, *Personal Narrative*, p. 43.

16. Theodore Gentilz, "Notes"; D. S. Kendall and C. Perry, *Gentilz*, p. 20; Corner, *San Antonio*, p. 17.

An unidentified visitor (1876) considered the portal "a wonderful piece of sculptural art" with St. Joseph on the right and the "Virgin Mother and the Infant Saviour" on the left (he had them in the wrong niches: the St. Joseph is actually St. Joachim and the Virgin Mother is St. Anne and the Child Mary). He identified the figure above the doorway as the "Virgin in the posture which . . . indicates the doctrine of the Immaculate Conception" (this is Our Lady of Guadalupe). He identified the three figures on the second stage of the portal as friars (the one in the center is St. Joseph with Child, flanked by St. Dominic on the left and St. Francis on the right). The portal sculptures were also admired by Corner (1890), who wrote that "its carving is surely 'a joy forever.' . . . The facade is rich with repletion with the most exquisite carving." He considered the drapery of all the figures, the numerous motifs, and the architectural and decorative details "wonderful." The doorway with all its details was "daring in its ornamentation," and the window above the archway "of surpassing workmanship."

According to Corner, there was no agreement regarding the identification of the portal figures. Nonetheless, he quoted Bishop John C. Neraz, who saw the figures of "[t]he Virgin, San José, San Benedict, San Augustine and San Francisco" (no iconographer in recent times has identified any of the figures as Saint Benedict or Saint Augustine).[14]

THE STATE OF THE FACADE SCULPTURES

The portal sculptures were heavily damaged during the 1840s and 1850s as a result of neglect and vandalism. Although the destruction started soon after troops were stationed at the mission in 1841, Kendall, who was there that year, reported that "the stone carvings have not been injured." Unfortunately, the damage began soon thereafter. Bollaert wrote that "the images of saints and other ornamental parts have been sadly mutilated by the soldiery during the wars." Three years later Gregg wrote that "it is painful to see that some wretched persons have wantonly mutilated them [the figural sculptures] by shooting at them." Bartlett also referred to the shooting as well as the deterioration due to the elements, noting that "the work of ruin has been assisted by the numerous military companies near here, who [found] in the hand and features of the statues convenient marks for rifle fire and pistol shots."[15]

By 1882 the figure of St. Anne was still undamaged, as seen in a drawing by Theodore Gentilz. Only the head of the Child Mary was missing (Fig. 4.11). Sometime later the entire sculpture was "gone," as indicated in his notes (no date): "*au S* [to the south] St. Ann (gone), *au N* [to the north] St. Joachim (*sans tête* [without the head])."

A photograph taken before 1890 shows the empty niche where the sculpture had been located (Fig. 4.12). The lower half of the sculpture appears in another photograph taken before 1890 (Fig. 4.13) and in photographs taken in the twentieth century before the sculpture was restored. Evidently at some point before 1890 the entire sculpture disappeared completely and then the lower part reappeared.

Corner was quite concerned about the destruction of the portal by persons who carried off pieces of the sculptures. He was appalled that men would "ruthlessly deface these for the sake of possessing a piece of the material."[16]

THE POLYCHROMY OF THE FACADE

Bartlett was the only one of the visitors to the mission in the 1840s who referred to the polychromy of the facade. Aside from the carved portal, the facade "was ornamented with a sort of stenciling in colors, chiefly red and blue. But few traces of this have withstood the rain." Corner also mentioned the painting as being "red, blue and yellow, but this is now very difficult to discern."[17]

WOODWORK

Several nineteenth-century visitors, among them Kingsbury, Bartlett, and Corner, referred to the winding stairway to the second story (the choir-loft level mentioned in the 1785 inventory) and the logs used from there to the belfry tower. None of the visitors, however, mentioned the wooden doors of the main portal (listed in the 1785 and 1824 inventories), nor did they refer to the metalwork: the iron cross with a weathervane on the belfry tower (listed in the 1785 and 1824 inventories) and the dome cross and the wire grilles on the four dome windows with glass panes (listed in the 1824 inventory).[18]

THE STATE OF THE INTERIOR

In 1841, when Kendall visited San José mission, the church interior was relatively undamaged. "The interior is plain. To the right is a handsome belfry tower, and before the altar a large stone cupola." Unfortunately, it suffered even greater damage than the exterior shortly thereafter. Bollaert (1843) noted that the church was "full of bats' nests, but mass is occasionally said to 8 or 10 Mexican families who live within the walls of the mission." Kingsbury concentrated more on the architectural details of the interior. He referred to the earth floor of the church and the raised stone flooring of the altar area and commented on the condition of the altar, located within

> an area of twenty-five or thirty feet square . . . covered with stone. . . . The altar still preserves its elaborate workmanship but the rich gilding is seen in only a few spots, which have eluded the corroding touch of time.

Kingsbury also commented on one of the surviving devotional sculptures found in the small chapel in the tower base to the right of the entrance:

> [The chapel] . . . at the right displays through a grated door, a statue of the Virgin, apparelled in an old, faded calico gown; and as well calculated, perhaps, to stifle any sentiments of devotion, and substitute those of derision, as any design that could be erected in a temple to the Almighty.

He found the "small chapels" along the sides of the nave of the church empty of any devotional figures.

Bartlett found "little of interest" in the interior. "The dampness [had] destroyed the frescoes upon the walls, and the altar [had] been stripped of its decoration." The unidentified visitor (1876) considered the interior

> a model of rude neatness. The nice, clever and evidently pious Mexican matron, who brought the key for our entrance, had hung the altar with gaudy patch-

17. Bartlett, *Personal Narrative,* p. 43; Corner, *San Antonio,* p. 17.

18. Kingsbury, "Notes from My Knapsack," p. 177; Bartlett, *Personal Narrative,* pp. 43–44; Corner, *San Antonio,* p. 18; for the metal crosses and the spiral staircase, see Fr. Díaz de León, "Inventory of the Church of Mission San José," pp. 150–151.

FIGURE 4.12. *West portal of the San José church. Photograph by N. H. Rose, before 1890. Rose Collection, CN96.229. Courtesy of the Daughters of the Republic of Texas Library.*

FIGURE 4.13. *West portal of the San José church. Photograph by A. L. Delfraisse, before 1890. Courtesy of the Witte Museum, San Antonio, Texas.*

19. Kendall, *Narrative,* vol. 1, p. 50; Bollaert, *William Bollaert's Texas,* p. 232; Kingsbury, "Notes from My Knapsack," p. 176; Bartlett, *Personal Narrative,* p. 43; unidentified visitor (1876), in Sturmberg, *History of San Antonio,* p. 126.

work quilts of her own manufacture. . . . Every part of the ruined chapel was arranged with neatness and decency.

There were also "some old pictures" which he could not plainly see in the dim twilight of the setting sun.[19]

THE SACRISTY

Visitors to the mission also mentioned the sacristy window. Bollaert wrote: "The ornaments on the doorway and window of the sacristy or vestry still show much exquisite work and labour that had been bestowed upon them." To Bartlett, "[t]he most perfect portion of the church is an oval window in the sacristy, which is surrounded with scrolls and wreathwork of exceeding grace and beauty." Although the unidentified visitor (1876) incorrectly identified the sacristy as the baptistry, he considered the window "almost equal to the main door in sculptural beauty." Corner noted that "its curves and proportions are a perpetual delight to the eye," and the doorway "is beautifully sculptured" (see Fig. 4.27).

Corner published a drawing of the holy water font in the sacristy. The carved stone font is embedded in the wall below a niche with a fan-like ogee arch (Fig. 4.30). Just above the font there is a rectangular shaped notched area on the left side of the niche. A metal container placed inside the font, as shown in the drawing, is no longer there.[20]

THE *Convento* (FRIARS' QUARTERS) AND OTHER BUILDINGS

The visitors to the missions also referred to the *convento* behind the church. According to Kendall, there was "a long range of rooms for the missionaries, opening upon a covered gallery or *portales* of nine arcades." Bollaert also mentioned the quarters, correctly identifying the friars as Franciscans "who resided at the oriel [east] side of the church in a fine suite of rooms, shaded by a broad corridor." A few years later, Kingsbury and Eastman erroneously attributed the mission to the Jesuits. Kingsbury referred to the *convento* behind the church as "a long wing, to which arched porticos are appended." Eastman wrote that "a few Mexican families now reside around it and in that portion of the church formerly occupied by the Priests—These old Missions were constructed by the Jesuits." According to Bartlett, the convent, as the friars' quarters were called, "remains in tolerable presentation and is at present inhabited by an American who cultivates the adjoining lands."

Although Kendall did not refer to Indian or Mexican houses, he indicated that "[n]umerous Mexican families still [made] it their residence" and that services for them were performed in the church. Gregg noted that "[i]n the cabins or huts of the square attached to the church [there were] about a dozen indigent families (Mexican), in all about 60 or 70 souls." Eastman indicated that "a few Mexican families reside around" the mission and in the quarters formerly occupied by the friars.[21]

THE RESTORED ARCHITECTURE AND THE EXTANT SCULPTURES, 1890 TO THE PRESENT

Nothing was done at the former mission after the north wall collapsed in 1868, and the greater part of the roof and the dome fell in 1874 (Figs. 4.5, 4.14, and 4.15). The situation remained unchanged until 1917, when the first restoration work was begun under the auspices of the Daughters of the Republic of Texas. Restoration work was continued in the following decades with different sponsors.

The Redemptionist Fathers (whose order was founded in 1732) took over the former mission in 1922 and remained there for the next nine years. In 1928 half of the bell tower collapsed but was immediately repaired (Fig. 4.16).

The Franciscan Fathers of the Province of the Sacred Heart of St. Louis arrived in 1931 at the invitation of Archbishop Arthur J. Drossaerts. The new friary they built east of the old *convento* was dedicated on October 24, 1931.

20. Bollaert, *William Bollaert's Texas,* p. 232; Bartlett, *Personal Narrative,* p. 43; unidentified visitor (1876), in Sturmberg, *History of San Antonio,* p. 126; Corner, *San Antonio,* p. 18.

21. Kendall, *Narrative,* vol. 1, pp. 50–51; Bollaert, *William Bollaert's Texas,* p. 232; Kingsbury, "Notes from My Knapsack," p. 177; Eastman, *A Seth Eastman Sketchbook,* p. xxii; Bartlett, *Personal Narrative,* p. 43; Gregg, *Diary and Letters,* p. 235.

FIGURE 4.14. *General view of the San José church. Photograph, after 1874. Courtesy of the Witte Museum, San Antonio, Texas.*

FIGURE 4.15. *Interior view of the nave of the San José church. Photograph by Harvey Patterson, ca. 1880. Courtesy of the Witte Museum, San Antonio, Texas.*

FIGURE 4.16. *View of the collapsed south tower of the San José church. Photograph taken after the tower collapsed in 1928. It was reconstructed shortly thereafter. Courtesy of the Estate of Harvey Smith, Jr.*

The complete restoration of the church and the rest of the mission was carried out in the 1930s under the auspices of the archdiocese and the Works Progress Administration, the San Antonio Conservation Society, and Bexar County. The restoration of the north wall, vaults, crossing dome, and architectural details was done under the direction of Harvey P. Smith from 1933 to 1937. Services were resumed in the church proper in 1937, following its rededication on April 18, 1937.

San José was designated a national historic site by the U.S. Department of the Interior on June 1, 1941, as the result of an agreement reached between the Texas State Parks Board, the archdiocese of San Antonio, and the U.S. government on the ownership and operation of the site. It became known as San José Mission State Park.

The west portal doors of the church were recreated in 1940, and figural and architectural sculptures of the west portal and the sacristy north and east doors were restored in 1949.

Archaeological excavations have been carried out at the mission (1984) and the *acequia* (1988, 1991). It is now part of the San Antonio Missions National Historical Park.[22]

22. For the restoration work on San José in the 1930s and 1940s, see Habig, *San Antonio's Mission San José,* pp. 174–184; see also *The Restored San José Mission Church,* no pagination (the booklet was published to commemorate the "Re-dedication of San José Mission Church"); for archaeological excavations, see I. W. Cox, *Archaeological Monitoring of the San José Acequia, Wastewater Facilities Improvement Program, San Antonio, Texas;* A. A. Fox and I. W. Cox, *Testing of the San José Mission Acequia, San Antonio Missions National Historical Park, Bexar County, Texas;* R. J. Hard, A. A. Fox, I. W. Cox, K. J. Gross, B. A. Meissner, G. Mendez, C. L. Tennis, and J. Zapata, *Excavations at Mission San José y San Miguel de Aguayo, San Antonio, Texas.*

THE MISSION

The facade of the San José church faces west (Fig. 4.17). The church is directly in front of the main entrance on the west wall. Its sacristy is adjacent to its south wall; behind the church, appended to the apse, is the *convento*. The entire cluster of buildings has an east-west orientation and is located in the north-eastern corner of the enclosure.

Although the church does not have a cruciform plan, it has a dome over the area where transepts would normally be found. The granary is located on the west wall to the left of the main entrance. The Indian houses were built along the four walls of the mission compound.

THE MISSION WALL

The reconstructed wall of San José has a north-south orientation, but its proportions differ from those of the Valero wall. The east-west walls are longer than those of Valero. The main entrance is on the west wall near the north-western corner of the enclosure. There were bastions at each of the four corners and soldiers' quarters at the northwest corner. Other entrances were located near each of the four corners of the wall.

FIGURE 4.17. *General view of the San José church facade. Architectural and figural sculpture. Courtesy of Kathy Vargas.*

THE CHURCH FACADE

The original design of the facade of San José church (1768–1782) remains intact, even though some of its constituents have been altered by restorations.

ARCHITECTURAL POLYCHROMY

Several reconstruction drawings in color of what remained of the polychromy on the facade were done by Ernst Schuchard in 1927 and 1932 (Fig. 4.4). He and Rufus Walker based their restoration work of 1949 on that early work (Fig. 4.18). The remaining geometric and floral motifs were originally painted over the entire facade.

The facade has an overall grid created with Greek crosses and the resulting squares filled with alternating quatrefoil frames. There were simulated masonry block frames on the tower base windows and along the outer sides and top of the tower bases. Quatrefoil shapes alternate on the tower base masonry blocks. The polychromed surfaces do not appear to have been used to divide the facade into three parts, as was done at Concepción. Traces of paint are still visible on the underside of some of the arches in the *convento* and around the facade window.

ARCHITECTURAL AND FIGURAL SCULPTURE

The architectural frame is comprised of a single bay which spans the two stories of the portal (Fig. 4.19). The entablature of the first story establishes its width, and the niche-pilasters provide its outer frame. Inner pilasters extend up to the entablature beyond the jambs of the doorway with a mixtilinear arch. The narrower second story has an oval window and an entablature with supporting pilasters which are in line with the inner dimensions of the main doorway. Mixtilinear brackets provide the frame for the ensemble and a transition to the cornice topped by a stone cross.

There are five free-standing figural sculptures and a sixth in high relief on the main portal. The figural sculptures, placed on pedestals, are approximately the same size. The sixth one is slightly smaller. Two of the free-standing figural sculptures are framed by niche-pilasters on the first story. Two on either side of the choir window are framed on their outer sides by mixtilinear brackets and on the inner sides by slightly projecting pilasters that extend beyond the oval window in the center of the second story. The fifth figure is placed directly above the choir window. The sixth sculpture, in high relief, is located directly under the projecting cornice of the entablature and above the mixtilinear arch of the doorway. A high-relief sculpture of the Sacred Heart with thorns is placed on the uppermost part of the portal just beneath the stone cross (Fig. 4.20).

Scallop shells form the arches of the two niche-pilasters on the first story and the frame for the Sacred Heart on the second story. Similar shells are placed beneath the pedestals with figural sculptures of the second story and in the capitals of the pilasters of the second story. Acanthus leaf forms are found throughout the entire portal within columnar and pedestal supports, spandrels, capitals, entablatures, and the choir window frame. Full-figure cherubim hold onto some of the acanthus leaf forms around the mixtilinear frame of the

FIGURE 4.18. *Geometric and floral designs. Right tower base; south wall of the San José church. Polychromy restored by E. Schuchard and R. Walker in 1949. Note the spiral stairway enclosed by the circular structure with a doorway and oval window adjacent to the south wall (woodwork). Stairs are made of oak up to the choirloft. Courtesy of Kathy Vargas.*

FIGURE 4.19. *Main portal of the San José church. Architectural and figural sculpture. Restored in part from 1933 to 1937 and 1949. The main portal doors are modern reproductions by Peter Mahrsbendel, 1940. Woodwork. Courtesy of Kathy Vargas.*

FIGURE 4.20. *Close-up of the Sacred Heart of Jesus with thorns and the cross on top of the San José church portal. Architectural sculpture. The cross is a modern addition. Courtesy of Kathy Vargas.*

main doorway and the oval window. Two cherub heads are placed on the lower part of the choir window frame. A base comprised of three cherub heads is used as a support for the figure above the same window.

STYLE CONSIDERATIONS AND RELATIONSHIPS

The use of a mixtilinear arch for the San José portal doorway and niche-pilasters flanking it as well as comparable surfaces on the second story is characteristic of the Late Baroque period in New Spain.[23] The breakup of the receding and projecting horizontals by the undulating verticals creates the dramatic effects of dark and light favored by the Baroque artists.

The Mexican churches of Guadalupe in Aguascalientes, La Valenciana in Guanajuato, and Lagos de Moreno in Jalisco have been suggested as sources for the portal design of the San José church in San Antonio. It is more likely that the source is closer at hand in the side portal of the San Agustín church in Zacatecas, Mexico, for it is there that we find the mixtilinear outer brackets of the second story, the mixtilinear arch of the doorway, and the niche-pilasters with their respective mixtilinear arches. Although the niche-pilasters are similar to those found in Guanajuato, there are no mixtilinear arches on the exterior surfaces of La Valenciana or in any of the other Guanajuato churches. The mixtilinear arches are relegated to the retables (altarscreens) and interior doorways of those churches. The facade of the Guadalupe church in Aguascalientes has the mixtilinear brackets at the second story but does not have the pronounced niche-pilasters. It has very prominent double *estípites* framing each niche on the first and second stories.

The Aguascalientes church of Guadalupe is part of the tradition that started at the cathedral in Mexico City and spread northward during the second half of the eighteenth century. It is based on polychromy and the use of the *estípite*, introduced by Jerónimo Balbás in the Capilla de los Reyes (1718–1737) in the cathedral in Mexico City. It was used soon afterward at the Cathedral Sagrario (1749–1768) by Lorenzo Rodríguez. It was also used in a number of churches around the same time in Tepozotlán, Guanajuato, San Luis Potosí, and other cities in north-central New Spain.

23. For the Late Baroque period in New Spain, see G. Kubler and M. Soria, *Art and Architecture in Spain and Portugal and Their American Dominions, 1500–1800,* p. 77. Kubler considered the portal of San José de Aguayo the "ultimate expansion of Rodríguez's School, via Aguascalientes (Guadalupe church 1767–89)" (p. 81).

The niche-pilasters of the San José church in San Antonio are similar to those seen on the portals of La Valenciana in Guanajuato (1765–1788) and the Guadalupe church in Zacatecas. Although there are token *estípites* flanking the niche-pilasters in Zacatecas, there are none at the San José church portal.

CONTENT AND MEANING

The discussion of the portal figural sculptures of the portal follows in boustrephedon or zigzag fashion from left to right on the first story up to the lower center and in the same manner on the second story. The first figure on the left holding a book in his left hand and a scroll(?) in his right is St. Joachim (Fig. 4.21). The second figure on the right is St. Anne with the Child Mary in her arms. The Child Mary holds an open book in her hands. The third figure over the main doorway, modeled on the miraculous image in the basilica of Guadalupe in Mexico City, is Our Lady of Guadalupe (Fig. 4.22). The first figure on the left of the second story is St. Dominic (Fig. 4.23). He holds a book in his right hand and may have held the staff associated with him in his left. The robe with the front panel extending from the upper to the lower part of the body and the cloak and capelet are clearly meant to represent the habit of the Dominican Order. The figure on the right represents St. Francis, for he has the attributes of the saint—the habit with the Franciscan cord, the cross, and the skull. The central figure is St. Joseph holding the Christ Child in his arms. He is always shown bearded.

FIGURE 4.21. *Details of the San José church portal: a. St. Joachim, b. St. Anne and the Child Mary. Figural sculpture. The head and the lower left and right arms of the St. Joachim figure are modern restorations; the entire upper half of the bodies of the St. Anne and Child Mary figures are modern restorations, 1949. Courtesy of Kathy Vargas.*

The figural sculptures and their placement on the portal convey several levels of meaning which can be subsumed under spiritual and temporal matters. As motifs, they provide religious, cultural, and ethnographic information. Symbols associated with the figures, such as the Sacred Heart of Jesus with thorns, provide a deeper religious meaning.

On the primary level, St. Joachim, St. Anne and the Child Mary, and St. Joseph and the Christ Child and their placement on the portal are reminiscent of the images known as the Tree of Jesse. Traditionally, these images have been interpreted as depictions of the genealogy of Christ. The representation of the ancestors of Christ in these images as the fruit of the tree that grows from Jesse, the father of David, is based on the Gospel of St. Matthew. Usually the Virgin Mary, holding the Christ Child in her arms, is placed in the uppermost part of the tree. This is based on the prophecy of Isaiah 11:1–2, "And there shall come forth a rod out of the stem of Jesse, and a Branch shall grow of his roots: And the spirit of the Lord shall rest upon him. . . ."

When the Crucifixion is included in these images, the meaning changes to

FIGURE 4.22. *Our Lady of Guadalupe. Detail of the San José church main portal. Figural sculpture, restored in part, 1949. Courtesy of Kathy Vargas.*

FIGURE 4.23. *Detail of the San José church main portal, second story. From the left, sculptures framing the choir window: St. Dominic, St. Joseph with Christ Child, and St. Francis. Architectural and figural sculpture and metalwork. Restored in part in 1949: the shell corbel, the two panels with twin acanthus leaf scrolls to the immediate right in the frieze, the acanthus leaf scroll below the corbel, the winged cherub on the left, the head of St. Joseph and Child Jesus. The wrought-iron railing was added before 1937. Courtesy of Kathy Vargas.*

the idea of revival of the "Tree of Life" through Christ's sacrifice. Other interpretations of the Tree of Jesse images have emphasized the genealogy of the Virgin Mary. This is signaled by the placement of the Virgin Mary holding the Christ Child in her arms instead of the Christ Child alone in the uppermost part of the image. Related images found in Spain, New Spain, and its northernmost provinces, including Texas, are known as Los Cinco Señores (The Holy Family) and La Mano Poderosa (The Powerful Hand). All of them include the parents and maternal grandparents of the Christ Child. The inclusion of other motifs and symbols distinguishes one from the other and determines the meaning of the image.

The San José portal includes the five members of the Holy Family in a manner that differs slightly from traditional images of the Tree of Jesse, Los Cinco Señores, and La Mano Poderosa. In the Tree of Jesse and La Mano Poderosa images, St. Joachim and St. Anne are always shown on the lowermost level of the image, followed by St. Joseph and the Virgin flanking and slightly below the Christ Child. In some of the Tree of Jesse images, as already noted, the Virgin Mary holds the Christ Child. In the images known as Los Cinco Señores, the focus is on the Christ Child held by the Virgin Mary in the center, flanked by St. Joseph, St. Joachim, and St. Anne.

In terms of hierarchy, the San José portal is similar to the Tree of Jesse and La Mano Poderosa images rather than Los Cinco Señores. The Christ Child, placed in the upper part of the portal, is held by St. Joseph instead of the

Virgin Mary. His maternal grandparents are placed in the lower part on either side of the main door. The Virgin Mary is shown as a child in her mother's arms at the same level and under the first entablature as Our Lady of Guadalupe in the pose of the Virgin of the Apocalypse. Aside from the similarities in arrangement, there are also parallels in meaning. References to the Crucifixion of Christ in the Tree of Jesse and La Mano Poderosa images are also found on the San José portal. The Sacred Heart of Jesus with the crown of thorns is placed above St. Joseph and the Christ Child.

In all representations of the Tree of Jesse, Jesse is shown in a recumbent or sitting position, but almost always asleep. The tree grows from different parts of his body, usually from his side or heart. The ancestors of the Virgin Mary are shown as busts or seated in the branches of the tree. The culminating part of the image is the seated figure of the Virgin Mary with or without the Christ Child. In some examples God the Father and St. Joseph are shown together in the upper part of the image.

Images of Los Cinco Señores, in contrast, can be described as intimate portrayals of a nuclear family unit. What makes these depictions different from an ordinary portrayal of a family, however, is the dove of the Holy Spirit and God the Father over the Virgin Mary and the Christ Child. Images of La Mano Poderosa have the five members of the Holy Family perched on the fingers of a large open hand instead of the branches of a tree found in the Tree of Jesse images. There is always a wound in the palm of the hand in these images.

The Crucified Christ grafted onto the Tree of Jesse, the wound of the Crucified Christ depicted in La Mano Poderosa, and the Sacred Heart of Christ with thorns on the San José portal all point to the overall meaning of these images. They refer to the blood of Christ and His sacrifice to revive the dead tree of life, to atone for the sins of the world.

The other figures on the portal point to other meanings that were important in the conversion effort. The placement of the image of Our Lady of Guadalupe above the doorway emphasizes the special meaning the image had for the people of New Spain (Creoles and Mexican Indians) in spiritual and ethnographic terms. She was the focus of their religious beliefs and their special relationship to the Virgin Mary following her appearance to Juan Diego as Our Lady of Guadalupe in 1531. In temporal terms, she was also a reminder that the mission was founded by Franciscan missionaries, whose administrative headquarters were located at the Colegio de Nuestra Señora de Guadalupe de Propaganda Fide in Zacatecas.

The figure of St. Joseph, to whom the church was dedicated, is a reminder of his special relationship with the Indians of Texas and New Spain. According to Norman Neuerburg, the cult of St. Joseph became very important in the New World. "The first church dedicated to St. Joseph in the New World was San José de los Naturales, the chapel of the Indians in Mexico City, founded in 1527. St. Joseph thus became a special patron of the Indians."[24]

Finally, the figures of St. Dominic and St. Francis to the left and right of St. Joseph represent the special relationship between the two saints, which was carried over into the two orders they founded.

In summary, the main theme of the portal is the genealogy of Christ and His sacrifice for humankind. The primary motifs, His parents and maternal grandparents, are included on each side of the main doorway and above the

24. For a discussion of the Tree of Jesse theme and La Parentela de María (the Parentage of Mary, called Los Cinco Señores in New Spain), see M. Trens, *María: Iconografía de la Virgen en el arte español,* pp. 98–114; see also A. M. Reyes, "Los Cinco Señores: Una pintura del siglo XVI en la Catedral de México," in *Estudios acerca del arte novohispano: Homenaje a Elisa Vargas Lugo;* N. Neuerburg, *Santos para el Pueblo, Saints for the People,* p. 58.

FIGURE 4.24. *Close-up of the wrought-iron cross on top of the San José church belfry. Metal work. Restored, 1934–1937. Courtesy of Kathy Vargas.*

choir window. The symbol of His Sacred Heart with thorns is included in the uppermost part of the portal. The reference to Christ's Crucifixion to atone for the sins of the world finds parallels in the images of the Tree of Jesse and La Mano Poderosa. The first stage of the portal also includes the well-known theme of the Virgin Mary as a Child being instructed by her mother, St. Anne. Our Lady of Guadalupe, the Virgin of the Apocalypse, is an avocation of the Virgin Mary but also serves to render homage to the administrative center of the Franciscans who founded the mission, the Colegio de Nuestra Señora de Guadalupe de Propaganda Fide. She was a reminder of the special relationship that the peoples of New Spain had with Our Lady of Guadalupe. The second stage refers to the two related orders of the Dominicans and the Franciscans as followers of the cult of St. Joseph, to whom the church was dedicated, and to his position as patron of the Indians.

It is very likely that the friars used the portal to instruct the Indians on the meaning of the Catholic church, the Franciscan Order, the Apostolic College of Zacatecas, and their special relationship with St. Joseph and Our Lady of Guadalupe.

RESTORATION OF THE FIGURAL AND ARCHITECTURAL SCULPTURES

In 1949 the forearms of St. Joachim, the upper half of the St. Anne and Child Mary figures, a number of cherubs around the figure of Our Lady of Guadalupe, the left hand of St. Dominic, the crucifix held in the right hand of the St. Francis figure, the head of St. Joseph, and the upper part of the Christ Child's body, with the exception of the right arm, were all restored (Figs. 4.21, 4.22, and 4.23).

The architectural sculpture of the lower part of the first-story niche-pilasters (the area between each support-base and the platform for the figural sculpture) was damaged (Fig. 4.19). The bases were reconstructed in the 1930s.

The stump of the stone cross which was originally on the upper part of the portal is shown in various states of deterioration in photographs taken from the mid-nineteenth to the early twentieth centuries and in nineteenth-century drawings, prints, and paintings (Figs. 4.12 and 4.14). The cross was in place in 1848, as shown in a drawing done that year by Everett (Fig. 4.6). A new stone cross was put in place in 1949 (Fig. 4.20).[25]

RESTORATION OF METALWORK AND WOODWORK

The original metal cross of the dome was already gone by 1848, as seen in Everett's drawing. This is also confirmed by published engravings and photographs taken throughout the nineteenth century (Figs. 4.7 and 4.8). The original belfry cross may have been used in its reconstruction in the 1930s (Fig. 4.24).

The iron balcony on the second story of the church facade is a modern addition (Figs. 4.19 and 4.23). The railing does not appear in nineteenth-century photographs of the facade (Fig. 4.12). According to the booklet used for the rededication of the church on April 17, 1937, "the ornamental details of the railing [were] made to follow the designs in the . . . Rose Window." It was undoubtedly put in place during the 1934–1937 restoration of the church.

The wooden doors of the main portal, listed in the 1785 and 1824 inventories, are no longer there. According to Habig, the doors disappeared sometime

25. For the restoration of the portal sculptures, see Habig, *San Antonio's Mission San José,* p. 179; see also "San Antonio Lives Again," *San Antonio Express Magazine* (April 16, 1950): 25.

FIGURE 4.25. *Damaged spiral staircase enclosure of San José. Photograph, early twentieth century. Onderdonk Collection. Courtesy of the Witte Museum, San Antonio, Texas.*

in the 1880s. The present ones are 1940 reproductions carved by Peter Mahrs-bendel (Fig. 4.19). The doors are based on a photograph taken around 1860 and on designs and research carried out by Harvey P. Smith, Sr.

Although technically found in the interior, the circular tower staircase is included here because it is visible from the outside of the church. It is comprised of heavy wedge-shaped steps of live oak overlapped to form a spiral and encased in a circular tower (Fig. 4.18). According to the *San Antonio Express Magazine* (1950), "the late Mrs. Henry Drought found the steps of the spiral stairway scattered about [in the 1920s], and replaced them with her own funds" (Fig. 4.25). The circular tower was undamaged when the south tower collapsed in 1928 (Fig. 4.16).[26]

26. "The Facade with Railing," in *The Restored San José Mission Church,* no pagination; Habig, *San Antonio's Mission San José,* p. 177; "San Antonio Lives Again," p. 24.

THE CHURCH INTERIOR

ARCHITECTURAL SCULPTURE

Although Fr. Salas (1785) referred to the "sculptured stone" doorway leading from the church nave to the sacristy, no further references to it were made in the other inventories or in the travelers' accounts published in the nineteenth century.

The carved rectangular doorframe is framed above by a cornice molding and by low pedestals at the base (Fig. 4.26). An elaborately carved motif spans the top center of the header and fills the space defined by the entablature, which extends into a hemispherical shape in the center. The same motif is used for the elevated bases of the niche-pilaster of the main portal and at the base of the sacristy rose window. The doorframe has double engaged pilasters

FIGURE 4.26. *San José church interior. Doorway to the north side of the sacristy. Architectural sculpture and woodwork. The door was buried in debris when the dome and roof fell in 1874. The sculptured moldings of the entablature were restored in the 1930s. Courtesy of Kathy Vargas.*

with rounded base molding on square blocks. The shafts without capitals continue around the header and lintel to echo the frame. A vine-like motif carved in low relief over the entire surface appears to be laced around a half-round molding in the center of the frame. There are additional motifs carved in low relief along the outer sides of the door jambs.

The doorway was buried in debris when the dome and roof fell in 1874. Within a few years the debris inside the church was cleared, as seen in a photograph by Harvey Patterson taken around 1880 (Fig. 4.15). The sculptured door frame is slightly damaged. The sculptured moldings of the entablature were restored in the 1930s (Fig. 4.26).[27]

WOODWORK AND POLYCHROMY

Part of the choir-loft balustrade was available in the 1930s for use as a model for the turned balusters of the recreated communion railing.

Fr. Salas (1785) referred to the painting on the arches of the church nave. He also reported "the three arches [*sic:* vaults] that [were] painted [in the sacristy]." The few remainders of the wall paintings in the church were reported by Bartlett in 1851. "The dampness has destroyed the frescoes upon the walls." The architectural and geometric designs in blue, yellow, and brown in the nave interior of the San José church were restored between 1934 and 1937. There are no traces of painting in the sacristy.[28]

THE SACRISTY

EXTERIOR SCULPTURES

The San José sacristy window has a mixtilinear beveled or quatrefoil frame, which is essentially a rectangle with two hemispherical extensions above and below and two extended ones (oval shaped) on the sides. The scrolls and floral patterns on the sides overlap the sides of the frame and extend vertically in both directions to encompass the architectural portal with pilasters and entablature, which is used as a backdrop for the window (Fig. 4.27).

The mixtilinear frame of the sacristy window is in keeping with the emphasis on these contours on the facade and others like it in Zacatecas and elsewhere in north-central New Spain.

Unlike the sculptured portal, which demonstrates a partial loss of visual cohesion, the sacristy window reveals no such disparity between structural and decorative aspects. There is a beautiful balance between the geometric and organic design programs. Schuetz attributed the sacristy window to Antonio Salazar. The window "was rejointed and made waterproof in 1949."[29]

The carved east door of the sacristy provides access from the *convento* (Fig. 4.28). The Roman arch, supported by multiple pilasters set on base blocks, has the appearance of being superimposed onto a carved portal with a large entablature. The arch has a shell over the keystone and acanthus leaves over the surfaces of the half columns and the voussoirs of the arch. There are winged angel or cherub heads superimposed on the capitals of the half columns. The acanthus leaf motif is continued on the pilasters leading up to the entablature, which is comprised of projecting and receding surfaces, all in the Baroque manner. The motifs on each side of the columns or pilasters of the doorway

FIGURE 4.27. *General view of the San José sacristy window with a wrought-iron grille. Architectural sculpture and iron work. Courtesy of Kathy Vargas.*

27. "Inventory of Fr. Salas," p. 217; *The Restored San José Mission Church,* no pagination.

28. "Inventory of Fr. Salas, 1785," pp. 217–218; Bartlett, *Personal Narrative,* p. 43.

29. Schuetz, "Professional Artisans," p. 31.

FIGURE 4.28. *Exterior view of the San José sacristy doorway from the* **convento.** *Architectural sculpture. Courtesy of Kathy Vargas.*

are related to similar motifs found as early as the sixteenth century in the Plateresque architecture of New Spain. These are extended *S*-shaped forms which became an integral part of the sculptural vocabulary used throughout New Spain.

The east doorway of the sacristy is similar to the north doorway leading from the church nave to the sacristy. The same craftsmen must have worked on both door frames, because the same motifs are found on the half columns included on the inner side of the lintel and jambs of the doorway. What differs is the cornice of the entablature, which extends beyond its horizontal direction into a hemispherical shape in the center (Fig. 4.26). The sacristy doorway was restored in 1949.

IRONWORK AND WOODWORK

The iron grille on the sacristy window, listed in the 1785 and 1824 inventories, is still in place (Fig. 4.27). Schuetz ascribed the grille to Francisco Poredano.[30] The sacristy doors were restored by Harvey Smith, Jr., in the mid-1960s (Fig. 4.28). The elaborately carved panels are original. The plain panels are replacements.

30. Ibid., p. 34.

INTERIOR ARCHITECTURAL SCULPTURE

The north and east interior doorways of the sacristy have shell-shaped arches similar to the one found in the Concepción infirmary window (Fig. 4.29). The sacristy window does not have a shell-shaped arch. In Corner's view (1890), "the fan-like fluted canopies of the window and recesses have a pretty architectural effect."

Some of the sculptured capitals of the sacristy pilasters have winged cherubs. They are similar to those of the church facade pilasters, which are in line with the door jambs and whose capitals support the entablature of the first stage of the portal. The carved holy water font in the sacristy is embedded in

FIGURE 4.29. *San José sacristy interior. East doorway. Architectural sculpture. Courtesy of Kathy Vargas.*

FIGURE 4.30. *San José sacristy interior. Holy water font. Stone sculpture. Courtesy of Kathy Vargas.*

FIGURE 4.31. *St. Joseph. Wood sculpture. Gilded estofado, glass eyes. a. Front view. b. Reverse side. Originally in Old Spanish Missions Center; now in sacristy altar. Courtesy of Kathy Vargas.*

the wall below a niche with a mixtilinear arch (Fig. 4.30). Although there are no references to this font in the colonial documents, two holy water fonts near the entrance to the church are listed by Fr. Salas (1785) and Fr. Díaz (1824).[31]

RESTORATION OF THE EXTANT SCULPTURES

There are presently five sculptures of St. Joseph—two in the sacristy and three in the Spanish Missions Center. At least one, possibly two, of the sculptures may be original to San José Mission. The St. Joseph originally placed in the main altar of the church is now by itself on a pedestal in the southeast corner of the sacristy. The other St. Joseph of similar size but in poor condition, now in the Spanish Missions Center, may also be originally from San José Mission.

The sculpture of St. Joseph presently located in the sacristy is the titular saint of the San José church (Fig. 4.31). The sculpture is gilded, with *estofado;* it has glass eyes and measures forty-one inches high, including the halo but not the pedestal. The Christ Child is missing.

According to Salas (1785), a sculpture of St. Joseph "a little more than a vara [over thirty-two inches] in size [was placed in] an old niche [in the main altar of the San José church] above the tabernacle, which is carved and gilded." The sculpture "has a silver diadem and staff." Fr. Díaz (1824) wrote that this same

31. Corner, *San Antonio,* p. 19; "Inventory of Fr. Salas," p. 217; Fr. Díaz de León, "Inventory of the Church of Mission San José," p. 151.

sculpture was "1½ varas [forty-nine inches] in height." He described the figure as wearing a "garment of carved, gilded, and painted wood, with a silver diadem and a silver lily staff, and with a Christ Child who [wears] a shirt of fine linen, a silk mantle and silver halo rays." Its baldachin of silver "with a base of the same [silver] and a back rest of mirrors [was] stored in the sacristy."

The second sculpture of St. Joseph now found in the Spanish Missions Center may be the one described in the 1824 inventory as "dressed and very disfigured, with only a silver diadem." The sculpture was found in the 1930s by Castañeda. It is gilded and has *estofado;* the Christ Child, loose but extant, is in very poor condition (Fig. 4.32).

The sculpture of the titular saint is seen in a late-nineteenth-century photograph of the sacristy altar (Fig. 4.33). It is located in the west window niche; below it are smaller sculptures behind an altar table with sculptures of another St. Joseph on the right and a robed figure on the left. The robed figure is no longer extant, but the St. Joseph figure is now in the Spanish Missions Center. The cross seen to the left of the robed figure is now on exhibition in the San José arts and crafts display area.

The sculpture of St. Francis presently located in the Spanish Missions Center has a carved head, neck, and arms and a cloth armature body and is dressed in a long brown tunic which corresponds to the habit of the Franciscan Order (Fig. 4.34). It is twenty-nine inches tall.

The sculpture was originally placed in the main altarpiece of the San José church. According to Fr. Salas (1785) and Fr. Díaz (1824), the sculpture of St. Francis placed in the main altar of the San José church was originally found in the Espada altarpiece. Fr. Sáenz (1772) listed a sculpture of a "very devout image . . . with his key." It was originally placed in "a carved and gilded niche one vara in height." A sculpture of St. John Capistran was placed above it.

FIGURE 4.32. *St. Joseph with "missing" Christ Child. Wood sculpture. Old Spanish Missions Center. Courtesy of Kathy Vargas.*

FIGURE 4.33. *Interior view of the San José sacristy toward the altar. West wall. Photograph by M. E. Jacobson, 1880s– 1890s. Gift of Mr. and Mrs. Earl Sammons, CN96.212. Courtesy of the Daughters of the Republic of Texas Library.*

FIGURE 4.34. *Two views of St. Francis. Wood sculpture. Carved head, neck, and arms; body is cloth armature; dressed in long brown tunic. Twenty-nine inches high. Old Spanish Missions Center. Courtesy of Kathy Vargas.*

FIGURE 4.35. *Our Lady of the Rosary with Christ Child. Wood sculpture. Forty-four inches high. Gilded* estofado *and glass eyes. Originally in the Old Spanish Missions Center; now in sacristy altar. Courtesy of Kathy Vargas.*

The sculpture of Our Lady of the Rosary and the Christ Child is presently located in the San José Sacristy (Fig. 4.35). The Virgin is gilded, with *estofado* and glass eyes. It is forty-four inches high. Also in the sacristy is a sculpture of St. Joseph and the Christ Child placed in the central part of the sacristy altar area. The gilded sculpture has *estofado* and glass eyes. It is forty-five and one-half inches high. According to M. K. Schuetz and R. K. Winn, the Christ Child is not the original one placed with the St. Joseph. The sculpture, originally located in San Fernando Cathedral, was taken to San José mission in 1973.[32]

32. "Inventory of Fr. Salas," pp. 217–218; Fr. Díaz de León, "Inventory of the Church of Mission San José," pp. 150–151; the sculpture of St. Joseph found by Carlos E. Castañeda and Charles Muskavitch and Mrs. Muskavitch ("known professionally as Gail Northe of radio fame") in the 1930s was reported in an article titled "Rare Objects of Art Found," *San Antonio Light* (date unknown, possibly 1937; copies of the undated newspaper clippings were provided by M. Schuetz, who obtained the copies from Sister M. Tharsilla Fuchs of Our Lady of the Lake College); Fr. Sáenz, *Inventory: 1772,* p. 6; M. K. Schuetz and R. K. Winn, "The Art of the Era," in *San Antonio in the Eighteenth Century,* p. 121.

5

La Purísima Concepción

Nuestra Señora de la Purísima Concepción de Acuña was moved from the Colorado River in 1731. The exact construction period for the present church of the mission is not known, but it probably was initiated in the late 1730s, as there is evidence of an earlier permanent church.[1] Recent excavations at the mission have revealed the remains of an old adobe church used before the present church was built. The stone and mortar church was under construction in 1745 and was finished in 1755. It has a cruciform plan with a dome at the crossing and two bell towers flanking the entrance, each with a chapel beneath; one is the baptistry and the other is dedicated to St. Michael. By 1789 the quarters for the missionaries, the granary, the workshops, and the Indian homes were also of stone.

The Indian population had begun to decline when the mission was turned over to the Zacatecan missionaries in 1773, making it difficult for them to run it.

The Original Art and Architecture, 1740–1824

THE CHURCH

When Fr. Ortiz visited La Purísima Concepción in 1745, the church was about half finished. The temporary church was in a large adobe hall with a flat roof, and the sacristy was in a separate room. He visited the mission again on June 4, 1756, and indicated in his report that the stone masonry church, dedicated on December 8, 1755, had a vaulted roof (like the adjacent sacristy), a transept (in the shape of a Latin cross), a dome, and two towers, each surmounted with an iron cross. He described the nave and transept and the furnishings of the church in some detail. The presbytery was raised by two steps above the main floor of the nave and was set off from the rest of the church by a communion railing made of turned wood.

The choir loft, with a "good" arch and vaulted ceiling, had grilles over the two windows facing west, and the four windows of the cupola drum had frames of waxed paper instead of glass panes.

Fr. Dolores, who visited the mission on April 19, 1759, and again in 1762,

1. For the eighteenth-century history of Concepción, see Habig, *The Alamo Chain of Missions,* pp. 129–147.

considered the church "very well painted and elegant." He noted the barrel vaulted roof of the stone and masonry church and the two towers with "very good" bells.

Fr. Sáenz described the church in great detail in 1772. The architectural units of the rubble and stone masonry church included the nave, transept, the sanctuary with altars, and the vaulted ceiling. Among its interior features were the "beautiful" ring (the entablature, framed by an architrave) and cornice on the inside of the "good" cupola (Fig. 5.1 and Tables 5.1 and 5.2). He described the buttresses, merlons, and cornices at the four exterior corners of the drum (which served as the base for the cupola and its "very small" octagonal lantern), the bronze grating over the glass panes of the four windows of the drum, the wrought-iron cross with a weathervane on top of the lantern, the two towers with four belfries, a cornice, and an octagonal vault each, and "for finals, their small well-made square lanterns, each with a cross and weathervane of iron," the well-made merlons of each tower, and the stone gutters.

FIGURE 5.1. *Interior view of the Concepción church looking toward the main altar. Courtesy of Kathy Vargas.*

TABLE 5.1. THE ARCHITECTURE OF LA PURÍSIMA CONCEPCIÓN, 1745–1759

STRUCTURES	1745	1756	1759
Church (nave)	under construction	30 × 7.25 v	no dim.
Transept		17 v	no dim.
Temporary Church	large		
Sacristy	no dim.	no dim.	no dim.
Upper Cell (Infirmary)			
Convento (friary)	2-story	almost ruined	——
Portería			
Arcaded Cloister			no dim.
Cells (rooms)	unspecified	3	unspecified
Offices	2		1
Obraje			no dim.
Refectory			
Cells/Alcove			no dim.
Guest Rooms/Alcove		unspecified	
New Friary		under construction	unfinished
Indian Houses	no dim.	no dim.	62
Rows			2
Barracks	no dim.	——	——
Workshops			unspecified
Masonry			tools
Carpentry			
Forge			tools
Storage			no dim.
Granary	no dim.	——	——
Outer Wall	no dim.	——	——
Gates			

Note: v = vara (32.909 inches); dim. = dimensions; *portería* = main entrance to the friary; *obraje* = spinning room.

Inside the front entrance of the church was a well-built vestibule made of painted and varnished wood. It had two inner doors with an iron bar. The floor was made of carefully laid brick. The door of the baptistry had an iron grating and a latticed window. The choir loft, with a vaulted ceiling, had a railing made of turned wood (Fig. 5.2). The entire church had "a wooden floor, artistically arranged in eleven sections, the boards resting on oak beams and stretching from beam to beam."

Fr. Morfi visited the mission on January 3 and 9, 1778, but did not mention the church in his diary entries for those days. However, in his *History of Texas* he noted the vaulted roof, transept, dome, and the two towers of the church, which he considered "beautiful."

Fr. López (1785) reported that the church and sacristy, located next to the *convento,* were "very notable for this country, because of the two towers and the beautiful cupola." According to Padilla (1820), the church had deteriorated

TABLE 5.2. THE ARCHITECTURE OF LA PURÍSIMA CONCEPCIÓN, 1762–1772

STRUCTURES	1762	1772
Church (nave)	32 × 8 v	30 × 8 v
Transept		no dim.
Sacristy	12 v	8 × 4.5 v
Upper Cell (Infirmary)		8.5 × 5.5 v
Convento (friary)	no dim. (vaulted)	——
Portería		
Arcaded Cloister		23 × 5 v ht. 3 arches
Rooms		
Office	unspecified	9 × 5 v (left side)
Obraje	no dim.	14 × 5.5 v (center?)
Refectory		6.5 × 3+ v (right side)
Cells/Alcove	unspecified	9 × 5 v/5 × 3 v
Guest Room/Alcove		8 × 3 v/5 × 3 v
Indian Houses	unspecified	24*
Rows	2	
Barracks		
Masonry	tools	——
Carpentry	tools	——
Forge	tools	8 × 4.5 v
Storage	no dim.	——
Granary	no dim.	——
Outer Wall/Gates	no dim.	no dim./4 gates**

Note: v = vara (32.909 inches); dim. = dimensions; *portería* = main entrance to the friary; *obraje* = spinning room.

*Two more houses were almost completed; six more were planned.

**There was a gate at each of the four cardinal points.

FIGURE 5.2. *Interior view of the Concepción church looking toward the choir loft. Courtesy of Kathy Vargas.*

FIGURE 5.3. *Reconstruction drawing of the Concepción church facade. Ernst Schuchard, 1932. Schuchard Collection. Courtesy of the Daughters of the Republic of Texas Library.*

due to the "damage of time," because there were no priests or Indians at the mission. The final references to the church during this period were made by Fr. Díaz (1824). The iron crosses were still on top of the two bell towers and the dome, and the choir loft had a railing of turned wood.[2]

THE FACADE

The earliest reference to the newly completed church facade was made by Fr. Ortiz (1756), who noted the stone sculpture of Our Lady of the Immaculate Conception inside a niche and a sculpture of two angels holding a monstrance in another niche (the first, a free-standing sculpture inside the pediment niche, is no longer there; the second is a low-relief sculpture within an oval frame placed in the center of the doorway arch). The sun and moon were painted on each side of the portal, and floral designs were painted over the entire facade (Fig. 5.3).

Fr. Sáenz (1772) described the facade in more detail. He noted the stone cross at the top of the facade flanked by merlons, a continuous cornice painted in several colors, the wooden lattice over the round window in the center, a stone crucifix above the sculpture of the Immaculate Conception in the pediment niche, and the doorway with a large iron bar, two wooden doors, and a small door with a latch key.

The two sculptures of the Immaculate Conception and the Crucifixion on the main portal of the church were still in place when Fr. Díaz prepared the final inventory of the mission in 1824.[3]

2. Fr. Ortiz, *Visita de las missiones,* pp. 27, 30; Fr. Ortiz, *Razón,* vol. 2, pp. 27–28; Fr. Dolores, "Inventories, 1759," p. 9 (quotation); idem, "Report," p. 335; Fr. Sáenz, "Testimony and Inventory," pp. 2 (trans. Donna Pierce), 12–13; Fr. Morfi, *History of Texas,* p. 94; Fr. López, "Documents," p. 41; Padilla, "Texas in 1820," p. 59; Fr. Díaz de León, "1824 Secularization Inventory: Concepción," p. 1.

3. Fr. Ortiz, *Razón,* vol. 2, pp. 27–28; Fr. Sáenz, "Testimony and Inventory," pp. 2–3; Fr. Díaz de León, "1824 Secularization Inventory: Concepción," pp. 1–2.

FIGURAL WALL PAINTING

Fr. Sáenz (1772) noted the wall paintings in the chapel of St. Michael (right tower base room), the main altar area, the arms of the transept, and the sacristy. There were paintings of

> the Crucified Christ and Our Lady of Sorrows . . . on the wall [of St. Michael's Chapel]. . . . A canopy of painting on the wall [of the main altar area used as a backdrop for a number of oil paintings] . . . a large image of Christ on the Cross with Magdalene and St. John the Evangelist [above the altar in the left transept], . . . an image of Our Lady of the Column with other paintings, all on the wall [of the right transept, and] a painted canopy [above] a framed canvas painting of Christ [on the wall of the sacristy].[4]

THE ALTARPIECES IN 1772

The main altarpiece was essentially completed by 1772, when the inventory of the mission holdings was prepared by Fr. Sáenz (all references to the altarpieces are taken from this document). The altarpiece had a gilded tabernacle with a lock and key from which hung "a beautiful cloth ribbon." Above the tabernacle was a "bronze crucifix [about 11 inches high], Our Lady of Sorrows, the inscription, and silver clips [corner guards]" (Fig. 5.4a and Table 5.3).

Above the cornice of the tabernacle there was a "very beautiful" sculpture of the Virgin of the Immaculate Conception with a silver crown and "her most holy Son in her arms." Its base had the world and a serpent depicted on it. The altar had a backdrop (reredos) comprised of a carved baldachin, gilded and painted to simulate rich fabric (estofado). Earlier, Fr. Dolores (1762) had noted the "elegant sculpture" with a silver crown placed in an oval frame in the main altarpiece.

A small table stood on the epistle (congregation's right) side of the altar, used as a credence table and for the viaticum (Eucharist given to a person who is in danger of death). There was a walnut chair for the priest, as well as "two portable carved [wood] communion railings."

Other sacred images listed in the earlier reports are the paintings of Los Cinco Señores (The Holy Family) and of the Holy Shepherdess and the Holy Pilgrim.

On one side of the "stylish" hanging lamp was a large silver cross with the image of Christ and on the other an image of Our Lady of the Immaculate Conception. Gilded sculptures of St. Francis and the Immaculate Conception were placed below and on the sides of the cross.

As in the case of the main altar, the transept altars were "completed" by 1772 (Fig. 5.4b and c). The altar tables of the left and right transepts were made of stone and lime (mortar). Each had a number of sacred images placed on it. The altarpiece in the left transept had a "good canopy of damask with floral design, silver lace, and silk fringe." The canopy was displaced with the use of thin rods. Inside the large niche above the altar was a "very devout" sculptured image of Jesus of Nazareth (no mention of this sculpture is found in any of the earlier reports and inventories). The sculpture, with adjustable parts, was made with hinges and richly dressed in an inner tunic of fine linen (chambray) with fine lace and an outer purple one with silver point lace. It also wore a cincture with buttons and long fringe, all embroidered, and a cord

4. Fr. Sáenz, "Testimony and Inventory," pp. 14, 16, 17, 18 (trans. Donna Pierce).

TABLE 5.3. THE ALTARPIECES OF LA PURÍSIMA CONCEPCIÓN

SACRED IMAGES	1756	1759	1762	1772
Conception w/Child	1+ v	no dim.	no dim.	no dim.
Christ Crucified	no dim.	——	——	large
Cinco Señores (M)	no dim.	no dim.	no dim.	no dim.
D. Shepherdess (P)	"varias imágenes"	no dim.	——	no dim.
D. Pilgrim (P)		no dim.	——	no dim.
Francis				no dim.
Crucifix				no dim.
Stations of the Cross	no dim.(N) left tr.	left tr.	both tr.	
OL of Sorrows	——	——	——	medium
Crucifixion (M) w/ Sorrowful Mother and John the Evangelist	no dim. "otros santos"	no dim. (as listed)	"varias pinturas"	large Magdalene and St. John
Jesus of Nazareth				large (niche)
Christ in Sepulchre				no dim.
OL of Sorrows	no dim. right tr.	1+ v right tr.	no dim. both tr.	no dim.
OL of the Pillar (P)	no dim.	no dim. (M)	"varias pinturas"	"pinturas"
OL of the Pillar	small	——	no dim.	no dim.
Joseph w/Child				2- v (niche)
Crucifix				.33 v
Last Supper (P) on door of glass case				no dim.
Nativity scene (in glass case): 3 figures				no dim.
Peter and Paul				no dim.
Conception (port.)*				no dim.

Note: (M) = mural; D. = Divine; (P) painting/s; OL = Our Lady; port. = portable altar; v = vara (32.909 inches); dim. = dimensions; "varias imágenes/pinturas" = several images/paintings; (N) = church nave; "otros santos" = other Holy Images; tr = transept.

*Used for the Rosary.

with buttons and silk fringe draped from the neck, as though the hands were about to be tied. The sculpture was used (undressed) on Holy Thursday for "a very moving" scene of the Flagellation and on Good Friday, with a cross placed on its shoulders for the procession. On the altar were a bier and a pillar as well as a red silk curtain for the sculpture. There were two votive offerings (*milagros*) made of silver—a small heart and a small arm—presented by some devout person. The sculpture was "donated by Phelipa [Felipa] de Villa Nueva y Terreros of Querétaro."

The altar also had a medium-sized sculpture of Our Lady of Sorrows with a diadem and dagger, both made of silver. A large figure of the Crucified Christ was painted on the altar wall, with Mary Magdalene and St. John the Evangelist on the sides. Hanging from rods was a "good" canopy of damask with floral design, silver lace, and silk fringe.

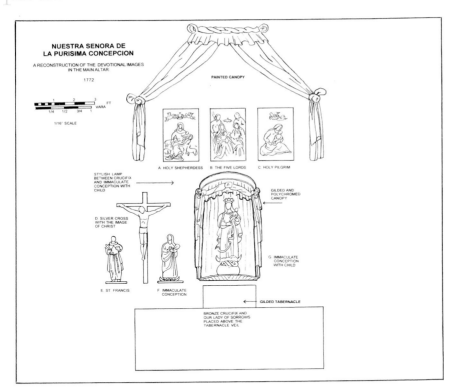

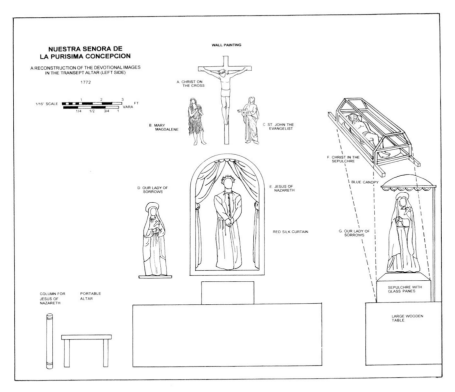

FIGURE 5.4. *Altarpieces of La Purísima Concepción, 1772: a. main altar. b. transept altar (left side). c. transept altar (right side). Drawn to the scale of the sanctuary. Diagrams by Jacinto Quirarte.*

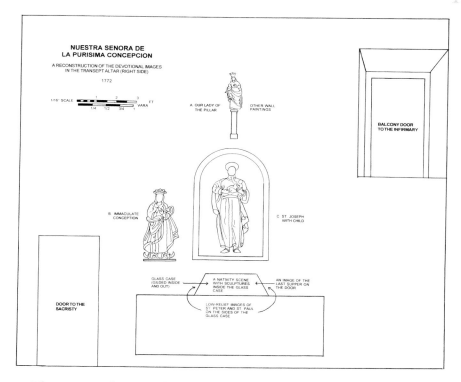

There were other sacred images not mentioned in the earlier reports and inventories, including a sculpture of a "very revered image of our Lord in the Descent from the Cross" inside an "artistic" urn (case) in the shape of a sepulchre with glass panes and "well painted." The urn was placed on a large wooden table that served as an altarpiece in the nave of the church. The sculpture of the Christ figure was dressed with a fine striped linen cloth. Two richly embroidered pillows, donated by a very devout woman, were placed beneath the head. The urn or glass case was protected from the dust with a purple cotton cloth. Placed over this was a sculpture of Our Lady of Sorrows with adjustable parts. The figure was dressed in a tunic of red damask and a blue mantle with stars. Its diadem and dagger were made of silver-gilded wood. This sculpture was used, among other things, for the devout service of the Descent from the Cross. It was kept beneath a blue canopy.

A number of sacred images in the altarpiece of the right transept were not mentioned in the earlier reports and inventories, including a cross with bronze corner plates, a bronze image of Christ, and a triangular-shaped glass case used as a repository on Holy Thursday. The case was gilded on the inner and outer surfaces and had a depiction of the Last Supper on the door, which had a "good" lock with a silver key. Inside the glass case was a scene of the Nativity with sculptures of the Virgin Mary, St. Joseph, and the Christ Child. On the sides of the case were sculptured images of St. Peter and St. Paul. In a niche above the glass case was a "most beautiful" sculpture of St. Joseph with a gilded wooden diadem, a white lily, and the Child Jesus in his arms. The sculpture was donated "by Juan Francisco Núñez del Prado." There was a sculpture of Our Lady of the Pillar above the niche with the St. Joseph figure. The entire wall was covered with paintings. Also on the altarpiece was a sculpture of the Immaculate Conception with a silver crown that was placed on a portable stand when it was used for the singing of the Rosary.[5]

5. Ibid., pp. 5–7, 8 (my translation), 9–11; Fr. Dolores, "Report," p. 335 (my translation).

THE ALTARPIECES IN 1824

According to Fr. Díaz (1824), the stone tables of the transept altars and the altarpiece of the main altar were still in place. On a large wooden table stood the wooden altarpiece, with sculptured floral motifs and a gilded oval in the center, on its platform. The tabernacle was carved and gilded inside and out and placed on a wooden base. Stone steps and a wooden railing led to the altar area.

The sacred images were no longer in the altarpieces of the church. They had been taken several years earlier and stored at San José Mission. Nonetheless, Fr. Díaz described them in detail. As in all other inventories, the titular saint of the church was listed first. The carved wood sculpture of the Immaculate Conception was gilded and painted to simulate the rich fabric of her garment. She still wore a crown of silver, noted by earlier observers, and the Christ Child in her arms had a silver halo of rays and a shirt of fine linen.

The clothed sculpture of Jesus of Nazareth wore a tunic of purple chintz, a silk cord around his neck, a crown of thorns, and a cross on his shoulders. The cross was stained green. The Crucified Christ, used for the Descent and Christ in the Sepulchre, wore a linen scarf. There was a "beautifully painted" image of the Crucifixion on canvas with a wooden frame. Three sculptures finished in the *estofado* technique were listed in the inventory: an Immaculate Conception with a silver crown and the Christ Child with silver halo rays, a St. Joseph with a halo of gilded wood and the Christ Child dressed in a shirt of Brittany linen, and a small St. Joseph. A sculpture of Our Lady of Sorrows with a "very lovely face" wore a silk dress and a silver halo. There was a small sculpture of the Immaculate Conception.[6]

CHAPELS

There is very little information on the architectural features of the tower base room in the reports and inventories of this period. They all focus on their function, furnishings, and the sacred images. Fr. Ortiz (1756) identified the room on the left as one enters the church as the baptistry and the one on the right as the chapel dedicated to St. Michael. All other reports include this identification. Fr. Ortiz noted the screen over the window of the chapel. Fr. Sáenz (1772) referred to the identical windows in the two tower base rooms. Fr. Díaz (1824) noted that the baptistry had a double door, with the upper half made of turned wood, and the room on the other side (the chapel dedicated to St. Michael) was used for storage.[7]

OTHER SACRED IMAGES

Fr. Ortiz (1756) reported seeing prints with depictions of the Stations of the Cross (Via Crucis) on the walls of the nave and a framed painting of the Crucified Christ on the main wall of the sacristy.

According to Fr. Sáenz (1772), the four pendentives were painted with images of St. Francis, St. Bonaventure, St. Anthony of Padua, and St. Bernardine of Siena (Figs. 5.1 and 5.5). Other sacred images included prints in painted frames with depictions of the Stations of the Cross, evenly distributed on the walls of the choir-loft (Fig. 5.2), a painting of Our Lady of Sorrows, a painting of a condemned soul in the room above the sacristy, and a crucifix

6. Fr. Díaz de León, "1824 Secularization Inventory: Concepción," p. 3.

7. Fr. Ortiz, *Razón,* vol. 2, pp. 29–30; Fr. Sáenz, "Testimony and Inventory," pp. 4–5, 7–12; Fr. Díaz de León, "1824 Secularization Inventory: Concepción, 1824," pp. 3–6.

FIGURE 5.5. *Diagram of the pendentive paintings, 1772. The paintings are no longer extant. Drawing by Jacinto Quirarte.*

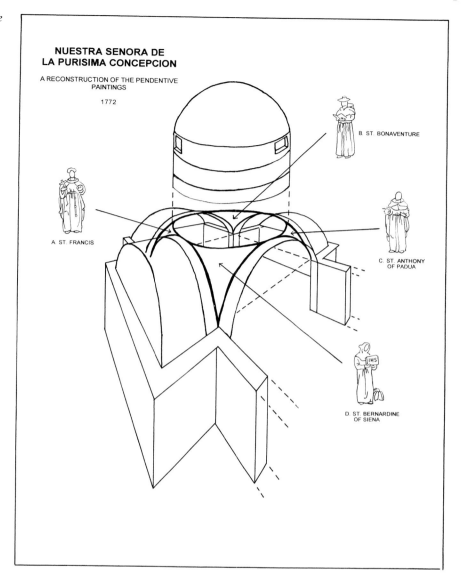

with a satin baldachin and a painting of Our Lady of Refuge on canvas with its frame and veil in a private room next to the refectory.[8]

CHURCH AND CHAPEL FURNISHINGS

The church and chapel furnishings included a baptismal font, a holy water font, a pulpit, confessionals, benches, and other items needed for divine services. All reports and inventories prepared during this time include references to these items.

The baptismal font in the baptistry (located in the left tower base room as one enters the church) is included in all of the documents prepared during this period. Fr. Ortiz (1756) reported that the "beautiful and well-carved" stone font had a smaller copper font inside it. The baptismal font made of copper was listed by Fr. Dolores (1759 and 1762), along with a reference to the appropriate items needed for baptisms in the latter. Fr. Sáenz (1772) noted

8. Fr. Ortiz, *Razón,* vol. 2, pp. 29–30; Fr. Sáenz, "Testimony and Inventory," pp. 4–5, 7–12.

that the round baptismal font had "various mouldings in the form of shells on a perforated pillar for drainage . . . a beautifully-made wooden cover," and a silk covering. Fr. Díaz (1824) did not refer to the baptismal font.

Fr. Ortiz (1756) noted that there was a large stone font for holy water with an old font of copper inside it. Fr. Dolores (1759) listed the holy water font made of copper. Fr. Sáenz (1772) provided the fullest description of the holy water font made of stone: "a large basin for holy water on a square column" near the chapel of St. Michael (it is now located inside the chapel). "The basin [was] more than a vara [over thirty-two inches] wide, . . . made from one piece of good stone and . . . decorated with four angels and various mouldings." Fr. Díaz (1824) described the same font as "a holy water font of carved stone."

Fr. Ortiz (1756) made the first reference to the pulpit and its various components, including the stairway made of carved and painted wood. Fr. Dolores listed the pulpit with a sounding board and an image of Christ with its baldachin in 1759 and included a simple reference to the pulpit in 1762. Fr. Sáenz (1772) noted that the pulpit had "a stone and wooden stairway and a voice guard with an iron grille, all beautifully done." According to Fr. Díaz (1824), the cedar pulpit, with stairs and sounding board, was anchored to the wall with an iron rod.

Fr. Ortiz (1756) reported that there were two "very good" new confessionals with curtains and iron bolts. Fr. Dolores (1759) listed the two confessionals and "several" benches and other furniture which "adorn[ed] and beautif[ied]" the church. He included the two confessionals and the benches in his report of 1762. Fr. Sáenz (1772) listed two "very beautiful and spacious confessionals . . . , and a [large] bench for the leaders of the pueblo [mission Indians] and three more for the aged and other Indians" so they could comfortably hear the catechism or sermons. Also located in the church were two "wooden tables, used in the pueblo for the Feast of Corpus Christi." Fr. Díaz (1824) listed the two confessionals in the church too. He noted that one of them had a double door and an iron handle with wood screens. Other furniture in the church included three small chairs and a bench for the officials of the pueblo before the steps of the sanctuary.[9]

SACRISTY

Fr. Dolores (1762) made the first reference to the vaulted roof of the sacristy. Fr. Sáenz (1772) also mentioned the vaulted roof as well as the room above the sacristy "with an alcove . . . and door that leads to [a small] raised area [tribune]." Fr. López (1785) incorporated the sacristy with the church when he evaluated the latter as "very notable . . . because of the two towers and the beautiful cupola." Fr. Díaz (1824) more clearly described the elevated tribune in the room above the sacristy which provides a view of the church. The second-story room "communicates with the church through a door to an elevated tribune." He noted that the sacristy had three carved cedar doors—two on the outside and one inside in the partition wall. The one leading to the *convento* was a large double door. The second story room had "served or [could] serve as a comfortable hospice for persons on retreat."[10]

9. Fr. Ortiz, *Razón,* vol. 2, pp. 31, 33–34; Fr. Dolores, "Inventories, 1759," pp. 9–10; idem, "Report," pp. 335, 337; Fr. Sáenz, "Testimony and Inventory," p. 8 (trans. Donna Pierce); Fr. Díaz de León, "1824 Secularization Inventory: Concepción," pp. 2–4 (quotation), 6–8.

10. Fr. Dolores, "Report," p. 335; Fr. Sáenz, "Testimony and Inventory," pp. 13, 39; Fr. López, "Documents," pp. 41–42; Fr. Díaz de León, "1824 Secularization Inventory: Concepción," p. 4 (translation modified).

SACRED ITEMS

The liturgical vestments, sacred vessels, and other items needed for divine services were stored in a number of different pieces of furniture, referred to as boxes with closets or cupboards. All these are duly noted in the reports and inventories prepared during this period.

Fr. Ortiz (1756) reported seeing the vestments and sacred vessels stored in three large locked boxes made of walnut. Fr. Dolores (1759) described the storage units as a box made of "very well" carved walnut and savin woods, with three large drawers, and two closets or cupboards with locks and keys. He noted the units used in 1762 as a cupboard and a cabinet. Fr. Sáenz (1772) listed a large cabinet with three large drawers in the center and a closet or cupboard on each side, painted in several colors and varnished. The drawers were gilded, and the closets or cupboards had iron handles, locks, and two keys for each missionary.[11]

THE *Convento* AND OTHER BUILDINGS

According to Fr. Ortiz (1745), the two-story *convento* had two offices downstairs and private rooms upstairs (Fig. 5.6). In 1756 he noted that a new *convento* was under construction because the old one was almost in ruins. The new one had three rooms for living quarters and offices. Fr. Dolores (1759) indicated that most of the vaulted roof of the unfinished stone masonry building was completed. It had private rooms, an office, and a workshop. By 1762 the *convento* had a vaulted roof and a porch, rooms and offices for the missionaries, and a large room for the textile shop.

Fr. Sáenz (1772) described most of the rooms and their functions. The *portería* (the main entrance to the *convento*) had three arches and a corridor (arcaded porch). A comparable corridor on the north side led to the cemetery. The refectory on the right side of the main entrance corridor had a vaulted roof, a door and window, and a small serving window that led to the kitchen. There was a private room next to the refectory, another room with a vaulted roof served as a guest room, and a room with a vaulted roof on the left side of the main entrance served as a workshop.

Fr. Morfi (1778–1783) noted that the sacristy had a vaulted roof that was "the same as [the roof of] the living room of the religious, which [was] large and comfortable, though not very high." Fr. López (1785) reported that the "spacious" *convento,* located on the east side of the walled-in area, was constructed with stone and lime (mortar). Almost every room had a vaulted roof, and the one-story building had one room on the second story.

According to Padilla (1820), the buildings of the *convento* were in the worst condition of those standing. The remaining buildings were just "heaps of rubbish."

Fr. Ortiz (1756) noted that most of the Indian houses were made of adobe; some were *xacales* (or *jacales:* huts). According to Fr. Dolores (1759), there were sixty-two houses for the Indians along two of the mission walls. Some were made of stone; others were *xacales.* Three years later he reported that the Indians lived in two rows of stone houses and *jacales:* twenty-four completed houses and two others that were almost finished. Only the partition walls

11. Fr. Ortiz, *Razón,* vol. 2, pp. 31, 33–34; Fr. Dolores, "Inventories, 1759," p. 9; idem, "Report," p. 335; Fr. Sáenz, "Testimony and Inventory," p. 13.

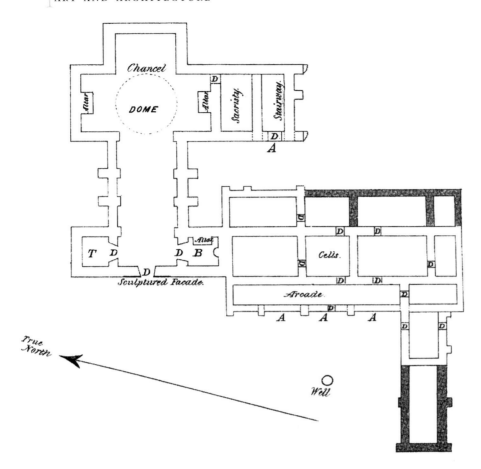

FIGURE 5.6. *Plan of the Concepción mission. Published by W. Corner, San Antonio (1890), between pp. 16 and 17.*

Concepcion Mission.

The shaded part is in ruins. The material is rough stone laid in mortar. B is the baptismal chamber. T is the room under the left tower. D stands for door, as A for arch. There is another room above the Sacristy.

The river is towards the west about ¼ mile.

Scale, 40 feet to the inch.

were lacking. There were plans to build six more houses to take care of the anticipated growth in population.

Fr. Morfi (1778–1783) also noted that the Indian houses were arranged in two parallel rows on either side of the *convento* (north and south walls), with the granary on the other side (east wall). Fr. López (1785) reported that a "rampart" served as a wall for the twenty-three Indian houses, built with flat roofs and of the same material as the mission wall (stone and mud). Although some of the houses were in a ruinous state, he believed it would not be difficult to repair them and indicated that there were plans to rebuild most of them.

THE CHURCH FACADE

ARCHITECTURAL POLYCHROMY

The first story of the facade is essentially an unrelieved surface from side to side except for the sculptured portal and windows (Fig. 5.10). The entire facade originally was divided into three sections with the use of color (Fig. 5.3). The tower bases defined with color framed the central portal, which was only slightly wider than each tower base. An added illusion of architectural division was created with a painted masonry design over the entire surface of the facade. All the windows of the portal and tower bases and the belfries were painted to simulate stone masonry frames and voussoirs (belfry arches). Diamonds and ovals were painted within the framed bands above and below each belfry tower. In addition, simulated fluted pilasters were painted near the corners of each side of the belfry towers (Fig. 5.11).

The lily motif was painted throughout the facade within the simulated

FIGURE 5.10. *General view of the Concepción church facade. Courtesy of Kathy Vargas.*

FIGURE 5.11. *Church belfry arch with traces of painted voussoirs. Courtesy of Kathy Vargas.*

FIGURE 5.12. *General view of the Concepción church portal. Courtesy of Kathy Vargas.*

masonry blocks. The sun and the moon were also painted on the upper part of the facade and the capital letters "MAR" placed above "AVE" in the center (Fig. 5.3).[22]

METALWORK

The metal cross over the main portal was made by Kurt Voss and placed there in the 1960s (Fig. 5.10). The original stone cross disappeared sometime in the nineteenth century, as evidenced by the watercolor done by Everett in 1846 and the print published by Bartlett in 1854 (Figs. 5.8 and 5.7).

Schuetz attributed the dome lantern cross mentioned in 1772 and 1824 to Cayetano Guerrero or Juan Banul. The present iron crosses of the two belfries and the dome lantern probably date from the late-nineteenth-century restoration of the church carried out by Bishop Neraz. Other metalwork mentioned in 1772 is no longer there (metal grilles over the four large dome windows with glass panes put there to protect them and a large iron gate at the main entrance of the mission).[23]

22. The Ernst Schuchard rendering of the painted facade done in the 1930s is in the collection of the Daughters of the Republic of Texas Library, Alamo Plaza, San Antonio, Texas.

23. The date for the Kurt Voss cross comes from a Harvey Smith, Jr., interview (personal communication, 1982); Schuetz, "Professional Artisans," p. 34.

ARCHITECTURAL AND FIGURAL SCULPTURES

The portal has a pediment placed on an entablature supported by two half columns which flank a polygonal (half-octagonal) arch. There is a small circular window directly above the pediment, with two identical windows on either side of the raking cornices of the pediment (Fig. 5.12). The two half columns of the first stage without capitals have the same width over the entire length of the shaft, which is divided into two decorative zones. The lower portion, over half the length of the shaft, is filled with fluting. The upper half has a floral pattern executed in very low relief. The shafts of the pediment niche columns are plain. The arch is in the shape of a shell, and the entire unit is surmounted by an entablature.

The church portal has only fragments of figural sculptures and polychromy left. The sculptures on the portal, such as the cross, the flowers on either side of it, and the right hand of the Crucified Christ figure, are still visible (Fig. 5.13). The rest of the figure as well as the sculpture of Our Lady of the Immaculate Conception, originally located in the pediment niche, disappeared in the 1840s.

Each spandrel has a winding rope (with knots) that fills the space not occupied by low-relief carvings within a medallion (Figs. 5.14 and 5.15). There is another low-relief carving within an elaborate oval frame over the center

FIGURE 5.13. *Detail of the Concepción church portal. Entablature, pediment, and window. Courtesy of Kathy Vargas.*

(keystone) of the doorway arch. The outer pilasters of the portal flanking the engaged columns have flowers arranged vertically and within double-framed diamond shapes. Each flower is comprised of four petals. The archivolt of the doorway arch has an inscription in two lines that extends over its entire surface.

STYLE CONSIDERATIONS AND RELATIONSHIPS

The polygonal arch of the main portal doorway is typical of such forms used throughout northern New Spain from about 1650 to 1750. Octagons were used in this region for domes, arches, window frames, and tower plans. Examples are found at the Guadalupe basilica built by Pedro de Arrieta between 1695 and 1709. According to Kubler, the earliest Mexican examples are the door of the Concepción church (1655) in Mexico City and the door of the Congregación church in Querétaro (1675–1680).[24] The Basilica of Guadalupe, north of Mexico City (1695–1709), has been suggested as a model for the half-octagon arch of the Concepción church doorway. Similar arches are seen in the first stage of the towers of the Morelia Cathedral (built by 1744).

The polygonal arch of Concepción in San Antonio is only one of several angular forms used in the church. The dome over the crossing rests on an octagonal drum, and the pyramidal roofs of the two belfries are octagonal in plan.

Although the main portal of the Concepción church does not have the standard Solomonic columns (used from 1680 to around 1730) or the profusely decorated surfaces comprised of foliated patterns, it belongs to the early Baroque style described by Toussaint as "sober or austere."[25] This style with a preference for octagonal or angular forms lasted from around 1650 to 1750.

Thus, the portal with its polygonal arch, flanked by fluted half columns, a niche within a pediment, and a circular window above, places the Concepción church at the end of the Baroque style of New Spain. The portal, with its unusually proportioned pediment and window above it, is a variation of this style, which usually had single or double pilasters or columns flanking the doorway and a niche or a window above.

According to Schuetz, the unusual proportion of the main portal pediment (too high for its width) is actually "correct" given the interests of the designers of the portal (Fig. 5.13).[26] She based her interpretation on a geometric analysis of the facade.

FIGURE 5.14. *Detail of the Concepción church portal. Franciscan emblem and cord in the left spandrel, the framed inscription, and the keystone medallion of the polygonal arch. Courtesy of Kathy Vargas.*

FIGURE 5.15. *Detail of the Concepción church portal. Franciscan emblem and cord in the right spandrel, the keystone medallion, and the framed inscription of the polygonal arch. Courtesy of Kathy Vargas.*

24. Kubler and Soria, *Art and Architecture in Spain and Portugal,* p. 77. According to Kubler, referring to the most distinctive traits of "northern" Mexican work from 1650 to about 1750, "the octagon is generally the favorite, in domes, in arches, in window frames, and in tower plans."

25. Toussaint, *Colonial Art in Mexico,* p. 275.

26. Schuetz, "Professional Artisans," pp. 26–27. For the unusual proportions of the pediment, see M. Schuetz, "Proportional Systems and Ancient Geometry," *Southwestern Mission Research Center* (1980): 2–7.

CONTENT AND MEANING

The references to the Franciscan Order on the portal are found within the spandrels (Figs. 5.14 and 5.15). The medallion on the left includes the crossed arms of Christ and St. Francis overlapping a Latin cross; each arm of the cross has a hand nailed to it. The outstretched arms in the form of a cross are a reference to the appearance of St. Francis at a provincial chapter of the order in Arles during a sermon by St. Anthony of Padua. The medallion on the right has the stigmata (marks in the semblance of the five wounds suffered by Christ upon the cross) of St. Francis, the emblem of the Franciscan Order. The Franciscan cord with four knots, a reference to the habit worn by the Franciscan friars, is interwoven with the medallion in each spandrel.

The low-relief carving of the medallion over the doorway (keystone) originally depicted two winged angels holding up a monstrance, a transparent receptacle in which the consecrated Host is held or viewed. The Host, a round piece of unleavened bread, is consecrated by the celebrant at the Eucharist or Mass in commemoration of the Last Supper and the sacrifice of Christ upon the cross.

The stylized flowers in the upper third of each half column and within the frieze may be the same as those flanking the Crucifixion within the pediment. These may represent the anemone, the flower depicted in scenes of the Crucifixion or with Our Lady of Sorrows, who is associated with the Passion of Christ. The triple leaf of this plant was used to symbolize the Trinity in the early days of the Church.

The inscription on the archivolt of the arch refers to Our Lady of the Immaculate Conception, to whom the church is dedicated. It reads: "A SV PATRONA Y PRINCESSA CON ESTAS ARMAS ATIENDE ESTA MISSION Y DEFIENDE EL PUNTO DE SV PUREZA" (With these arms, this mission attends to her patron and princess and defends the state of her purity).

The lily painted within the simulated masonry blocks is a symbol of the Virgin's purity and of her Immaculate Conception. The painted letters "MAR" placed above "AVE" in the center are the words spoken to the Virgin by Gabriel when he appeared to announce that she had been chosen to bear the Son of God: "Ave Maria, Gratia Plena." The painting of the sun and the moon below the monogram probably refers to the Crucifixion represented in the pediment rather than to the Virgin Mary, the "woman clothed with the sun, and the moon under her feet" (Revelation 12:1). When represented in scenes of the Crucifixion, the sun and the moon indicate the sorrow of all creation at the death of Christ.[27]

INTERIOR

ARCHITECTURAL SCULPTURE

There is a sculptured font embedded in the wall of the St. Michael chapel (Fig. 5.16). According to the 1772 inventory, it was originally located in the baptistry of the left tower as a free-standing font placed on a carved pedestal. The rim of the font has a low-relief carving of a knotted Franciscan cord. The frieze has an elaborate scene carved in high relief with rounded rather than sharp edges, which characterize the work of an accomplished sculptor. The

27. M. G. Ferguson, *Signs and Symbols in Christian Art,* pp. 50, 120–121.

scene has a figure with outstretched arms shown in frontal view, holding ribbons in both hands. The carving is not as delicate or as accomplished as the carving of the portal.

According to Schuetz, the "innocent rendering" of some of the anatomical features of the figure indicates that the work was "copied from a book illustration by an Indian who did not quite grasp the symbolism."[28] She assumed that the artisan, whom she identified as Nicolás, intended to depict a small angel but did not use the standard proportions of a cherub and did not include the wings. Nonetheless, she suggested that it may have been copied from a print published as the frontispiece in the 1726 edition of the *Diccionario de autoridades de la Real Academia.*

Another holy water font, shaped like a shell, is now embedded in the sacristy wall. A third font seen in an early photograph of the church interior was later taken off its columnar support, and both were placed in one of the *convento* rooms.

There are further examples of architectural sculpture in the other buildings of the mission, including a mixtilinear arch in the stairwell of the infirmary

FIGURE 5.16. *Crucifixion and Our Lady of Sorrows and font in St. Michael's Chapel, south wall. Painting and stone sculpture. The font can be seen below the painting. Courtesy of Kathy Vargas.*

FIGURE 5.17. *Mixtilinear arch in the infirmary. Interior view of the stairway and arch. Courtesy of Kathy Vargas.*

28. Fr. Sáenz, "Testimony and Inventory," p. 4; Schuetz, "Professional Artisans," p. 27.

and the ogee window in the infirmary proper at the top of the landing of the stairwell (Figs. 5.17 and 5.18). A window seat in the infirmary with a shell-shaped header (Fig. 5.19) was described as "a window with alcove" by Sáenz in 1772.

FIGURAL WALL PAINTING

There are vestiges of figural painting in the two belfry tower base rooms flanking the main entrance to the church. The wall painting in the St. Michael chapel (right side as one enters the church), depicts the Crucifixion and the Sorrowful Mother beneath it (Fig. 5.16). A stone holy water font, as already noted, was embedded in the wall directly below the painting at a later date. The font caused damage to the painting of the Sorrowful Mother.[29]

The face of the Virgin was destroyed. There is a red and yellow shell niche painted as a backdrop for the Virgin. Above the Virgin is a painting of an architectural header (an entablature) with balusters on each side. The header functions as a low frame for the Crucified Christ painted directly above and in the center. The balusters are in very good condition. The Crucifixion is faded

FIGURE 5.18. *Ogee window in the infirmary. Top landing of the infirmary stairwell. Courtesy of Kathy Vargas.*

FIGURE 5.19. *Shell window in the infirmary. Courtesy of Kathy Vargas.*

29. Corner, *San Antonio*, p. 16.

FIGURE 5.20. *Reconstruction drawings of all the extant wall paintings by Ernst Schuchard (1933). Schuchard Collection. Courtesy of the Daughters of the Republic of Texas Library.*

but otherwise in good condition. Along the base of the cross is a long, wide banner with a faded inscription. This and all other vestiges of painting at the mission were copied by Ernst Schuchard in the twentieth century (Fig. 5.20-4).

ARCHITECTURAL DECORATION

There is a painting of a three-sided floral frame in grisaille with a scalloped pediment on top on the east wall of the church. Two large flowers flank the pediment. Nothing was painted inside the frame, which has vestiges of a floral pattern (Fig. 5.20-1).

A painting of a floral border with red flowers surrounds the arch on the south wall of the baptistry to the left of the entrance to the church (Fig. 5.21). A vase of flowers with two birds was painted above the arch. All the motifs are painted in grisaille with some red highlights. The painting is in reasonably good condition (Fig. 5.20-7).

Other designs were painted on the north wall of the baptistry. They are almost identical to the vase with the flowers and birds but larger and a little more faded. There is a geometric medallion painted (in red, yellow, gray, and black) on the vaulted ceiling of the baptistry (Fig. 5.22). A hole made in the center for the bell rope damaged one side of the medallion (Fig. 5.20-8). Along the wall and vaulted ceiling are alternating red and black scallops, which go all the way around to create a continuous band of heart shapes (Fig. 5.20-5).

The vestiges of painting in the *convento* include several doorways with red and blue rectangular stones painted around the lintels and jambs. A cross with flowers at its base is painted above one header, with two vases holding flowers on each side and at the corners of the lintel (Fig. 5.20-10). Along the center line of the barrel vault is a red and yellow frieze with a red sun painted in the center of it (Fig. 5.20-2). The same band of color meets at the end wall, extends down along the border of the vaulted ceiling with the wall, and then goes all the way around the room in a series of colored bands at cornice level (Fig. 5.20-11).

FIGURE 5.21. *Floral designs: detail. Painting. Baptistry, south wall. Courtesy of Kathy Vargas.*

FIGURE 5.22. *Geometric medallion (damaged). Painting. Baptistry. Courtesy of Kathy Vargas.*

CONTENT AND MEANING

The anemone flower has red spots on the sepals, a symbol of the blood of Christ. The triple leaf of the plant symbolized the Trinity during the early days of the Church. These flowers may be the ones flanking the sculptured crucifix within the pediment of the portal and the cross painted over one of the doorways in the *convento*. It may also be the flower intended in the fantastic double flowers attached to the bifurcated ends of the banner at the base of the painting of the Crucifixion in the St. Michael chapel. The profile views of the anemone are seen at the corners of the *convento* doorway and in the frame on the east wall of the church. The four lobed flowers depicted in frontal view in the flowerpots flanking the cross over the *convento* doorway and in the flowered door frame of the baptistry (to the left of the church entrance) may also represent the anemone.[30]

Finally, the ceiling painting of the baptistry has eight outer elements comprising the geometric design. Appropriately, many baptismal fonts are octagonal in shape. Eight is the number of the Resurrection, a reference to the eighth day after Christ's entry into Jerusalem, when He rose from his grave.

30. For a discussion of the anemone flower, associated with the depictions of the Crucifixion, see Ferguson, *Signs and Symbols in Christian Art,* p. 27.

6

San Juan Capistrano

San Juan Capistrano was moved from the Colorado River to San Antonio in 1731. The church and the living quarters for the missionaries were built before 1745.[1] The church was made of brush plastered with mud and roofed with straw and had a tower with two bells. A stone church was finished by 1756. The construction of a larger church was begun sometime after 1777, but the building ceased in 1787 because there were not enough laborers available and building materials were scarce. The mission was partially secularized in 1794 and became a *visita* or submission of San Francisco de la Espada. A number of Spaniards settled at San Juan, far outnumbering the few Indians who remained. Full secularization occurred in 1824.

The Original Art and Architecture, 1740–1824

THE MISSION

According to Fr. Sáenz (1772), the church had walls of stone and mud and four windows. Half the roof, made of beams and boards, was new. The other half was "made of a good type of solid carved wood." Fr. Morfi (1778–1783) considered the church "neat and in good order" but did not think it compared with the churches of Concepción and San José. Fr. López (1785) reported that the church, sacristy, *convento,* and granary were built near a corner of the square or walled-in area (Fig. 6.1 and Tables 6.1 and 6.2). He also noted that another church was left half finished because there were few Indians and there was little money to complete it. According to Padilla (1820), the church was still unfinished, but there was a chapel where religious services were held. Although the mission buildings were almost in ruins, many people still lived there. Fr. Díaz (1824) noted that the main entrance of the church had a single door with a key and the belfry (*campanario*) had a metal cross and two bells with clappers.[2]

THE MAIN ALTARPIECE IN 1772

The main altarpiece was essentially complete by 1772, when the inventory of all the mission's holdings was prepared by Fr. Sáenz (Fig. 6.2). There were

1. For the eighteenth-century history of Capistrano, see Habig, *The Alamo Chain of Missions,* pp. 185–191.

2. Fr. Juan José Sáenz de Gumiel, "Inventory [of San Juan Capistrano]," p. 6; Fr. Morfi, *History of Texas,* p. 98; Fr. López, "Documents," p. 43; Padilla, "Texas in 1820," p. 60; Fr. José Antonio Díaz de León, "1824 Inventory: San Juan."

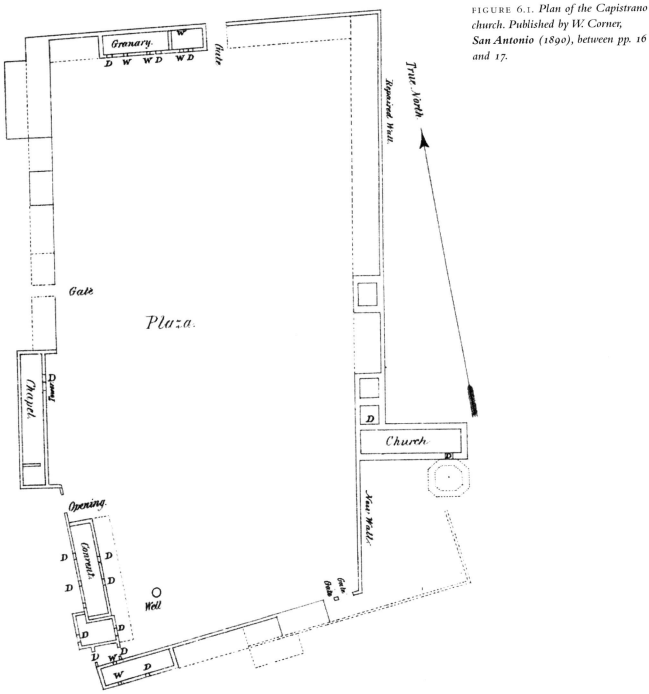

Granary.

W

D W W D W D

Gate

Repaired Wall.

True North.

Plaza.

Gate

Chapel.

D

Church

D

D

New Wall.

Opening.

Convent

D   D

D   D

Well

Gte in Gate

D   D

D W D

W   D

San Juan Mission.

Solid lines show existing works, dotted lines, old and ruined
ones. The river is to the west about 100 yards, flowing in a southerly
direction. D is for door, W is for window. The Granary and Church
are partly in ruins.

Scale, 80 feet to the inch.

TABLE 6.1. THE ARCHITECTURE OF SAN JUAN CAPISTRANO, 1745–1759

STRUCTURES	1745	1756	1759
Church	large hall	24 × 5.66 v	24 × 5.5 v
Sacristy		no dim.	no dim.
Convento (friary)		1-story	——
Patio			
Portería			
Rooms/Arcade			
Offices			
Common Room			
Granary	no dim.	no dim.	——
West Bldg.	unspecified	1-story	unspecified
Arcaded Cloisters	2		
Rooms	no dim.	3	3
No. 1	no dim.	no dim.	no dim.
No. 2		no dim.	no dim.
No. 3		no dim.	——
Guest Room		——	no dim.
Obraje			no dim.
Distribution Room*			
South Bldg.		unspecified	unspecified
Rooms	others	3	——
Offices	no dim.	No. 1	3
Refectory		No. 2	no dim.
Kitchen		No. 3	no dim.
Obraje			no dim.
Storage**		no dim.	——
Others			no dim.
Carpentry	no dim.	——	tools
Forge	no dim.	——	——
Masonry			tools
Indian Houses		unspecified	——
Streets		2	
Outer Wall			4 walls

Note: v = vara (32.909 inches); dim. = dimensions; *portería* = main entrance to the friary; *obraje* = spinning room.

*The distribution room was next to the *obraje* (spinning room).

**The storage room was near the kitchen.

"three painted risers" on the large wooden table of the altar. Above the risers was a carved and gilded niche. A large table on the Epistle (congregation's right) side was used as a credence table, and a cedar bench next to the presbytery was used for the local officials of the mission.

There was a sculpture of St. John Capistran with a diadem of gilded wood and a staff (although listed as new by Fr. Sáenz, this was undoubtedly the same sculpture mentioned earlier by Fr. Ortiz in 1756 and by Fr. Dolores in 1762). It was placed above a niche in the center of the altarpiece made of carved and

TABLE 6.2. THE ARCHITECTURE OF SAN JUAN CAPISTRANO, 1762–1772

STRUCTURES	1762	1772
Church	25 v (temporary church)	20 × 5 v
Sacristy	no dim.	5.33 × 3.5 v
Convento (friary)		
Patio		no dim.
Portería	no dim.	no dim. (faces north)
Rooms/Arcade		2 rooms/5 v each arch
Offices		5 × 5 v (faces north)
Common Room		12 × 5 v (faces north)
Granary	no dim.	40 × 6 v (faces north)
West Bldg.	unspecified	unspecified
Arcaded cloister	no dim.	24 v long, 5 arches
Cells	4	4
No. 1	no dim.	8.5 × 5- v (faces east)
No. 2	no dim.	8.5 × 5 v (faces east)
Guest Room	no dim.	5 × 5 v
No. 4	unspecified	no dim.: barber shop?
Obraje	no dim.	11 × 5 v
Distribution Room*		no dim.
South Bldg.		
Rooms	2	4
Kitchen	no dim.	5 × 5 v
Refectory	no dim.	11 × 5 v
Storage		5 × 5 v
Carpentry	tools	——
Forge		8 × 4 v (new)
Masonry	tools	——
Indian Houses	straw huts—stone houses planned	15 new houses 8 × 4 v each
Outer Wall		under construction
Walls		

Note: v = vara (32.909 inches); dim. = dimensions; *portería* = main entrance to the friary; *obraje* = spinning room.
*Distribution room was next to the *obraje* (spinning room).

gilded wood (Table 6.3). The niche had a "very attractive [sculpture] of St. Francis with its glass case and key."

According to Fr. Sáenz, there was a sculpture of Our Lady of the Rosary with the Christ Child on her left hand on the Evangelical or Gospel (congregation's left) side of the altarpiece above the three risers. She had a silver crown and six strands of fine small pearls around her neck and four strands of similar pearls in her left hand. Her clothing was made of carved wood with simulated silk brocade (*estofado*). She stood on a base with three cherubim. The Child had a silver crown and two strands of small pearls around his neck and held ordinary rosary beads with a silver cross in his right hand. On the Epistle (congregation's right) side of the main altarpiece was an "old" sculpture of St. Joseph with a silver diadem and the Christ Child on his left hand. The St. Joseph stood on a beveled pedestal.

A small urn made of painted wood stood in the center of the altarpiece in place of the tabernacle. A sculpture of Our Lady of the Assumption was placed inside the urn in a recumbent position over some "used" cloths with her head on a small pillow made of fine linen. She had a silver crown and silver sandals and was dressed with two small white linen tunics and, over these, a green tunic of ribbed silk with fine gold trimming and a small cloth tunic with mother-of-pearl background. Her mantle was made of blue cloth with lace edging and fine silver trim.

FIGURE 6.2. *The altarpieces of San Juan Capistrano, 1772. Drawn to the scale of the sanctuary wall. The sacred images are no longer extant, with the exception of image C. Diagram by Jacinto Quirarte.*

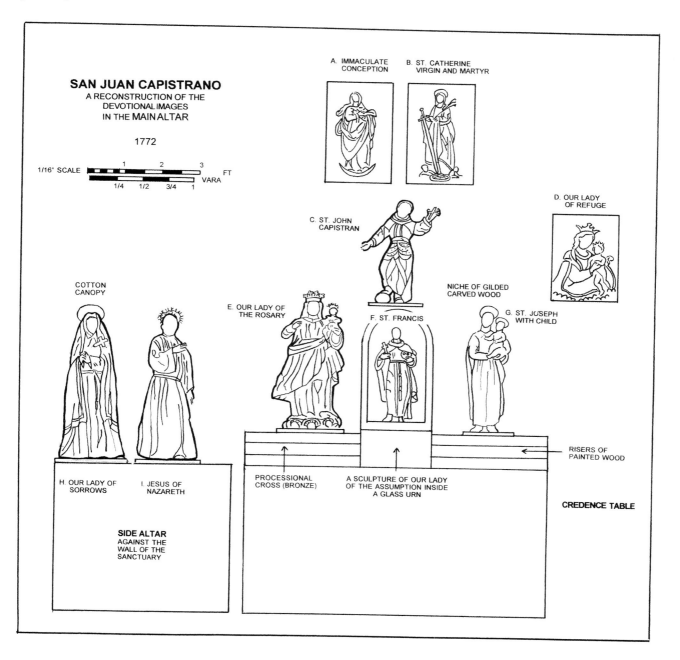

Table 6.3. The Altarpieces of San Juan Capistrano

SACRED IMAGES	1745	1756	1759	1762	1772
Capistrano (P)	1 v	——	——	——	——
Joseph	.5 v	——	——	——	——
Infant Jesus	small	——	——	——	——
Capistrano		1 v	1 v	no dim.	1 v
A few paintings		no dim.	no dim.(8 P)	no dim.(w/P)	
Francis		.3 v	.3 v	——	no dim.
OL of the Rosary w/Child		1 v	1 v	no dim.	1+ v
Joseph		1 v	——	——(w/P)	no dim.
OL of Refuge (P)		1 v	1+ v	——	——
Other Images			no dim.	——	——
OL of Sorrows			.5 v	no dim.	no dim.
Jesus Christ					no dim.
Capistrano					no dim.(new)
			port.	main	main
Jesus of Nazareth			2 v	no dim.	no dim.
	port.				port.
OL of Sorrows	large	——	——	——	——
OL of the Assumption (Port.)					.66 × .5 v (urn)
Procession Cross					no dim.

Note: (P) = painting/s; OL = Our Lady; v = vara (32.909 inches); dim. = dimensions; port. = portable altar; main = main altarpiece.

There was a Jerusalem cross near the altar stone, and two canvas paintings over the main altar, one of the Immaculate Conception and the other of St. Catherine, Virgin and Martyr. The two paintings were not specifically listed in the earlier reports and inventories, although Fr. Ortiz (1756) referred to "a few easel paintings" and Fr. Dolores (1762) to "a number of easel paintings" in each of the three altarpieces of the church.

A painting of Our Lady of Refuge hung over the main altar and a bronze processional cross on the Gospel (congregation's left) side of the altar. "There [was] also a very inspiring [sculpture] of Christ." The cross and the Christ figure were not listed in any of the earlier reports and inventories.[3]

THE JESUS OF NAZARETH ALTAR

The Jesus of Nazareth sculpture with a crown of thorns was first listed and described in the inventory of 1759 by Fr. Dolores. The sculpture was dressed in a "tunic white inside and [purple lustring cloth] outside; silk cincture, crown, cross, and hair over the shoulder all new." Fr. Dolores simply listed the sculpture in his 1762 report. According to Fr. Sáenz (1772), the sculpture was dressed in a coarse linen tunic and one of purple damask lined with linen ("almost new") over it. A long cincture of silk fringed with ribbons and pearls was hung by a silver cord from around the neck. Its "new hair" was "neatly arranged."

3. Fr. Sáenz, "Inventory [of San Juan Capistrano]," pp. 6–8; Fr. Ortiz, *Razón,* vol. 2, p. 14; Fr. Dolores, "Report," p. 337 (the information for the Dolores report on Capistrano was provided to Fr. Dolores by Fr. Manuel Rolan and Fr. Benito Varela); Fr. Ortiz, *Visita de las missiones,* pp. 6–7.

Fr. Sáenz (1772) noted that a sculpture of Our Lady of Sorrows was on the Gospel (congregation's left) side of the altar. The figure, with rays and dagger made of silver, was dressed in an outer tunic of thin silk and a mantle of shiny blue satin with silver branches and completely edged by silver scallops. The baldachin for the sculpture was made of delicate cotton.[4]

THE MAIN ALTARPIECE IN 1824

By 1824 there were still a few sacred images in the main altarpiece. The altarscreen had a niche in the center and a bracket pedestal on each side.

The sculpture of St. John Capistran had a garment of carved, gilded, and painted wood (*estofado*), a halo of gilded wood, and a silk banner. Although its location was not given, it is likely that it was still in the center of the altar above the niche that had once contained the St. Francis sculpture. The other sacred images remaining at Capistrano were a St. Francis, a Jesus of Nazareth with a tunic of purple chintz and a crown of thorns, a "small" metal crucifix, and two sculptures of Our Lady of Sorrows. One had a silver halo and was dressed in a white silk tunic with gold trim and a mantle of Chinese silk. The hilt of the dagger was made of silver and the remainder of iron. The other sculpture of "medium size" was "very deteriorated." It was dressed in a cloth tunic and white damask mantle with fake gold spangles and a shirt of rough linen.[5]

CHURCH FURNISHINGS

According to Fr. Sáenz (1772), the baptismal font with a well-fitting cover, both made of copper, had a bronze Christ over it. The font was clamped on a table of solid walnut attached to the wall, and near it was "a beautifully carved ebony box." The pulpit was made of walnut (the base, stair steps, and hand rail) and beveled savin (the box). In front of the church door was a "beveled" confessional made of savin wood, and next to it "a large missal stand for singing the Prophecies and for officiating at High Masses."

Fr. Díaz (1824) listed a copper pan for holy water on top of a wooden base and a confessional with an armchair in the center. The choir loft, roofed with beams, had a wooden staircase and a railing. The altar railing of turned wood had a door in the center.[6]

THE SACRISTY

The only reference to the architecture of the sacristy was made by Fr. Sáenz (1772). The sacristy had new walls of stone and mud and a roof made of oak beams and carved mesquite boards. One of the walls had thin ceramic tiles. The room had a window and two new doors, one with a lock and key, facing the patio of the *convento,* and the other with only a bolt, leading to the sanctuary of the church. The liturgical vestments were stored in a case.[7]

SACRED ITEMS

Fr. Ortiz (1756) reported that the sacred objects and ornaments used for divine services were stored in the sacristy in the three drawers (with keys) of a "good" walnut table. Fr. Dolores (1759) referred to another storage unit in the sacristy: a piece of furniture with three large drawers and a closet or cupboard on one

4. Fr. Dolores, "Inventory, 1759," p. 6; idem, "Report," p. 6 (translation modified); Fr. Sáenz, "Inventory [of San Juan Capistrano]," pp. 8–9.

5. Fr. Díaz de León, "1824 Inventory: San Juan Capistrano," p. 3.

6. Fr. Sáenz, "Inventory [of San Juan Capistrano]," pp. 9–10; Fr. Díaz de León, "1824 Inventory: San Juan Capistrano," pp. 1–2.

7. Fr. Sáenz, "Inventory [of San Juan Capistrano]," pp. 7–9; Fr. Díaz de León, "1824 Inventory: San Juan Capistrano," p. 5.

side, completely lined with red sheepskin. All the sacred vessels were stored in another cupboard, placed on a table.[8]

THE *Convento* AND OTHER BUILDINGS

According to Fr. Sáenz (1772), the plan of the four-room *convento* was in the form of a cloister with a well in the center "that always [had] water." The new main door (*portería*) was strong and wide enough to allow a man to enter on horseback. The ceiling of the first room was "made of dark oak beams and mesquite boards with a finishing that spared no cost." The second room had a new ceiling, strong walls, and a window on the south side. The two rooms had a corridor with five "arches, which beautif[ied] it." The rebuilt roof was not plastered due to bad weather. In the guest room there was a window on the south side with a wrought-iron guard.

The textile shop had a door with a lock and key on the east side and two windows. The room next to the main entrance and textile shop also had a door with a lock and key. This room was used to assign work and distribute the cotton and wool clothing to the Indians. The kitchen faced north, with a window on the south side. A room near the kitchen had a "door and window in good condition" and a new, well-made roof. Supplies for the baker were stored in the room, as well as "stocks for fugitives and delinquents" and a large altar table and a small one. A community room had two lofts with wooden staircases and benches all around, "made of beams resting on mortar and rough stone supports." It had a window and a door with lock and key on the north side. Fr. Morfi (1778–1783) noted that the *convento* contained four rooms with a gallery, two offices, a refectory, a kitchen, and a workshop (textile). According to Fr. López (1785), the *convento,* granary, church, and sacristy were built near a corner of the square.

Fr. Sáenz (1772) noted that there were fifteen houses for the Indians, "well-made" with doors and windows and roofs kept in good condition. New houses were under construction within an almost square area "with a strong wall which [served] as a rampart against the enemy." Fr. Morfi (1778–1783) wrote that the Indian houses did not compare with those at Concepción and San José. According to Fr. López (1785), the Indian houses were built up against the mission wall.

There is very little information in the documents on the granary and the workshops for carpentry, blacksmithing, textiles, and masonry. Fr. Sáenz (1772) noted that the granary, actually a shed, had a door facing north, a wall made of vertical boards, and a "well-thatched" roof. He also listed the forge, which was the same size as the Indian houses. It had a new door with a lock and key and a roof made of thin flat stones and mortar.[9]

THE MISSION WALL

Fr. Dolores (1759) noted that the church and sacristy were inside the walled-in area of the mission. According to Fr. López (1785), the mission wall, with Indian houses built against it, had three entrances, one somewhat larger than the others. The other structures of the mission—the *convento,* granary, church, and sacristy—were built near a corner of the square.[10]

8. Fr. Ortiz, *Razón,* vol. 2, pp. 15–16; Fr. Dolores, "Inventories, 1759," p. 6.

9. Fr. Sáenz, "Inventory [of San Juan Capistrano]," pp. 25–28, 30, 37; Fr. Morfi, *History of Texas,* pp. 98–99; Fr. López, "Documents," p. 43.

10. Fr. Dolores, "Inventories, 1759," p. 7; Fr. López, "Documents," 43.

FIGURE 6.3. *General view of the Capistrano church. Photograph by E. K. Sturdevant, ca. 1886. Courtesy of the Witte Museum, San Antonio, Texas.*

†HE FORMER MISSION, 1840–1890

The mission church was abandoned until 1840, when occasional visits were made by a priest from San Antonio.[11] From 1873 on, Fr. Francis Bouchu visited Capistrano from his home at Mission Espada.

THE MISSION CHURCH

According to Kendall, the church was "a plain, and simple edifice with little ornament." Bollaert saw the church "in ruins; part of the belfry and walls only remaining." Gregg reported that the mission was "nearly in ruins. The church, originally very inferior, has the roof now fallen in." Bartlett noted: "This was never a building of much pretensions, and is in a more ruinous state than San José" (Fig. 6.3).[12]

The roof of the church was blown off by a hurricane in 1886 (Fig. 6.4).

ARCHITECTURAL POLYCHROMY

Corner described the content and condition of the fragments of painted architectural and figural painting in the nave of the church (Fig. 6.5).

The frescoes are almost obliterated by exposure to the weather and the wonder is that they have not long since been washed entirely off by heavy rains. They are a curious mixture of Old and New World ideas. Detail of Moorish design, a Roman arch, an Indian figure and pigments.[13]

11. For a description of Capistrano in the late 1880s and historical notes, see Corner, *San Antonio*, pp. 20–24; for the nineteenth-century history of Capistrano, see Habig, *The Alamo Chain of Missions*, pp. 178–181; M. Schuetz, *The History and Archaeology of Mission San Juan Capistrano, San Antonio, Texas*, vol. 1: *Historical Documentation and Description of the Structures*, pp. 61–63.

12. Kendall, *Narrative*, p. 51; Bollaert, *William Bollaert's Texas*, pp. 232–233; Gregg, *Diary and Letters*, p. 235; Bartlett, *Personal Narrative*, vol. 1, p. 44.

13. Corner, *San Antonio*, pp. 20–21.

FIGURE 6.4. *General view of the Capistrano church. Half of the roof was gone. Photograph by A. L. Delfraisse, late nineteenth century. Courtesy of the Witte Museum, San Antonio, Texas.*

FIGURE 6.5. *Interior view of the Capistrano church entrance showing vestiges of wall paintings. Photograph, 1895. Gift of Jack C. Butterfield, CN 96.208. Courtesy of the Daughters of the Republic of Texas Library.*

OTHER MISSION BUILDINGS AND MEXICAN FAMILIES

According to Kendall, the "adjacent buildings [were] poor and out of repair." The granary was the only building in the square, and in the northwest corner there were the remains of a small stone tower. Bollaert noted that a few Mexican families resided at the former mission in "their favorite mud ranchos." Although the roof of the church had fallen in, Gregg wrote that "in the attached square there [were] still living near a dozen families—some 50 or 60 souls, of very poor Mexicans."[14]

THE RESTORED MISSION AND EXTANT SCULPTURES AND PAINTINGS, 1890 TO THE PRESENT

The roof blown off by the hurricane in 1886 was repaired in 1907. The church was rededicated in January 1909 and has been used since that time for services. Other restoration and archaeological work was carried out at the former mission in 1968 and 1988.[15] It is now part of the San Antonio Missions National Historical Park.

THE CHURCH AND THE OTHER BUILDINGS

The longitudinal axis of the Capistrano church, still standing, faces north, and the entrance is on the side of the east wall (Fig. 6.3). The nave runs parallel and is part of the west wall of the mission. Its orientation is consistent with the *convento* and workshops located along the west wall. The original doors of the church entrance are no longer there. The present door dates from the 1970s. An unfinished church and its sacristy, which was to have an octagonal plan, were located near the northeastern corner of the old wall. The church facade faced northwest (Fig. 6.1).[16]

IRONWORK

A stone cross was placed over the belfry for a short time at the turn of the century. This is seen in a 1910 photograph.[17] The belfry iron cross, reinstalled sometime after that date, is attributed to Cayetano del Valle or José Antonio Conde and is dated to the early 1800s by Schuetz (Figs. 6.6 and 6.7).[18] The iron door handles are modern and date from the 1970s reconstruction of the church.

ARCHITECTURAL DECORATION

The remains of architectural decoration are still visible around the door of the Capistrano church in late-nineteenth-century photographs (Fig. 6.5). The architectural and figural paintings in the Capistrano church described by Corner are no longer visible.[19] The interior was whitewashed when the church was restored in the twentieth century.

14. Kendall, *Narrative,* vol. 1, p. 51; Bollaert, *William Bollaert's Texas,* pp. 232–233; Gregg, *Diary and Letters,* p. 235.

15. M. Schuetz, *The History and Archaeology of Mission San Juan Capistrano, San Antonio, Texas,* vol. 2: *Description of the Artifacts and Ethnohistory of the Coahuiltecan Indians;* D. A. Turner, *Excavations at San Juan Capistrano, 41 Bx 5, Bexar County, Texas.*

16. Habig, *The Alamo Chain of Missions,* pp. 187–188; Turner, *Excavations at San Juan Capistrano,* pp. 2–5.

17. "Mission San Juan, 1910 (Crocker)," Daughters of the Republic of Texas Library, Alamo Plaza, San Antonio.

18. Schuetz, "Professional Artisans," p. 34.

19. Corner, *San Antonio,* pp. 20–21.

FIGURE 6.6. *General view of the Capistrano church. Courtesy of Kathy Vargas.*

FIGURE 6.7. *General view of the Capistrano church* **campanario** *with an iron cross. Courtesy of Kathy Vargas.*

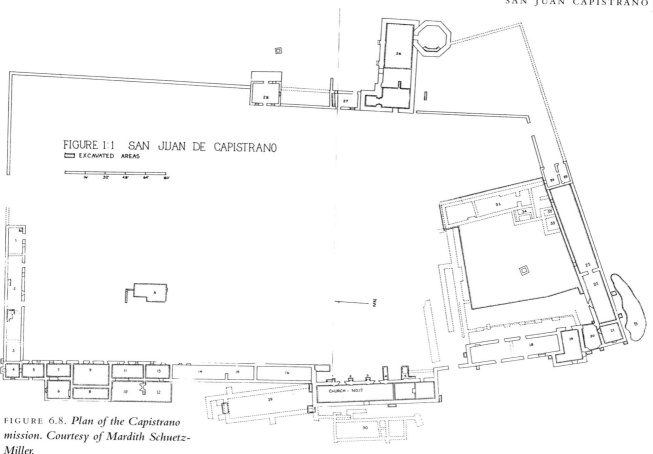

FIGURE 1:1 SAN JUAN DE CAPISTRANO
EXCAVATED AREAS

FIGURE 6.8. *Plan of the Capistrano mission. Courtesy of Mardith Schuetz-Miller.*

THE MISSION WALL

The old wall had an east-west orientation. The southern ends of the west and east walls of the much larger newer enclosure were grafted onto the old wall (Fig. 6.8). The wall on the west was anchored to the northern corner of the old west wall, thereby causing a change in direction of the wall at the southern end, and the east wall was extended right through the eastern end of the old wall. The southeastern portion of the old wall was dismantled, creating an irregularly shaped enclosure. There were gates on the north and west walls and at the southeastern corner.

According to J. E. Ivey and M. B. Thurber, the *convento* structure formed the southwestern corner of the mission wall.[20] Following this initial building phase, the early north and east walls were built. These walls were demolished, followed by the construction of the present north and east walls of the mission compound.

EXTANT SCULPTURES AND PAINTINGS

The altarpiece with Solomonic columns, presently located in the altar area of the Capistrano church, is a modern addition (Fig. 6.9). It was donated by Gilbert Denman along with all the sculptured and painted images with the exception of the sculpture of St. John Capistran placed in the center of the altarpiece.

20. J. E. Ivey and M. B. Thurber, "The Missions of San Antonio: A Historic Structures Report and Administrative History: Part 1, The Spanish Colonial Missions," p. 73.

The Capistran sculpture has actual chainmail affixed to the lower plates of the carved cuirass, and the armor is decorated with brass bosses (Fig. 6.10). The figure carries a crucifix in its left hand, and its right foot rests on the severed head of a Turk. It is thirty-four and three-fourths inches high.

St. John (1385–1456), born at Capistrano, Italy, had a vision of St. Francis while imprisoned during a civil war in Italy. He later joined the Franciscan Order (1415) and became a noted preacher and evangelist in central Europe. He is also renowned for leading an outnumbered army against the Turks and winning a decisive victory.

Fr. Dolores (1759) listed a "carved and very beautiful" sculpture of St. John Capistran, one vara (over thirty-two inches) tall, placed on a pedestal "beneath a baldachin of striped satin." Fr. Sáenz listed the St. John Capistran as "a new sculpture, one vara in size, with a diadem of gilded wood and a banner [standard]." Fr. Díaz listed the sculpture as "more than ½ vara [over sixteen inches] in height . . . [with] a garment of carved, gilded and painted wood, a halo of gilded wood, and a silk banner."

FIGURE 6.9. *Interior view of the Capistrano church nave toward the main altarpiece. Courtesy of Kathy Vargas.*

FIGURE 6.10. *Main altarpiece with St. John Capistran in the center flanked by polychromed sculptures and a sculpture of the Crucifixion directly below St. John Capistran. Only the titular saint was originally found in the church. Courtesy of Kathy Vargas.*

The other sculptures in the altarpiece are St. Francis of Assisi on the left and Jesus Christ on the congregation's right. There is a crucifix below the St. John Capistran. The small predella paintings represent the miraculous apparition of Our Lady of Guadalupe.

A sculpture of Jesus of Nazareth is presently located on a bracket pedestal on the left wall near the altar area (Figs. 6.9 and 6.11). The figure of the suffering Christ belongs to the events of the Passion of Christ and is usually shown with the crown of thorns. The sculpture was described by Fr. Dolores (1759) and by Fr. Sáenz (1772): Fr. Dolores noted that its clothing, crown, cross, and hair were all new. According to Fr. Sáenz, the figure wore "a crown of thorns made of wood and new hair," with "a linen tunic underneath and on the outside one of purple damask, which is almost new and completely lined with linen." Fr. Díaz wrote that the figure wore "a tunic of purple chintz." He listed it as "1½ varas in height [and still wearing] . . . a crown of thorns."

A sculpture of Our Lady of Solitude is presently located on a bracket pedestal on the right wall near the altar (Fig. 6.12). It may be the sculpture that

FIGURE 6.11. *Jesus of Nazareth. Sculpture. Courtesy of Kathy Vargas.*

FIGURE 6.12. *Our Lady of Solitude. Sculpture. Courtesy of Kathy Vargas.*

Fr. Díaz (1824) described as a dressed sculpture at Espada Mission "1¾ varas [fifty-six inches] high" with "a white tunic underneath and an outer one of black silk and a mantle of the same material with gold trim, its wimple and towel of fine linen, a Jerusalem rosary with a silver cross, [and] gilded silver halo encircled with stars of the same [metal]."

Fr. Díaz listed two sculptures of Our Lady of Sorrows. One of the sculptures (½ vara high) was described by Fr. Dolores in 1759. It may be the same one described by Fr. Sáenz in 1772. According to Fr. Díaz, the larger sculpture, "1 vara [over thirty-two inches] in height," was dressed "with a white silk tunic with gold trim and a mantle of Chinese silk. The hilt of the dagger is silver and the remainder is iron. The halo is gilded silver." According to Fr. Dolores, a sculpture of Our Lady of Sorrows "½ vara high" was placed on the epistle side of the sanctuary. It was dressed in "a tunic of red cloth, blue mantle, [and a silver halo. Its silver dagger was] joined to the rosary." Fr. Sáenz noted that the sculpture had a crown of "silver rays and dagger of silver." The outer tunic was made "of thin silk, and the mantle of shiny blue satin with silver branches." It was placed in a silver niche, and its baldachin was made of delicate cotton.

The allegorical figure of the Virgin Mary symbolizes the seven sorrows in her life and belongs with the events of the Passion of Christ. She wears a red gown and blue mantle, usually has one or seven daggers or swords representing her sorrows, and is shown clasping her hands.[21]

21. Fr. Dolores, "Inventories, 1759," p. 5; Fr. Sáenz, "Inventory [of San Juan Capistrano]," pp. 6, 8 (translation modified); Fr. Díaz de León, "1824 Inventory: San Juan Capistrano," p. 3.

EASEL PAINTINGS

A number of easel paintings found in other locations are now housed in the Mission Capistrano Museum. One is a painting of St. Francis, found in the San Fernando School by Carlos Castañeda and others in the 1930s (Fig. 6.13). It measures fifty-four by forty-two inches and shows a standing St. Francis gazing down toward his right, with the stigmata clearly visible on his hands. His left hand is held up in the open position, and the right is held slightly above waist level and palm down. The painting is cut off a little distance below the knee so that the lower part of the legs and the feet are not visible. Otherwise it would be a full-length portrait of the saint.

Although Castañeda believed the painting was originally from Espada, it is more likely that it was originally found at Valero. Fr. Sáenz (1772) listed two framed canvas paintings in the main altar of that church, one of St. Francis and the other of St. Clare. Although he did not include dimensions for the two

FIGURE 6.13. *St. Francis. Painting. Courtesy of Kathy Vargas.*

paintings, it is likely that the St. Francis painting was among those listed as early as 1756 by Fr. Ortiz for the Valero church. Fr. Ortiz (1756) reported seeing a painting (subject not identified) on the stairs of the Valero church that measured two varas (over sixty-four inches) in height. The dimensions are close to those of the painting found by Castañeda. Fr. Ortiz also found another painting of St. Francis Xavier of the same size in the choir loft altarpiece. Many of the sacred images were transferred to the San Fernando church in 1793 when Valero was secularized.[22]

22. Fr. Ortiz, *Razón,* vol. 3, pp. 12, 18; Fr. Sáenz, *Inventory: 1772,* p. 9; G. Ashford, "Old Spanish Paintings May Return Home," *San Antonio Express-News* (Sunday, December 21, 1965); an earlier article in the *San Antonio Light* (before 1937) reported the discovery of the St. Francis painting and several other works in the rafters of the San Fernando Cathedral auditorium.

Reconstruction of the San José mission church facade in color. Painting by Ernst Schuchard, 1932. Schuchard Collection. Courtesy of the Daughters of the Republic of Texas Library.

Reconstruction of the Concepción mission church facade in color, by Ernst Schuchard, 1932. Schuchard Collection. Courtesy of the Daughters of the Republic of Texas Library.

Reconstruction of all the extant wall
paintings at Concepción mission, by
Ernst Schuchard, 1933. Schuchard
Collection. Courtesy of the Daughters
of the Republic of Texas Library.

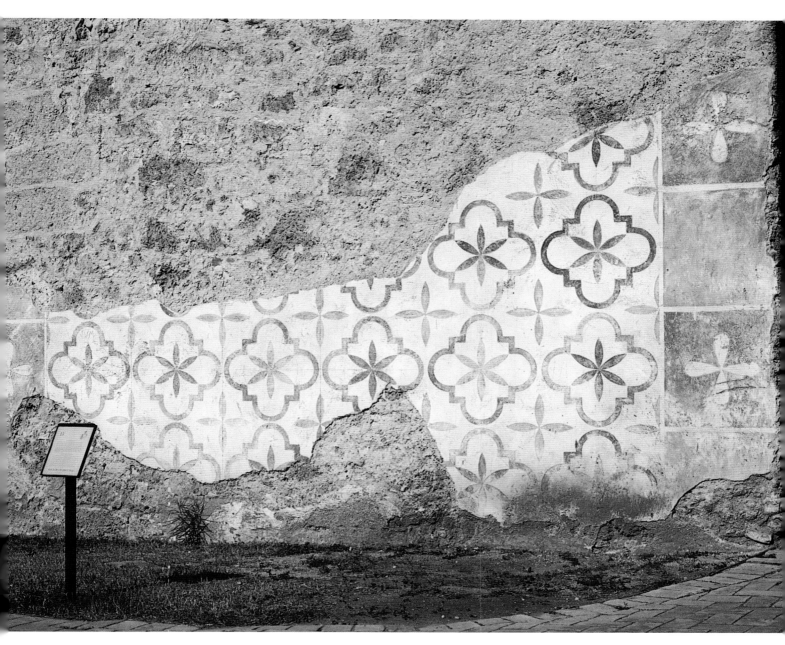

General view of the San José church south tower. Polychromy restored by E. Schuchard and R. Walker in 1949. Courtesy of César Martínez.

Opposite page: St. Joseph with Child. Detail of the San José church main portal. Courtesy of César Martínez.

Interior view of the San José church dome and pendentives. Architectural polychromy: vaulted ceiling. Courtesy of Tim Summa.

Sacristy window, San José mission. Courtesy of César Martínez.

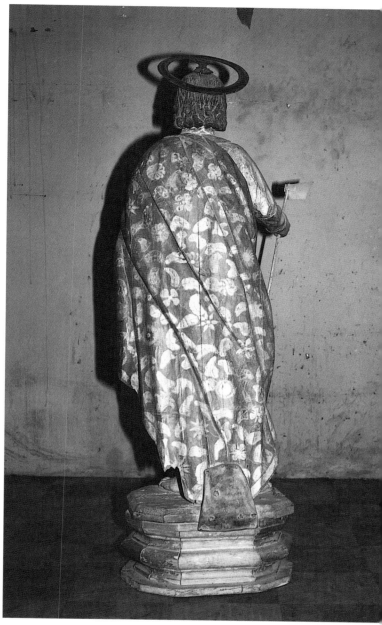

St. Joseph. Wood sculpture. Gilded **estofado,** *glass eyes. Old Spanish Missions Center. Photograph by Kathy Vargas.*

Above left: Our Lady of the Rosary.
*Wood sculpture. Gilded **estofado** and*
glass eyes. Old Spanish Missions
Center. Photograph by Kathy Vargas.

Above right: St. Francis. Sculpture.
Photograph by Jacinto Quirarte.

7

San Francisco de la Espada

San Francisco de la Espada was founded in 1731. It was the most isolated of the San Antonio missions and as a result had to face many Apache raids. Like the other missions, it had a very fortified appearance, with its quadrangular plan, fortified entrances, rifle ports, and a circular bastion with openings for both rifle and small cannon fire. In 1745 the sacristy was being used as a church while the stone and mortar church was under construction.[1] The church roofed with wooden beams was finished by 1756 along with a granary and a two-story building for the living quarters for the missionaries, all made of stone.

The church had a cruciform plan and a small transept. A larger church under construction by 1762 was completed by 1777, but it had to be torn down because it threatened to fall. There was no rebuilding because the Indian population continued to decline after 1762.

The Original Art and Architecture, 1740–1824

THE CHURCH

The Espada church was rebuilt several times. The sacristy was used as a temporary chapel during all those periods of construction. According to Fr. Ortiz, a new stone and mortar church was under construction in 1745. Fr. Dolores (1762) reported that the finished church was torn down because it was unsafe. Fr. Sáenz (1772) observed that the stone and masonry sacristy used as a temporary church had a roof constructed with beams and mortar. One of its two doors led to the *convento,* and the other to the church that remained to be built.

Fr. Morfi referred to the church in his diary entry for December 31, 1777, as "[b]eautiful and adorned" and to an old corral for the cattle as "no good." In his *History of Texas* he wrote that the church "was demolished because it threatened to fall down and services [were] being held in an ample room that [had] a choir and a sacristy, all very neat." This was undoubtedly the room mentioned by Fr. Dolores (1762) as "a large and proper room" with a choir loft.

1. For the early history of La Espada, see Habig, *The Alamo Chain of Missions,* pp. 207–220.

TABLE 7.1. THE ARCHITECTURE OF SAN FRANCISCO DE LA ESPADA, 1756–1772

STRUCTURES	1756	1759	1762	1772
New Church			under construction*	——
Temporary Church**	14 × 5.3 v	no dim.	no dim.	14 × 5.33 × 7 v (sacristy)
Temporary Sacristy				5.5 × 4 × 5 v
Convento (friary)	2-story	——	2-story	unspecified
Arcaded Cloister		no dim.	no dim.	——
Rooms: 1st floor	2	——	3 rooms	——
Offices	no dim.		no dim.	6 × 5.75 × 5 × 5.75 v
Obraje		no dim.	no dim.	17 × 5 × 5 v
Storage				6 × 5.75 × 5.75 v
Storage	no dim.	no dim.	——	——
Kitchen				no dim.
Common				5.5 × 3 v
Cells: 2nd floor	2	2	4	unspecified
No. 1	no dim.	——	no dim.	13.5 × 5.75 × 5.75 v
Guest Room	no dim.	——	no dim.	6 × 5.75 × 5.75 v
No. 3			no dim.	no dim.
Alcove				5.75 × 5 × 6 v
No. 4			no dim.	——
Brick				no dim.
Storage				21 v long
Forge		no dim.	tools	——
Masonry			tools	tools
Carpentry			tools	
Indian Houses	unspecified *xacales*	unspecified***	stone houses	——
Rows		2	3	——
Granary	no dim.	no dim.	no dim.	40 × 7 v

Notes: v = vara (32.909 inches); dim. = dimensions; *obraje* = spinning room.

*Construction had stopped due to lack of good stone. Work continued in 1762. The church was torn down after it was completed because it was considered unsafe.

**The temporary church was listed in the 1745 inventory, but no dimensions were given.

***The Indians lived in *xacales*. Stone houses were under construction in 1756.

According to Fr. López (1785), the church and sacristy on the west side of the square were constructed with stone and lime (mortar) (Fig. 7.1). They all had "sufficient room for all purposes." Although Padilla (1820) did not refer to the church, he indicated that the buildings of the mission were in a state similar to that of the buildings at Capistrano, but people were still living at the mission (Table 7.1).

Fr. Díaz (1824) reported that the roof of the stone church, made of wood beams and mortar, was in bad condition. The simple belfry with an iron cross contained three bells, one of them without a clapper. The entrance to the church had double doors with keys. The choir loft had a wooden railing and a stone staircase. There was a door to the sacristy inside the church.[2]

2. Fr. Ortiz quoted in ibid., p. 207; Fr. Dolores, "Report," p. 339; Fr. Sáenz, "Inventory of Espada Mission," pp. 1–2; Fr. Morfi, *Diario y derrotero,* p. 98; idem, *History of Texas,* p. 99; Fr. Dolores, "Report," p. 339; Fr. López, "Documents," p. 44; Padilla, "Texas in 1820," p. 60; Fr. José Antonio Díaz de León, "Inventory [of the Church of Mission de S. Francisco de la Espada, February 29, 1824]," p. 11.

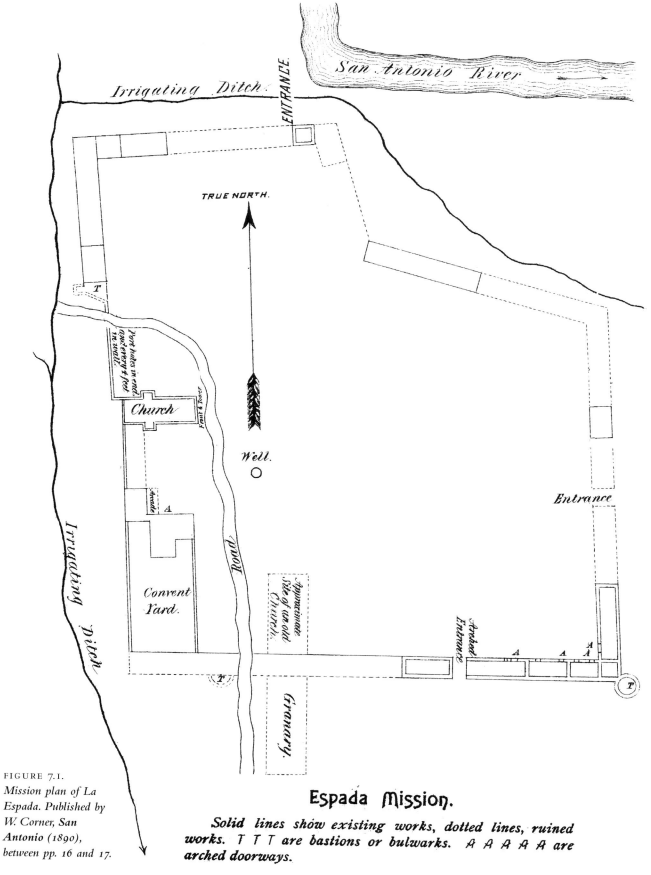

San Antonio River

Irrigating Ditch.

ENTRANCE.

TRUE NORTH.

Irrigating Ditch

*Port holes in end,
and every 4 feet
in wall.*

Front & Tower

Church

Well.

O

Road

Arcade

4

Convent
Yard.

*Approximate
Site of an old
Church.*

Granary.

Entrance

Arched
Entrance

A A A
A

T

T

Espada Mission.

**Solid lines show existing works, dotted lines, ruined
works. T T T are bastions or bulwarks. A A A A A are
arched doorways.**

Scale, 100 feet to the inch.

FIGURE 7.1.
*Mission plan of La
Espada. Published by
W. Corner, San
Antonio (1890),
between pp. 16 and 17.*

THE ALTARPIECES OF THE CHURCH IN 1772

According to Fr. Sáenz, the altar table in the temporary church was placed on a wooden platform (Fig. 7.2). The gilded tabernacle (first listed in 1762) with its key was in the center of the altarpiece and inside it a curtain with a silver rod. A cross with the crucifix and base made of bronze was placed on the altar. It was listed for the first time.

A carved sculpture of St. Francis was placed on a gilded base inside a carved wooden niche above the gilded tabernacle (Table 7.2). It wore a silver diadem and held a crucifix in its hand.

There were also four carved sculptures flanking the St. Francis: an image of the Most Holy Mary with Child on a gilded base wearing a silver crown and a necklace of fine pearls with a small gold cross and stones to match, a St. Joseph holding the Child Jesus on a gilded base wearing a gilded diadem, a St. Anthony of Padua holding the Child Jesus, and another St. Francis holding a skull and a crucifix.

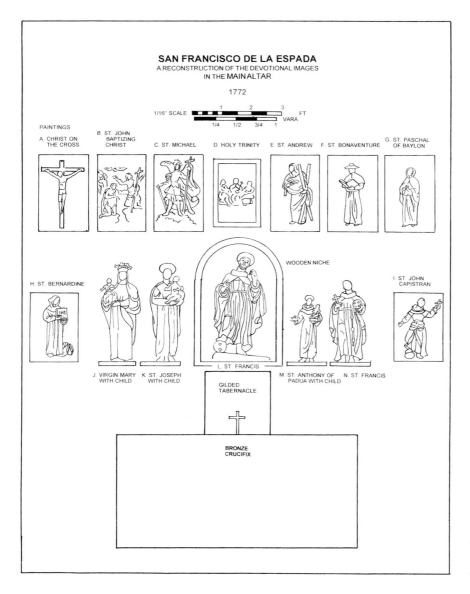

FIGURE 7.2. *The altarpieces of San Francisco de la Espada, 1772. Drawn to the scale of the sanctuary wall. Diagram by Jacinto Quirarte.*

TABLE 7.2. THE ALTARPIECES OF LA ESPADA

SACRED IMAGES	1745	1756	1759	1762	1772	1824
Francis	1± v	1– v	no dim.	no dim.	1± v	1.5 v
Bernardine (P)	1 v	———	1 of 4	———	no dim.	———
Capistrano (P)	1 v	———	1 of 4	———	———	———
OL of Sorrows	.75 v	no dim.	no dim.	———	———	medium
Holy Christ		1 v	no dim.	———	———	———
OL Pasaviense (P)		no dim.	1 of 4	———	———	———
OL of Refuge (P)			1 of 4	———	———	———
OL of the Rosary				no dim.	———	———
Mary w/Child					1.25 v	———
Joseph w/Child					1.25 v	———
Anthony of Padua w/Child					.75 v	———
Francis w/Skull and Crucifix					1 v	———
The Trinity (P)					1 v	———
Crucifixion (P)					1 v	———
Baptism of Christ (P)					1 v	———
St. Michael (P)					1 v	———
Andrew (P)					1 v	———
Bonaventure (P)					1 v	———
St. Paschal Baylon (P)					1 v	———
					sacristy	main
OL of Sorrows					.5 v	no dim.
Crucifixion					.5 v	.5 v
Conception						1 v
Jesus of Nazareth						1.5 v
OL of Solitude						1.75 v
Mary w/Child						.5– v
Joseph						.5– v

Note: (P) = painting/s; OL = Our Lady; v = vara (32.909 inches); dim. = dimensions; main = main altarpiece.

Seven paintings were listed for the first time in 1772. One was a "fine" painting of the Most Blessed Trinity in a carved gilded frame, above the niche of the St. Francis figure. The other six in wooden frames on the sides of the Holy Trinity were Christ on the Cross, St. John Baptizing Christ, St. Michael, St. Andrew, the Seraphic Doctor St. Bonaventure, and St. Paschal Baylon.

The other framed paintings of St. Bernardine of Siena and St. John Capistran, "somewhat old but still good," were also listed in the inventory.[3]

THE INVENTORY OF 1824

Fr. Díaz listed two altar tables. The main altar table had "two medium-sized [altars] on each side of it" as well as the gilded tabernacle with a key mentioned in 1762 and 1772.

3. Fr. Sáenz, "Inventory of Espada Mission," p. 4; Fr. Dolores, "Report," p. 339.

Only two of the many sacred images mentioned in the earlier reports and inventories were in place in 1824: the sculptures of St. Francis and a "medium-sized" image of Our Lady of Sorrows. The St. Francis had a garment made of carved, gilded, and painted wood. It still had a diadem and held a bronze crucifix. Newly added were four small silver votive offerings. The Lady of Sorrows, "somewhat disfigured," had a small halo and dagger, both made of silver.

The 1824 inventory for the first time mentioned a Jesus of Nazareth, with a crown of thorns, a halo of three rays of silver, and a cross on his shoulders, dressed in a white inner tunic and an outer one made of coarse silk; a crucified Christ; a carved sculpture of Our Lady of Solitude, dressed in a white inner tunic and an outer one made of black silk and a mantle of the same material with gold trim, a hood of fine hemp, a towel of the same material, a rosary of Jerusalem linked with a silver cross, and a halo of gilded silver rays surmounted with silver stars. It listed several sculptures finished in the *estofado* technique: an Immaculate Conception with a silver crown made of yellow metal and a necklace of imitation pearls; a sculpture or carved image of St. Joseph with a diadem of gilded wood, a silver staff with flowers of gilded wood, and the Child Jesus; a St. Anthony of Padua; and two smaller sculptures of the Most Holy Mother and St. Joseph.[4]

SACRED ITEMS AND CHURCH FURNISHINGS

The ornaments and liturgical vestments were stored in the four drawers of a walnut table, used as the main altar in 1756 and 1759. By 1762 the liturgical vestments, sacred vessels, and other items were stored in a cabinet. The table with four drawers that had been used as the main altar earlier was in the sacristy in 1824. According to Fr. Díaz, it was used to store vestments and a number of silver, copper, and other ornaments.

Fr. Dolores (1762) referred to a baptismal font, a confessional, and benches in the church. Fr. Díaz listed a basin for holy water on a stone base and a wooden confessional.[5]

THE SACRISTY

According to Fr. Sáenz (1772), a room used as a sacristy had a window and a door with a lock and key. It was reached through a door on the Epistle (congregation's right) side of the main altar of the church. Fr. Díaz indicated that the sacristy had a door without a key and a roof in ruins.[6]

THE SACRISTY ALTARPIECE

The sacristy altarpiece had a wooden table with a Jerusalem cross. Above the altar was a sculpture of Our Lady of Sorrows, originally located in the main altarpiece, with a gilded base and silver sword. Its dress and mantle were "presentable." In the front part of the altar was a crucifix placed inside a red velvet canopy. There was also a silver processional cross with gilded images of Jesus Christ and his Most Pure Mother on a "well-made" wooden pedestal.[7]

4. Fr. Díaz de León, "Inventory [of La Espada]," pp. 2–4 (trans. Donna Pierce).

5. Fr. Ortiz, *Razón,* vol. 1, pp. 37–38; Fr. Dolores, "Inventories, 1759," p. 3; idem, "Report," p. 339; Fr. Díaz de León, "Inventory [of La Espada]," p. 12.

6. Fr. Sáenz, "Inventory of Espada Mission," p. 14; Fr. Díaz de León, "Inventory [of La Espada]," p. 2 (trans. Donna Pierce).

7. Fr. Sáenz, "Inventory of Espada Mission," p. 5.

THE *Convento* AND OTHER BUILDINGS

According to Fr. Sáenz, the second floor of the *convento* was reached by one of two small stairways. Access to the entrance was through a room located next to one of the four workshops. It was roofed with beams, mortar, and brick. The *convento* was divided into one large room and two smaller ones. The first room had a roof constructed with beams and mortar, two framed windows with shutters and bolts, and a door with a lock and key. The second room had a framed window with a bolt and a door with a latch and key. The third room, roofed with beams, mortar, and brick, had an alcove.

Fr. Morfi noted in his *History of Texas* that the *convento* had four rooms on the second floor and three on the first.

According to Fr. Ortiz, stone houses for the Indians were under construction in 1756. Pending the completion of the houses, the Indians lived along the banks of the river in *xacales*. Fr. Dolores reported that the stone houses for the Indians, located along two walls, were roofed with beams and painted. By 1762 the Indians lived in stone houses arranged in three rows. Fr. Morfi stated that the three rows of Indian houses formed a square with the *convento*. Fr. López indicated that the Indian houses built against the mission wall were constructed with stone and mud.

Fr. Dolores referred to the workshops and storage rooms and reported that there was a textile workshop and a large stone granary. According to Fr. Sáenz, there were four workshops. One of them (textile?) next to the kitchen was made of stone with a brick floor and a roof of beams, plaster, and mortar. A hut made of logs and reeds with a door and a key was used to dry and store brick. Another served as a granary.

As in all his other observations, Fr. Morfi evaluated the layout of the buildings of the mission. In his view, the *convento,* galleries, workshop, and large granary laid out in a straight line were "ill-arranged and plain." Fr. López reported that the granary on the south side of the square was constructed with stone and mud.[8]

THE MISSION WALL

Fr. Dolores noted that two of the walls and Indian houses alongside them were completed. Another wall with the *convento* built against it was still under construction.

Fr. Morfi wrote that a stone wall closed the portion of the square where there were no houses. Fr. López reported that the mission had a wall constructed with stone and mud, built around a square, like all the others.[9]

THE FORMER MISSION, 1840–1890

Following complete secularization in 1824, no attention was paid to the mission until 1840, when repairs were made so that occasional services could be held.[10]

8. Fr. Sáenz, "Inventory of Espada Mission," pp. 46, 50, 51; Fr. Morfi, *History of Texas,* p. 99; Fr. Ortiz, *Razón,* vol. 1, p. 39; Fr. Dolores, "Inventories, 1759," p. 3; idem, "Report," p. 340; Fr. López, "Documents," p. 44.

9. Fr. Dolores, "Inventories, 1759," p. 3; Fr. Morfi, *History of Texas,* p. 99; Fr. López, "Documents," p. 44.

10. For the nineteenth-century history of La Espada, see Habig, *The Alamo Chain of Missions,* pp. 221–227.

FIGURE 7.3. *Mission Espada, ca.
1911–1912. C. O. Lee, photographer.
Gift of Allen Richards. Courtesy of the
Daughters of the Republic of Texas
Library, CN96.192.*

From 1858 to 1907, Fr. Francis Bouchu undertook major restoration for the chapel, rebuilding all the walls but the front one.

THE MISSION CHURCH AND OTHER BUILDINGS

Kendall described the mission and indicated that there were people still living there. "The Church, however, [was] in ruins. Two sides of the square consist[ed] of mere walls; the other sides [were] composed of dwellings as in other instances."

To Bollaert, "it [was] not quite in so ruinous a state as that of San Juan Capistrano." Gregg considered the "[c]hurch originally most inferior of any of them—now all in ruins—only front wall standing." Corner discussed the restoration work carried out by the Rev. Fr. Bouchu:

> Under his rule the Mission Chapel has almost entirely renewed, the front only retaining a portion of its ancient work.[11]

11. Kendall, *Narrative,* vol. 1, p. 51; Bollaert, *William Bollaert's Texas,* p. 233; Gregg, *Diary and Letters,* p. 235; Corner, *San Antonio,* p. 22.

METALWORK

There is a reference in the 1824 inventory to a "[s]imple belfry with iron cross and three bells, one of these without the clapper." Corner referred to "[i]ts three bells [which] clang out three times a day" and added that there were "several pretty little bits of wrought iron work in this and the other missions" but gave no details (Fig. 7.3).[12]

The Restored Mission and the Extant Sculptures, 1890 to the Present

New doors and windows, a wooden ceiling, a new roof, and a new brick floor were added in 1911. The only original part of the church is the front wall or the facade (Fig. 7.4). Fr. Bouchu added all the other walls during the years from 1858 to 1907. The Sisters of the Incarnate Word ran a school at the former mission from 1915 and 1967. The latest restoration dates from the 1960s.

Archaeological excavations have been carried out at the former mission (1976, 1981) and the southeast corner of the plaza (1992). It is now part of the San Antonio Missions National Historical Park.[13]

THE MISSION WALL

The irregularly shaped original wall of Espada had a north–south orientation, with gates at each of the four walls. The main entrance was on the south wall. The west gate was fortified, and there were bastions at the southeastern corner and near the southwest corner of the enclosure.

THE CHURCH, SACRISTY, AND *Convento*

The old Espada church reported in 1756 (the present reconstructed church except for the portal) faced east. It was located in the center of the west wall. The other church, completed before 1762 but later demolished, had a north–south orientation. The *convento* building and the patio were located in the southeastern corner of the enclosure.[14]

THE CHURCH FACADE

Although there is no exterior figural sculpture on the facade of the church, there is some carved stone on the portal arch (Fig. 7.5). As is well known, some writers have considered the unusual character of the *herradura* (horseshoe) arch to be the result of ignorance on the part of the masons, who presumably did not know how to fit the stones together. Paul Goeldner thought the voussoirs were "incorrectly reassembled in a restoration."[15] Eugene George examined the geometric relations of the arch to determine what was originally intended in the design of the Espada church (Fig. 7.6). He considered it "probable that the elements of the arch at Espada were precut complete on the site" and concluded:

12. Fr. Díaz de León, "Inventory [of La Espada]," p. 1 (trans. Donna Pierce); Corner, *San Antonio*, pp. 22, 23.

13. For the twentieth-century history of La Espada, see Habig, *The Alamo Chain of Missions*, pp. 231–233; for Espada archaeology, see A. A. Fox and T. R. Hester, *Archaeological Test Excavations at Mission San Francisco de la Espada*; A. A. Fox, *Test Excavations at Mission San Francisco de la Espada*; and F. K. Meskill, *Archaeological Testing within the Southeast Corner of the Plaza at Mission Espada San Antonio, Bexar County, Texas.*

14. Fr. Dolores, "Report," p. 339 and n. 14, p. 357; Fr. Ortiz, *Razón,* vol. 1, p. 35.

15. Paul Goeldner, comp., *Texas Catalogue: Historic American Buildings Survey* (San Antonio: Trinity University Press, 1974), p. 193.

FIGURE 7.4. *General view of the Espada church facade. Courtesy of Kathy Vargas.*

Instructions left by the maestro for placement of the voussoirs, however, might not have been fully comprehended. Having never seen an arch with elements that first spring outward from an opening prior to curving inward, the workcrew must have been baffled.[16]

METALWORK

A cross with scrolls appears on top of the *espadaña* sometime during the latter part of the nineteenth century, as seen in photographs taken during that time (Fig. 7.3). According to Harvey Smith, Jr. (personal communication, 1982), Kurt Voss told him that the present cross is hand forged and probably dates from the pre-1850 period (Fig. 7.4). Schuetz dated the cross to the early 1800s and suggested that it was made by Cayetano del Valle or José Antonio Conde, who also made the *campanario* cross of Capistrano (Fig. 6.7).[17]

16. Eugene George, "Espada Doorway: A Lesson in Harmony," *El Campanario,* Texas Old Missions and Forts Restoration Association, vol. 11, no. 3 (September 1980): 15–18; reprinted from *Perspective* 9, no. 1 (May 1980).

17. Schuetz, "Professional Artisans," p. 34.

FIGURE 7.5. *Main portal of the Espada church. Courtesy of Kathy Vargas.*

FIGURE 7.6. *Main portal of the Espada church. Three elevations by Eugene George. Courtesy of Walter Eugene George.*

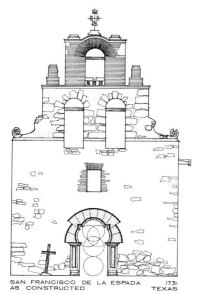

SAN FRANCISCO DE LA ESPADA 1731
AS CONSTRUCTED TEXAS

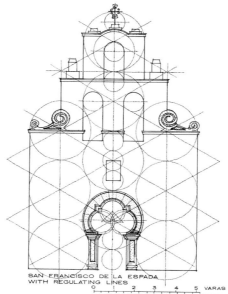

SAN FRANCISCO DE LA ESPADA
WITH REGULATING LINES

0   1   2   3   4   5 VARAS
0 1 2 3 4 5 6 7 8 9 10 11 12 13 14 FEET

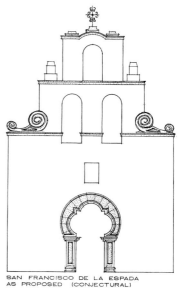

SAN FRANCISCO DE LA ESPADA
AS PROPOSED (CONJECTURAL)

FIGURE 7.7. *Main altar area of the Espada church. Courtesy of Kathy Vargas.*

FIGURE 7.8. *St. Francis. Sculpture. Courtesy of Kathy Vargas.*

THE CHURCH INTERIOR

ARCHITECTURAL SCULPTURE

Two crudely carved stone holy water fonts embedded on the wall of the entrance to the Espada church. There are no references to architectural sculpture in the interiors of the Capistrano and Espada mission churches in the colonial documents or in the published accounts of the nineteenth-century travelers.

EXTANT SCULPTURES AND PAINTINGS

The sculpture of St. Francis, the titular saint, is placed on a stone pedestal centrally located high over the main altar of the church (Figs. 7.7 and 7.8). It has glass eyes and teeth and a silver repoussé halo. The figure's right foot rests on a skull, and it holds a crucifix in its left hand. It is forty-three inches high. A thorough cleaning in 1970 revealed only patches of the original painted and gilded surface. The present finish is recent. This may be the sculpture repaired and regilded by Fr. Bouchu in the late nineteenth century. The tunic worn by St. Francis was painted brown sometime after 1907. (See Epilogue for more information.)

According to Fr. Dolores, there was "an altar of Our Father St. Francis over a carved and golden [gilded] tabernacle." Fr. Sáenz noted that above the tabernacle was "a niche 1½ varas [forty-nine inches] high with a carved image of St. Francis with a gilded base, silver diadem and a crucifix in his hand."

There are sculptures of Jesus of Nazareth and Our Lady of Sorrows (Figs. 7.9 and 7.10). The first, located on the left side of the main altar, does not have a crown of thorns or a halo. The wood sculpture, sixty-six inches high, has glass eyes and is fully clothed. The second sculpture, located on the right side of the main altar (as seen by the congregation), is a complete sculpture from the waist up and an armature support beneath that area. It has glass eyes and teeth and is fully clothed. It is also sixty-six inches high.

Fr. Sáenz listed a sculpture of Our Lady of Sorrows on a gilded base in the sacristy altarpiece. It had a silver sword, and its gown and mantle were "presentable." There was a red velvet baldachin over it that measured 1½ varas (forty-nine inches) high. A crucifix, ½ vara (sixteen inches) high, was placed on the upper part of the baldachin. This is not the sculpture presently found in the Espada church main altar area.

Fr. Díaz described a Jesus of Nazareth as

FIGURE 7.9. *Jesus of Nazareth. Sculpture. Courtesy of Kathy Vargas.*

FIGURE 7.10. *Our Lady of Sorrows. Sculpture. Courtesy of Kathy Vargas.*

1½ varas in height with a white interior tunic and an outer [one] of coarse silk cloth, a crown of thorns, and a halo of three rays of silver. He also has a cross on his shoulders.

This is not the sculpture now located in the Espada church altar area.

Fr. Díaz also described a sculpture of Our Lady of Solitude, 1¾ varas (over fifty-six inches) high, that sounds more like what is presently located on the right side of the altar area in the Capistrano church. It was dressed in

a white tunic underneath and an outer one of black silk and a mantle of the same material with gold trim, its wimple and towel of fine linen, a Jerusalem rosary with a silver cross, [and] a gilded silver halo encircled with stars of the same [metal].[18]

18. Fr. Dolores, "Report," p. 339; Fr. Sáenz, "Inventory of Espada Mission," p. 3 (translation modified); Fr. Díaz de León, "Inventory [of La Espada]," pp. 2, 3 (trans. Donna Pierce and Jacinto Quirarte), 11 (trans. Donna Pierce).

8

El Espíritu Santo

The Mission of Nuestra Señora del Espíritu Santo de Zúñiga was founded in 1722 by the Marqués de Aguayo and the Querétaran missionaries to serve the Taranames, Tamiques, Piquicanes, and Manos de Perros in the vicinity of the old fort St. Louis built by La Salle.[1] The mission and the garrison were moved to the Guadalupe River in 1726 because of the continuing problems with the Indians and soldiers at Presidio Nuestra Señora de Loreto. The mission and the presidio were moved one more time in 1749, to the lower San Antonio River around present Goliad, Texas.

Rivalries between the Querétaran and Zacatecan missionaries in the Espíritu Santo region as well as difficulties with the various Indian tribes and troubles between the soldiers and the Indians led to efforts by the missionaries in the mid-eighteenth century to establish another mission in their midst.

The Original Art and Architecture, 1740–1824

THE CHURCH

According to Fr. Hierro, the chapel of El Espíritu Santo was large and "decent." Fr. Solís, who inspected the mission from March 6 to March 11, 1768, considered it better than El Rosario even though it was smaller. He was impressed with the ornaments, sacred vessels, and other items used for "Divine worship," which he described as "very clean, very neat and in due arrangement."

According to Fr. López, the church and the sacristy were constructed with stone and lime (mortar) and had flat roofs. He added that considerable sums had been spent annually before the economic downturn of the mission "on public worship, as evidenced by the value of the church, its furnishings, and its ornaments, none of which [were] very old." The sacred images and other ornaments constantly needed to be replaced "on account of the strong south winds from the salt marshes."[2]

1. For information on Espíritu Santo in the eighteenth century, see W. H. Oberste, "Texas Missions of the Coastal Bend, Espíritu Santo, El Rosario, El Refugio, Part I"; for a brief survey, see J. W. Wakefield, *Missions of Old Texas,* pp. 124–126.

2. "The Fr. Guardian Simón Hierro Report," in Bolton, *Texas in the Middle Eighteenth Century,* p. 100; Fr. Solís, "Diary," p. 45; Fr. López, "Documents," p. 44.

TABLE 8.1. THE ALTARPIECES OF ESPÍRITU SANTO

SACRED IMAGES	1783	CONDITION, CONTEXT, FUNCTION
Holy Trinity (silver frame)	no dim.	
OL of Balvaneda (Valvanera)	no dim.	
Crucified Christ (2)	medium	
Jesus of Nazareth (hinges)	no dim.	used on Good Friday
Unidentified Holy Image	small	
Conception	no dim.	
Joseph	no dim.	
Crucifix (brass)	small	
OL of Refuge	no dim.	old
OL of Sorrows	no dim.	
OL of Sorrows (P)	small	
Veronica (P)	small	
OL of Sorrows	no dim.	old
OL of Guadalupe (P)	no dim.	
OL of Guadalupe (P)	no dim.	
Juan Diego	no dim.	placed next to the old (P) of OL of Guadalupe

Note: OL = Our Lady; (P) = painting; dim. = dimensions.

THE ALTARPIECES IN 1783

The Fr. Cárdenas inventory begins with the church and continues with the other mission buildings. He listed the sacred images of the church and provided a brief description of each one but did not give dimensions or their location in the altarpieces (Table 8.1).

A side altar had a carved sculpture of the Holy Trinity and a glass case in a niche with a gilded frame, covered with a yellow muslin curtain. There was a sculpture of Our Lady of Valvanera as well as two medium-sized carved sculptures of the Crucified Christ (one was probably part of the main altar). One was placed under a muslin canopy, the other in a wooden niche with a glass case. A sculpture of the Holy Christ (probably Jesus of Nazareth) with hinges (adjustable arms and legs) was used on Good Friday. There was also a small metal sculpture (saint not identified) with silver rays.

The gilded wood tabernacle had two keys (one made of silver, the other of iron), a tabernacle veil with trimmings, and a silver cross in the center.

Two "beautiful" sculptured images, one of the Most Pure Virgin with cloth garments, a silver crown, and several strings of pearls and the other of St. Joseph with his staff and silver rays and a silver reliquary, were placed inside a niche adorned with a curtain of scarlet cloth, eight small mirrors, and one large mirror in a frame. There was also a small Holy Christ of brass and an old painting of Our Lady of Refuge.

A sculpture of Our Lady of Sorrows wore two garments, one in color (not specified), the other black. It had rays (a diadem?) and a silver sword. Two small paintings depicted Our Lady of Sorrows under a silk canopy and St. Veronica. There was also a carved sculpture of Our Lady of Sorrows and a painting of Our Most Holy Superioress (Our Lady of Guadalupe) as well as another old painting on canvas of Our Lady of Guadalupe with a sculpture of Juan Diego.

Along with the many candlesticks made of tin, gilded wood, and copper and a lectern of gilded wood, there was a canopy of gilded wood with glass inlaid with tin and a number of mirrors to adorn the altar.[3]

THE *Convento,* WORKROOMS, AND INDIAN HOUSES

Fr. Hierro considered *convento* and storerooms "good." Fr. Solís noted that the workshops and dwelling for the missionaries, soldiers, and Indians were "adequate and decent." According to Fr. López, the *convento* with rooms and an office was next to the church and the sacristy. All of them were constructed with stone and lime (mortar) and had wooden roofs. He also noted that the Indian houses were built against the walls of the rectangular-shaped mission square. Some had flat roofs; others had hay or grass roofs (Fig. 8.1).[4]

THE FORMER MISSION, 1840–1890

Espíritu Santo was visited by McClintock, Bartlett, and Olmsted in the 1840s and 1850s. They all commented on its condition and the people they found there.[5]

THE MISSION, THE MISSION WALL, AND THE CHURCH

McClintock found the mission in worse shape than any he had seen: "a more dreamy and desolate [place], I never beheld." He described the church as a fort and the walled-in area as a fortress.

> The fort, or church, for it served both purposes, is enclosed within a wall containing, perhaps, one third of an a[c]re. In this wall there are many port holes. The angles were defended by strong towers. It has been a place of considerable strength but is now in ruins.

Bartlett visited the Presidio San Loreto and Espíritu Santo but assumed that both were missions. Most of his comments, however, relate to the presidio rather than to Espíritu Santo. They are included here because they provide a clear picture of the condition of these closely linked units.

Bartlett found the presidio ("the former mission") in ruins and commented on the ruined state of the "mission" enclosure. "A high wall seems once to have surrounded the church, but much of it now lies prostrate." He found "[t]he church . . . the only building in any tolerable preservation." He saw the church building serving a double purpose, as a church and a castle:

3. Fr. Joseph Mariano Cárdenas, "Inventory—1783, Mission of Espíritu Santo de la Bahía" (November 17, 1783), in Oberste, "Texas Missions of the Coastal Bend: Part I," Appendix, pp. 1–3.

4. "The Fr. Guardian Simón Hierro Report," p. 100; Fr. Solís, "Diary," p. 46; Fr. López, "Documents," p. 44.

5. McClintock, "Journal," pp. 153–154; Bartlett, *Personal Narrative*, pp. 25–27, 30; Olmsted, *A Journey through Texas,* pp. 262–266; for information on Espíritu Santo in the nineteenth century, see J. B. Frantz, "La Bahía," in J. Day, J. B. Frantz, B. Proctor, J. Schmitz, L. Tinkle, and D. H. Winfrey, *Six Missions of Texas,* pp. 53–57.

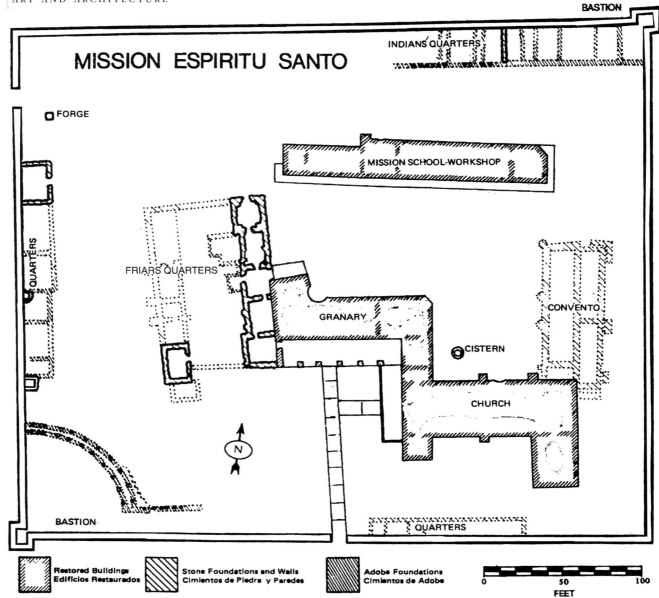

MISSION ESPIRITU SANTO

INDIANS'QUARTERS

FORGE

MISSION SCHOOL-WORKSHOP

QUARTERS

FRIARS QUARTERS

GRANARY

CONVENTO

CISTERN

CHURCH

N

BASTION

QUARTERS

Restored Buildings
Edificios Restaurados

Stone Foundations and Walls
Cimientos de Piedra y Paredes

Adobe Foundations
Cimientos de Adobe

0   50   100
FEET

FIGURE 8.1. *Plan of the Espíritu Santo mission. After the plan by the Goliad State Historical Park.*

Its massive walls on every side, which measure four feet in thickness, are cemented with waterlime; and to its great strength is owing its fine state of preservation.

Bartlett described the church and gave its dimensions. He called the vaulted roof "a single stone arch from wall to wall," supported by buttresses, and noted the defensive measures taken by those inside the enclosure: "a parapet rises above the roof, behind which cannon were formerly planted."

Bartlett also described the living quarters of Judge Pryor Lea, his host, who had actually taken up residence in the presidio church:

He had partitioned the church with a slight frame-work about ten feet high, which was covered with calico or brown cotton, the top being open; making it a very comfortable place for a greater portion of the year.

According to Bartlett, the Espíritu Santo church "was surrounded with the ruins of lesser ones." He noted that it was smaller than the church of the presidio and that it had been changed into "a comfortable dwelling . . . with restored walls, openings for windows, and a modern roof." It was "occupied by a gentleman from New York, who [lived] in a style of elegance that we are quite unprepared to meet with in Western Texas."

The "gentleman from New York" was not there when Olmsted visited the mission. He met a priest at the mission, who had been assigned to the church by the bishop. Olmsted found the mission in ruins. "There are the remains of a large fort, with bastions, which appears to have been about two hundred feet square." He described the buildings inside the enclosure of the mission:

> Several stone buildings stand about it, all now in ruins. Behind one of the bastions, in a corner of the inclosure, is the church. It is also of limestone, and in similar style to those of San Antonio.

Like Judge Lea at the presidio church, the priest had assigned space in the mission church for a chapel and another for living quarters. The chapel was set up at one end of the church, which he had whitewashed and "covered with calico; over it, an old and battered image, it was now impossible to guess of what, had been set up, and several glass candlesticks were placed before it."

The priest used a former chapel for his living quarters. The room was lighted by a round window high up the wall. Olmsted described the furniture and commented on "a heap of some hundred of well-bound books, over which the mould was beginning to creep" (the titles of the many books in the mission library were included in the inventory prepared by Fr. Cárdenas in 1783).[6]

THE SACRED IMAGES

The priest told Olmsted that the Americans had destroyed all the sacred images and damaged the church.

> It was once a very fine church, but the Americans destroyed it as much as they could. See, there we had a gallery, with the oriel over it; they burned it. All the pictures they burned; the carvings they cut with knives—ah it is all ruins![7]

OTHER PRESIDIO BUILDINGS AND MEXICAN HOUSES

Bartlett found "some twenty or more ruined buildings of stone, with nothing but their walls standing" at the presidio. He assumed one of them, given its dimensions, must have been constructed for barracks. "Its walls like the church are massive." He found that two or three houses had "been restored, provided with new roofs, and made into very comfortable dwellings—better, indeed, than modern builders would think of erecting."

Olmsted indicated that there were in the village "about twenty jacals, large, and of a comparatively comfortable character, scattered over two hills." This is probably the old town adjacent to the presidio.[8]

6. McClintock, "Journal," pp. 153–154; Bartlett, *Personal Narrative,* 25–27; Olmsted, *A Journey through Texas,* pp. 262–265; Cárdenas, "Inventory—1783," pp. 6–8.

7. Olmsted, *A Journey through Texas,* p. 264.

8. Bartlett, *Personal Narrative,* pp. 25–27; Olmsted, *A Journey through Texas,* p. 262.

THE RESTORED ARCHITECTURE AND THE EXTANT SCULPTURES AND PAINTINGS, 1890 TO THE PRESENT

Extensive archaeological work and some restoration of the mission was carried out in the mid-1930s by the Works Progress Administration and Civilian Conservation Corps. A thorough study of documents and the other Texas missions gave the excavation crews the necessary background to carry out the work. Espíritu Santo is now a state historical park.

THE MISSION WALL AND THE MISSION BUILDINGS

The original wall with stone foundations has an orientation that is slightly off true north, with its north-south walls running northwest-southeast. There were bastions on the northeast and southwest corners and an entrance in the center of the south wall (Fig. 8.1).

FIGURE 8.2. *View of the sacristy and the apse of the Espíritu Santo church. Photograph by Jacinto Quirarte.*

FIGURE 8.3. *General view of the Espíritu Santo church facade. Photograph by Jacinto Quirarte.*

The restored church and sacristy are located in the southeast corner of the mission enclosure. Twin tower bases flank the facade of the church, which has a hall-type or rectangular plan without a transept. It faces almost directly west. The sacristy is attached to the southeast side of the church (Fig. 8.2). The *convento* was attached to the northeast corner of the church. In the center of the enclosure is the restored granary. The original *convento* and its patio stood in front of it. The restored workshops are near the north east-west wall. The Indian houses were located along all the north, south, and west walls.

THE CHURCH

The facade of the church has a narrow portal flanked by two wide tower bases (Fig. 8.3). The one on the right and its belfry were completed. The one on the left was constructed up to a level that is half the height of the facade. There are four merlons at the octagonal base of the belfry and one on the left side of the facade that echoes the others on the right. The facade is surmounted by a segmented pediment with a stone cross in the center.

THE PORTAL

The reconstructed portal has a Roman arch flanked by shallow pilasters with shell and scroll motif capitals (Fig. 8.4). Balusters in line with the pilasters surmount the equally shallow entablature. There is a medallion above the

FIGURE 8.4. *General view of the main portal of the Espíritu Santo church. Photograph by Jacinto Quirarte.*

capstone of the arch, and one in each of the spandrels. The low-relief motifs in the spandrels depict the crossed arms and the stigmata and meandering cord of the Franciscan Order. The second stage has a small niche framed by pilasters and a steep pediment with a round choir window directly above it. There is a sculpture of the Virgin in the niche with the arch in the shape of a shell. The shafts of the pilasters have diamond shapes with floral motifs, and the base of the low-relief cross in the pediment has a floral motif on either side.

Very few portions of the portal are original, as can be seen in recent photographs (Fig. 8.5). The darker stone of the original architectural details is seen in portions of the entablature and the merlons above it, the projecting conical-shaped base for the sculpture in the niche, parts of the pediment, and the circular window. The reconstructed portions are very light in color. The iconographic if not the formal model for the reconstruction is found at La Purísima Concepción in San Antonio.

THE NORTH WALL DOORWAY

An almost square window with an iron grille is located on the north wall of the church above a doorway with a wide simple frame which has a framed relief sculpture of a human skull with crossbones directly above it (Fig. 8.6). When placed at the foot of the cross in depictions of the Crucifixion, the skull with crossbones is a reference to the cross on Golgotha (Calvary), "the place of the skull" (John 19:17). According to medieval tradition, the cross rested upon the skull and bones of Adam, suggesting that through the cross humankind was absolved of all sin and the promise of eternal life was regained.

FIGURE 8.5. *View of the upper part of the main portal of the Espíritu Santo Church. Photograph by Jacinto Quirarte.*

FIGURE 8.6. *Side portal of the Espíritu Santo church with a framed relief of skull and crossbones and a window with an iron grille. Photograph by Jacinto Quirarte.*

EXTANT SCULPTURES AND PAINTINGS

Some of the original sacred images of Espíritu Santo now form part of a modern altarpiece with *estípite* columns (Fig. 8.7). Others are placed in free-standing niches located on the walls of the church nave. The altarpiece has three panels and two stages.

The extant sculptures and paintings and their present location are discussed in the order of their listing in the 1783 inventory prepared by Fr. Cárdenas.

The relief of the Holy Trinity in the upper central panel of the altarpiece is probably the one listed by Fr. Cárdenas as "a carved statue of the Holy Trinity in its niche, [with] a silver frame." The sculpture of Our Lady of Valvanera in a niche in the lower right panel of the altarpiece may be the "carved statue of Our Lady of Balvaneda." The sculpture of the Crucified Christ placed under a canopy in the lower central panel may be one of the "two medium-sized carved statues of Christ Crucified." The sculpture "under a muslin canopy" is in the altarpiece. The other one in a "wooden niche with a glass case" is now placed in a free-standing niche located on the left side of the nave (looking toward the altar area) between the side door and the entrance of the church (Fig. 8.8).

The "statue of Our Lord, used on Good Friday," with hinges (adjustable arms and legs) is probably the sculpture located on the left side of the nave as one enters the church (Figs. 8.9 and 8.10). It is a life-size clothed sculpture of Jesus of Nazareth with hair, a crown of thorns, and a rope tied around the hands.

The "two beautiful sculptured images," originally placed inside "a niche adorned with a curtain of scarlet cloth, eight small mirrors and one large one with its frame," are no longer near the "tabernacle veil with trimmings and a silver heart in the center." They are probably the two sculptures placed on wall brackets inside a large free-standing niche located on the right side of the nave (looking toward the altar area) (Fig. 8.11). The lower one is probably "the most pure Virgin with garments of cloth, with a silver crown and various strands of pearls." The clothed sculpture of the Virgin no longer has the origi-

FIGURE 8.7. *View of the main altar of the Espíritu Santo church. Photograph by Jacinto Quirarte.*

above the doorway. It refers not only to the apostolic college under which the mission was administered but also to the special meaning Our Lady of Guadalupe had for the people of New Spain and its northernmost provinces.

The focus on the neophytes could be accomplished with the inclusion of Our Lady of Guadalupe over the doorway of the San José portal and the St. Joseph sculpture on the final stage of the same portal.

The quatrefoil motif painted in the alternating simulated masonry blocks on the San José facade may have a symbolic meaning. In Gothic decoration the quatrefoil referred to the Four Evangelists.

References to St. Francis with the emblems associated with him are found in the spandrels of the main doorway frame of La Purísima Concepción. Medallions in the spandrels contain the interlocking arms of Christ and St. Francis on the left and the stigmata of St. Francis on the right as one enters. The Franciscan cord functions as a link from one medallion to the other.

THE RECONSTRUCTED ALTARPIECES

A review of all the reconstructed altarpieces demonstrates that each one contained the titular saint to whom the church was dedicated. This is clearly seen in the inventory of the holdings of the failed San Xavier missions. Most of the altarpieces also included sculptures and paintings of the Crucifixion with its companion images of the Virgin Mary and St. John the Evangelist. Sometimes St. Mary Magdalene was included with the arrangement of the Crucified Christ. Various manifestations of the Virgin Mary were also found in the altars, such as Our Lady of Sorrows, Our Lady of Solitude, Our Lady of the Rosary, Our Lady of Guadalupe, and Our Lady of Refuge. Among the saints were St. Francis, St. Anthony of Padua, St. Joseph, St. Dominic, St. Clare, St. Margaret, and others.[2]

THE TITULAR SAINTS OF THE MAIN ALTARPIECES

There is no indication in any of the documents reviewed of how a particular saint was selected for a given mission. It is likely that this was decided by the founding missionaries in consultation with their colleagues in the Apostolic Colleges of Querétaro and Zacatecas. The primary consideration was clearly related to the most strongly supported doctrines of the Franciscan Order.

There seems to be no apparent pattern as to when a sculpture or a painting was called for in the founding of the missions. We have no data on the relative cost of sculptures and paintings, but it is likely that the former were more expensive than the latter. That would explain why paintings of the titular saints are found in San Xavier and El Orcoquisac, where more tentative efforts were made to found missions. Capistrano had a painting in 1745 but a sculpture of the titular saint by 1756. In any case, the sacred images of the titular saints in the main altarpieces could be sculptured, usually in the *estofado* technique, or painted, usually on canvas, and framed.

The titular saints in the Querétaran missions were in almost all cases sculptures, as demonstrated by the 1745 inventory of these missions of San Xavier and San Antonio (with the exception of San José de Aguayo). Sculptures of the titular saints were found in the main altars: a St. Anthony of Padua for

2. For a general source on the saints, see Benedictine Monks, *The Book of Saints,* especially pp. 64 and 180 for information on St. Clare of Assisi and St. Margaret of Cortona; for information on the Virgin Mary, see Trens, *María: Iconografía de la Virgen;* see also J. Pelikan, *Mary through the Centuries.*

Valero, an Immaculate Conception for La Purísima Concepción, and a St. Francis for Espada. Capistrano had a painting of St. John Capistran. Also reported in 1756 were the paintings of the titular saints of the San Xavier missions: St. Francis Xavier for San Xavier, St. Ildefonso for San Ildefonso, and Our Lady of the Purification (February 2) for La Candelaria.

The Zacatecan missions also had sculptures or paintings of the titular saints listed in the inventories: a St. Joseph for San José in 1753, Our Lady of the Rosary for El Rosario in 1783, and Our Lady of Refuge for El Refugio in 1793. A single painting of a titular saint, Our Lady of Light, was found at El Orcoquisac in 1766.

THE EIGHT PRINCIPAL SAINTS

There are eight principal saints, called "the chiefs of the Seraphic Order."[3] The first and fourth of the eight were honored in the naming of the Espada and Valero missions: St. Francis, patriarch and founder, and St. Anthony of Padua, who is the saint most renowned in the order for miracles next to St. Francis. The second of the eight was honored with a sculpture on the facade of Valero: St. Clare, Madre Seráfica, the first Franciscan nun and founder of the Poor Clares. The first, third, fourth, and fifth of the eight were honored in the paintings of the pendentives over the crossing of the Concepción church: St. Francis, St. Bonaventure, the great prelate of the order, St. Anthony of Padua, and St. Bernardine of Siena, the great preacher and reformer. The latter saint was also honored in a low relief sculpture of his monogram placed on the frame of the Valero church choir window.

THE CRUCIFIXION

The Crucifixion is the key focus of the altarpiece used in celebrations of the Mass before the altar. When the Crucifixion is placed in the center of the altarpiece it is seen as a mystery and used as a transcendent image. In this case the Virgin Mary is shown standing on the right side of the Crucifixion, and St. John the Evangelist on the congregation's left. Most of the altarpieces had this arrangement with free-standing sculptures. The Virgin Mary in this position is known as the Stabat Mater or Sorrowful Mother.

If the Crucifixion is treated as an event, as a living scene, then the Virgin, St. John the Evangelist, and the others traditionally included assume entirely different poses. The Virgin can be seen in a fainting attitude, on the verge of collapse. The others may be shown grieving and experiencing great pain, as in traditional depictions of the Descent from the Cross or the Deposition. These events were reenacted in processions during Holy Week. Dressed sculptures with movable arms and legs were placed on portable altars or palanquins and used for these special events, such as the Descent from the Cross. A sculpture of Christ Carrying His Cross, known as Jesus of Nazareth, was used in such processions. At other times it was placed in a special altarpiece inside the church or in the sacristy. This was also done with sculptures of the grieving Virgin Mary, identified as Our Lady of Sorrows or Mater Dolorosa.

The main altar at Valero in 1756 and at Concepción in 1745 had a large cross with the crucified Christ. There was a painting of the Crucifixion at Espada in 1772.

3. Clara Erskine Clement, *Legendary and Mythological Art* (London: Bracken Books, 1994), p. 26; originally published as *A Handbook of Legendary and Mythological Art* (New York: Hurd and Houghton, 1876).

JESUS OF NAZARETH

Next to sacred images of Our Lady of Sorrows in the altars are the sculptures of Jesus of Nazareth. This is a reference to Christ's Passion or two of the mystical sorrows related to the Rosary: the Procession to Calvary and the Crucifixion. It was through the Via Dolorosa that Christ bore His Cross, and Mary is said to have fainted at the sight of His sufferings.

Sculptures of Jesus of Nazareth were found at all five missions in San Antonio and at Espíritu Santo. At Valero the sculpture was placed in the choir altar in 1762. At Concepción it had movable arms and legs and was placed in a large niche in the left arm of the transept in 1772; at Capistrano it was used on a portable altar in 1759. The sculptures are simply listed in the inventories of 1824 at Espada and San José and in the inventory of 1783 for Espíritu Santo.

CHRIST IN THE HOLY SEPULCHRE

The original figure of Christ in the Holy Sepulchre goes back to the Middle Ages, when such figures were used to reenact the Entombment and Resurrection of Christ. The Christ in the Holy Sepulchre would remain intact on the left side of the church nave until Holy Week, when the articulated figure could be used to reenact the Passion and Crucifixion of Christ. There was a Christ in the Holy Sepulchre at Concepción with an articulated sculpture of Our Lady of Sorrows.

THE VIRGIN MARY

The Virgin Mary was shown in many of her aspects as the contemplative Virgin, either joyful or sorrowful, or as the protector of the faithful. As Our Lady of the Immaculate Conception and Our Lady of Guadalupe, she is the joyful Virgin. As Our Lady of Sorrows and Our Lady of Solitude, she is the sorrowful Virgin. As Our Lady of the Rosary, the Divine Shepherdess, Our Lady of Light, and Our Lady of Refuge, she is the protectress Virgin. Another representation of the Virgin was Our Lady of Pasaviense, a devotional figure whose origins are found in Germany.

The Virgin Mary is most prominently shown in scenes of the Crucifixion, either in wall paintings or in arrangements of sculptures that also include St. John the Evangelist. As the Sorrowful Mother, the Stabat Mater, she stands on the right of the Crucifixion, and St. John is on the left. Usually shown wrapped in a dark violet or blue mantle, the figure expresses great sorrow. The Virgin Mary is also shown by herself in the main altar and in other altars as Our Lady of Sorrows, Mater Dolorosa. She is depicted seated or standing, with bowed head, clasped hands, sorrowful face, and streaming eyes.

STABAT MATER AND MATER DOLOROSA

Every mission had a sacred image of Our Lady of Sorrows, and some had images of the Sorrowful Mother. The first was often placed on a portable stand by itself and used in processions for the weekly prayer of the Rosary. The other was shown in relation to the Crucifixion of Jesus Christ.

There were sculptures of both at Valero. According to Fr. Dolores, the sculpture of the Sorrowful Mother was placed in the main altar next to the crucified Christ with St. John on the other side, and a sculpture of Our Lady of Sorrows was placed on a portable altar in 1762. The Sorrowful Mother wore a mantle, and the latter wore two garments, one of cloth with trimmings and the other of velvet. She also wore a crown and a dagger.

At San José there was a sculpture of Our Lady of Sorrows with its diadem and dagger in the main altar in 1753. At Concepción there were two paintings of the Crucifixion flanked by images of St. John the Evangelist and the Sorrowful Mother. One, still extant, is found in the chapel to the right of the main entrance to the church. The tower base room is dedicated to St. Michael. The other was painted on the wall of the left side of the transept. Below it, on the altar table, there was a sculpture of Our Lady of Sorrows with a diadem and a silver dagger in 1772.

There was a sculpture of Our Lady of Sorrows at Capistrano in 1745 and a second one by 1824. One wore a red tunic, a blue mantle, a silver diadem, and a silver dagger joined to the rosary. The other, with a crown of rays and a dagger made of silver, was dressed in an outer tunic of thin silk and mantle of shiny blue satin with silver branches and completely edged by silver scallops. At Espada there was an armature sculpture of Our Lady of Sorrows in 1749, placed on a portable stand and used for the Rosary. It wore a dress and a silver diadem and silver dagger.

Espíritu Santo had two sculptures and a painting of Our Lady Sorrows in 1783. One of the sculptures was "carved"; the other was clothed in two garments and wore a diadem and a silver sword.

There were no images of the Sorrowful Mother or Our Lady of Sorrows at El Rosario or El Orcoquisac in 1766.[4] A sculpture of Our Lady of Sorrows stood in one of the altars at Refugio with a sculpture of the Crucifixion in 1796. Our Lady of Sorrows wore a diadem of gilded tin rays, a cincture, a veil, and a dagger. Flanking her were sculptures of St. John and St. Mary Magdalene. In this case Our Lady of Sorrows also seems to function as the Sorrowful Mother next to the Crucifixion. Both St. John and St. Mary Magdalene are traditionally included in scenes of the Crucifixion.

OUR LADY OF THE ROSARY

Our Lady of the Rosary was particularly favored by the Dominicans because the Virgin was supposed to have appeared to St. Dominic and given him a rosary. The Virgin is always shown holding the rosary and often accompanied by her three types of mysteries or meditations, the joyful, the sorrowful, and the glorious. These form the basis for the series of prayers of the Rosary—a devotion to the Virgin Mary—centered on the events in the life of Christ and the Virgin.

There was a sculpture of Our Lady of the Rosary holding the Child Jesus at San José in 1753. Both wore silver crowns and were placed on a portable altar. In 1756 there were sculptures of Our Lady of the Rosary at Capistrano and at Espada. The Espada sculpture was used on a portable stand. The most prominent example of Our Lady of the Rosary is found at El Rosario. It was a carved wood sculpture with garments of alpaca-like cloth, adorned with flowers.

Images of Our Lady of the Rosary were consistently used on portable altars for the devotion to the Virgin Mary or the prayers of the Rosary.

4. For Nuestra Señora del Rosario, see Fr. Mariano Antonio de Vasconcelos, ["Inventory of Mission Rosario, 1783"], in Oberste, "Texas Missions of the Coastal Bend: Part I," Appendix 13.0263, pp. 1–7. For Nuestra Señora de la Luz del Orcoquisac, see Fr. José Marenti, "Inventory to [Melchor Afán de] Rivera" (1766), in J. V. Clay, C. D. Tunnell, and J. R. Ambler, *Archaeological Excavations at Presidio San Agustín de Ahumada*, p. 15. See also Bernardo de Silva, "Inventory of the Goods of Nuestra Señora de la Luz de Orcoquiza, September 12, 1766," pp. 1–7.

OUR LADY OF REFUGE

The pictorial source for Our Lady of Refuge or Santa María Refugium Peccatorum, Refuge of Sinners, comes from a painting made in Frascati, Italy, in the early eighteenth century. Copies of the prototype painting were soon brought to Mexico by the Jesuits. One of them appeared as a gift to the Apostolic College of Our Lady of Guadalupe in Zacatecas. She became the patron of the missions connected with the college.

According to William Wroth, Our Lady of Refuge is depicted in these images "in half-length holding the Christ Child, amid billowing clouds." Paintings of Our Lady of Refuge were found at Capistrano in 1756, at Espada in 1759, and at Espíritu Santo in 1783.[5]

THE DIVINE PILGRIM AND THE DIVINE SHEPHERDESS

The Divine Pilgrim, of Franciscan origin, is particularly venerated in Galicia (a province of Spain) and is the patron of Pontevedra. Devotional images show the Divine Pilgrim in a rural setting protecting the Christ Child, as she seeks refuge in Egypt. This is a reference to an episode of the well-known theme of "The Flight into Egypt," after an angel appeared to Joseph in a dream to warn him of the danger to Jesus' life from Herod, who planned the Massacre of the Innocents (Matthew 2:13), and advised him to flee to Egypt. The Divine Pilgrim's attributes of a shepherdess relate her to the Divine Shepherdess, also of Franciscan origin.

The devotion to the Divine Shepherdess, the patron of the Franciscans, began in Spain in the early eighteenth century and spread quickly throughout the Spanish world. The Virgin, dressed as a shepherdess, is shown feeding roses (symbols of the Rosary) to the sheep (symbols of souls) gathered around her. The sheep have the initials of the Virgin Mary on their bodies. Two angels holding the Virgin's crown hover above her head. The twelve stars around her head allude to the dogma of the Immaculate Conception defended by the Franciscans. In some versions the Virgin is shown holding the Christ Child, also dressed as a shepherd. In the background there is always a scene of an angel coming down from heaven to protect a lone sheep from a wolf attack, a metaphor for the work carried out by the missionaries.

The main altarpiece of La Purísima Concepción included a painting of the Divine Pilgrim and one of the Divine Shepherdess.

OUR LADY OF GUADALUPE

Our Lady of Guadalupe miraculously appeared to an Indian named Juan Diego in 1531 at El Tepeyac, a hill located north of Mexico City. This is the same place where Toci (Mother of Gods) and Tonantzin (Our Mother) were venerated before the Conquest. The people of viceregal Mexico continued to congregate at the site to venerate Our Lady of Guadalupe. Given her "Indian" character, she became identified with all the people of viceregal Mexico— Indians, Creoles, and mestizos—and eventually with Mexican nationality, because she personifies the coming together of the Indian and European to create the mestizo. She therefore has political as well as religious meaning.

The Zacatecan missions, appropriately, contained paintings of Our Lady of

5. William Wroth, *Christian Images in Hispanic New Mexico,* Colorado Springs Fine Arts Center, Taylor Museum (Seattle: University of Washington Press, 1982), p. 205.

Guadalupe: two at San José and two at Espíritu Santo. One of them, "an old Painting" at Espíritu Santo, had a sculpture of Juan Diego associated with it.[6]

OUR LADY OF VALVANERA

There is a sculpture of Our Lady of Valvanera dating from around the tenth century in the Benedictine Church in Valvanera, Spain. The Virgin is shown enthroned, holding the Christ Child with her right hand on her lap and an unknown object in her left hand. More recent depictions of Valvanera show her holding an apple or a pomegranate. The image of the enthroned Virgin is known as Sedes Sapientiae, the seat or throne of wisdom.

By the end of the sixteenth century, the devotion to Our Lady of Valvanera had spread throughout the Spanish dominions in the New World. The cult of Valvanera was instituted in Mexico City during the first half of the seventeenth century. The church constructed in her name was completed in 1673. There is a painting of Our Lady of Valvanera at Espíritu Santo.[7]

LOS CINCO SEÑORES

The theme of Los Cinco Señores, usually represented in an intimate setting, has the look of a "family" picture. But its meaning as the supernatural presentation of the Virgin's Immaculate Conception is transmitted by the dove of the Holy Spirit hovering over the Virgin Mary and Child. Other members of the family include her husband, St. Joseph, and her parents, St. Anne and St. Joachim.

One of the earliest representations of Los Cinco Señores found in New Spain is the sixteenth-century painting known by that title (Cathedral of Mexico, Mexico City). Amada Martínez Reyes identified this theme in European art as La Santa Parentela (Holy Parentage) or Linaje de la Virgen (Lineage of the Virgin).[8] When it was brought to New Spain, it became known as Los Cinco Señores, a descriptive reference to the number of persons depicted in the scene. The painting includes the seated figures of Mary and Anne in the center of the painting, both attending to the standing figure of the Christ Child. The dove of the Holy Spirit and God the Father hover above them. Joseph is seen on the left behind Mary, and Joachim is on the right behind Anne.

Appropriately, the painting of this theme was originally placed in the main altar of the church dedicated to the Immaculate Conception of the Virgin Mary in San Antonio, Nuestra Señora de la Purísima Concepción.

6. Fr. Joseph Mariano Cárdenas, "Inventory—1783 of Mission Espíritu Santo de la Bahía," in W. H. Oberste, "Texas Missions of the Coastal Bend, Espíritu Santo, El Rosario, El Refugio," p. 3.

7. Ibid., p. 2.

8. Amada Martínez Reyes, "Los Cinco Señores," pp. 77–82.

Summary and Conclusions

The earliest Spanish contacts with the Gulf Coast of Texas were made from the islands of the Caribbean. Later expeditions to explore and settle the various regions of Texas came from the realm of Nueva Vizcaya and the provinces of Nuevo México, Nuevo León, and Coahuila (Nueva Extremadura). The provinces were established at different times as the Spaniards moved their settlements northward from central New Spain.

Nueva Vizcaya and Nuevo México served as bases for the exploration and settlement of west Texas in the seventeenth century. Similar expeditions into central and east Texas were mounted in the late seventeenth century from Nuevo León and Coahuila, once part of the eastern limits of Nueva Vizcaya. The province of Texas was once part of the northern limits of Coahuila.

The province of Texas was established and abandoned several times due to the rivalries between Spain and France for control of the territory in the seventeenth and eighteenth centuries. The first settlements in east Texas were established in 1690 to counter French influence in the area but abandoned three years later when it waned. A new French presence in Texas led to its occupation by the Spaniards in 1715. The east Texas missions were again abandoned when they were attacked by the French in 1719 at the outset of the war between France and Spain. The region was reoccupied for the last time by the Spaniards in 1722, when they also founded and erected missions and presidios in central Texas as well as on the Gulf Coast to consolidate their claim to the territory. Other missions were founded in central and east Texas and on the Gulf Coast during the remainder of the eighteenth century.

Most of the missions did not survive for a variety of reasons. Some of them were founded on a temporary basis by the early explorers who led expeditions into unknown territory. They were used to lay claim to the new lands as markers for the establishment of more permanent missions at a later date. Some of the missions intended as permanent settlements were abandoned soon after their founding as the result of a hostile environment, Indian raids, or attacks by other Europeans who were competing with the Spaniards for control of the northern frontier. Others were abandoned because of internal conflicts between the soldiers and missionaries and the Indians.

Until 1772 the Texas missions were administered by the apostolic colleges in Querétaro and Zacatecas. Each sent inspectors periodically to carry out the monitoring of the missions. After 1772 the missions came under the administrative control of the apostolic college in Zacatecas. The missions, partially secularized in 1792, began to deteriorate soon thereafter. The San Antonio missions were fully secularized in 1824. The remaining Gulf Coast missions were secularized a few years later.

The Original Art and Architecture

THE MISSION COMPLEXES

The walls of each mission served to protect the missionaries and the mission Indians. Their size and shape varied. The positions of the main entrances were governed by the location of the mission and the terrain around it, so they could be on any of the four walls of the enclosure. As a result, buildings such as the granary could be located on any of the walls, even though they were often built next to the main entrance to the mission. The Indian houses were consistently built inside the enclosure along one or more walls.

The relationship of the church to the other buildings of the mission complex also differed from that found in the sixteenth-century *conventos* of central New Spain. The church was no longer placed alongside the other buildings, such as the living quarters of the friars and the workshops. It was more often seen as an appendage to the mission complex than as a key focal point for the cluster of buildings in the *conventos.*

At Valero the church was appended to the southeast corner of the *convento,* which was entirely outside the mission wall. The main entrance to the walled-in area was on the south wall. At San José de Aguayo the church was within the northeast corner of the reconstructed mission wall, with the Indian houses alongside it and the main entrance and the granary on the west wall. At Concepción the church and the other mission buildings were within the eastern end of the mission enclosure with entrances on the east, west, and south walls. The granary was next to the east entrance. The present church of Capistrano and the other mission buildings were located along the southeast part of the mission wall, with the main entrance and the granary on the north wall. The Espada church was located on the west wall of the irregularly shaped enclosure, with the friary on the southwest wall and the entrances on the north and east walls. The granary was actually outside the south wall. At Espíritu Santo the main entrance on the south wall led to the granary located in the center of the enclosure, with the church and sacristy located in the southeast part of the enclosure.

THE MISSION CHURCHES

The missionaries used whatever materials were available in each region to build the mission churches. Adobe and stone were used in west Texas (Nuevo México) and logs in east Texas. Access to trained craftsmen from other settlements in northern New Spain made it possible to build more elaborate structures with stone masonry in central Texas.

The architectural features of the churches, church facades, and other mission buildings were determined by the availability of resources (funds, workers, and materials) and the reigning style at the time of construction. The decorative programs of the Texas mission churches and other buildings belong to the Baroque and Ultra-Baroque styles of central New Spain. Their plans and elevations also relate to those found in central New Spain. The *espadaña* (an extension of the facade wall with openings for bells) was the standard elevation of the sixteenth-century *convento* church in central New Spain. A good example is seen at the Augustinian church of Acolman, northeast of Mexico City. The *espadaña* was used at San Francisco de la Espada. The *campanario* (a bell wall) was used at Capistrano, where it was added to one of the walls of the nave.

Other churches have belfry towers and a dome over the crossing of the nave and transept, characteristic of cruciform (in the form of a Latin cross) churches found throughout New Spain in the seventeenth and eighteenth centuries. This type of plan and elevation was used for the church of La Purísima Concepción. A similar plan was used for San Antonio de Valero. Its unfinished elevation was probably intended to be like that of the Purísima Concepción church. Although San José and Espíritu Santo do not have a transept, both have a dome over the area that would normally have been the crossing of the nave and the transept in the form of a Latin cross.

Wrought-iron crosses were placed on top of the *espadañas, campanarios,* bell towers, and domes of the churches. Stone crosses were relegated to the top of the church facades, as seen at San José de Aguayo. Although the Concepción church now has an iron cross over the facade, it originally had a stone cross.

Some of the Texas mission facades were polychromed, as in the case of La Purísima Concepción and San José de Aguayo. The portals of both churches had figural and architectural sculptures, as did the portal of San Antonio de Valero. The portal of La Espada had architectural sculpture only.

THE SACRED IMAGES

Each mission had a sculpture of its titular saint, usually brought in from the administrative center in Querétaro or Zacatecas. The titular saint was accorded a prominent position in temporary as well as permanent altarpieces, when the permanent building was under construction and the altar was set in a temporary chapel.

Sculptures of St. Francis and other Franciscan saints were included in the altars, as well as sculptures of Jesus Christ, the Virgin Mary, and Saint John the Evangelist. Numerous others were added as the missions became more firmly established. Many of the sculptures were made with *estofado* and *encarnación*. Others were armatures to which heads, hands, and feet done with the *encarnación* technique were added. The same method was used with hinged sculptures. Both types were elaborately dressed, as can be seen in the detailed descriptions of some of the inventories. The latter sculptures were also used in special Feast Day celebrations, when they were placed on portable altars and carried in the processions.

REPORTS, INVENTORIES, AND DIARY ENTRIES

Fr. Morfi was sensitive to more than the routine demands of an inspection tour. He marveled at the quality of the portal sculptures and the skill with which the San José church was built. He admired its proportions and plan. But aside from his report, assessments of form other than the routine references to being "curioso" (curious, probably meaning well made or novel) and "beautiful" are rare in the colonial documents.

Some of the other missionaries occasionally described the unusual quality of a sacred item as "beautiful" or indicated in their reports or inventories that it moved them or enhanced their religious feelings. Fr. Sáenz (1772) referred to a "very beautiful" Our Lady of Sorrows at Valero and a "very beautiful" sculpture of the Virgin of the Immaculate Conception at Concepción. He saw "a very moving" scene of the Flagellation in the left arm of the transept of the Concepción church.

Fr. Cárdenas (1783) saw two "beautiful" sculptures at Espíritu Santo, one of the Immaculate Conception with cloth garments and the other of St. Joseph with his staff. Fr. Silva (1796) saw "a beautiful image of excellent workmanship of Our Lady of Guadalupe . . . that resembles the original." This was part of the Calvary altarpiece, located in the second room of the temporary church of El Refugio.

Fr. Díaz (1824) saw a "beautifully painted" image of the Crucifixion on canvas and a sculpture of Our Lady of Sorrows with a "very lovely face" at Concepción.[1]

THE FORMER MISSIONS

Most of the missions were secularized between the years 1824 and 1830 and abandoned shortly afterward. The unfinished church of Valero had been converted to military use following the secularization of the mission in 1793. Almost immediately following secularization and the turmoil of the 1830s, vandalism began to take its toll. The destruction was to continue for another forty to fifty years. The sculptures in the niches flanking the portal of the Valero church were still in place in the 1830s but disappeared shortly thereafter. The gilded altarpiece and side altars of the San José church were still extant as late as 1846, when Kingsbury reported seeing them, but they disappeared shortly thereafter. The gilded altarpieces of the Concepción church and the figural sculptures of the main portal vanished around the same time. The pendentive paintings of the Concepción church disappeared or were painted over when the church was restored in the late nineteenth century. The main portal doors of the San José church vanished in the 1880s.

The deterioration caused by neglect, misuse, vandalism, and natural disasters was reversed toward the end of the nineteenth century when restoration and reconstruction efforts were begun. These initial efforts eventually developed into the major restoration and reconstruction projects of the twentieth century at San José de Aguayo and others.

1. Fr. Morfi, *History of Texas*, pp. 94–97; Fr. Sáenz, *Inventory of the Mission San Antonio de Valero*; idem, "Testimony and Inventory," pp. 6, 8; Fr. Cárdenas, "Inventory—1783," pp. 1–3; Fr. Manuel Julio de Silva, "Brief Resume of the Inventory [of Our Lady of Refuge in the Province of Texas, September 8, 1796]," in W. H. Oberste, "Texas Missions of the Coastal Bend, Part II: Our Lady of Refuge Mission: 1793–1830," pp. 8-IV–9-IV; Fr. Díaz de León, "1824 Secularization Inventory: Concepción," p. 5.

TRAVELERS, ARTISTS, AND PHOTOGRAPHERS

A number of sympathetic travelers, including Bollaert, Gregg, and Bartlett, began to write about the vandalism in the 1840s and 1850s. Eastman and Gentilz and other artists began to draw and paint the mission churches in the 1840s, and the first photographs of the missions were taken in the 1850s. Photographers continued to record the condition of the mission art and architecture for the rest of the century.

Some of the travelers of the mid-nineteenth century reacted sympathetically to the mission architecture. Their comments focus on the state of the buildings, their abandonment, and use or abuse of the interiors and their contents. They reacted negatively, however, to the few sculptures they found in the churches, as in the case of Kingsbury (1846), who described the sculpture of the Virgin to the right of the entrance to San José church:

> Apparelled in an old, faded calico gown; and as well calculated, perhaps, to stifle any sentiments of devotion, and substitute those of derision, as any design that could be erected in a temple of the Almighty.

The situation began to change in the late 1880s with the work of Corner, who could not say enough positive things about the mission art and architecture. His admiration was boundless. Robert Sturmberg's book, published in 1920, signals the beginning of the popular writings on the missions.[2]

THE RESTORED ART AND ARCHITECTURE

Almost all the Texas missions were altered in the twentieth century with reconstructions or restorations. The only one that remained intact is the church of Concepción. The San José church was extensively reconstructed, as was the church of Espíritu Santo. All the others fell into ruins, and nothing remains of them. The missions in west Texas and east Texas were reconstructed.

The facades of Valero, Concepción, and San José retain the essential components of the original units. San José still has the architectural and figural sculptures which were restored in the 1930s and 1940s. The figural sculptures of Valero disappeared long ago, and those of Concepción were severely damaged in the nineteenth century. Only fragments remain. The same is true of the polychromed surfaces of the Concepción and San José church facades. The architectural sculpture of the Espíritu Santo church portal was restored and reconstructed in the twentieth century. An original relief is found on the north wall doorway of the church: a skull with crossbones.

Most of the church doors are modern restorations or reconstructions. Few of the original wrought-iron pieces are still extant, except for the well-known grille of the San José sacristy window. The wrought-iron cross of the Capistrano church belfry and possibly those of the San José church tower and dome may date from the colonial period.

Some of the figural and decorative floral paintings on the walls of the tower base rooms of the Concepción church are still visible. There are

2. Bollaert, *William Bollaert's Texas,* p. 232; Gregg, *Diary and Letters,* p. 235; and Bartlett, *Personal Narrative,* vol. 1, p. 43; Eastman, *A Seth Eastman Sketchbook,* Pls. 43–47; Kendall and Perry, *Gentilz,* Pls. 7, 12, 14, 16, 17, 19–21; Kingsbury, "Notes from My Knapsack," p. 176; Corner, *San Antonio,* p. 17; Sturmberg, *History of San Antonio,* pp. 124–125.

fragments of other paintings in the refectory of the same mission: geometric and floral borders over doorways and along the upper portion of the walls. The geometric border paintings on the arches and vaulted ceiling of the San José church are modern reconstructions.

EXTANT SCULPTURES AND PAINTINGS

A number of sculptures and oil paintings are still extant in the Texas missions, although they are no longer in their original locations. Now seen in isolation or in recently added altarpieces, the sculptures and paintings were meant to form a part of a larger arrangement. Like so many similar sculptures and paintings in central New Spain, these suffer as a result of dislocation. They should be seen in relation to their frame (the *retablo*), which provided a formal and thematic support.

A few of the original polychromed sculptures (*encarnación* and *estofado*) from the San José church remain at the sacristy of the church. A polychromed sculpture of St. Joseph is presently located in an altar area flanked by poly-chromed sculptures of Our Lady of the Rosary with Christ Child (badly damaged) and a St. Joseph with the Christ Child. A clothed sculpture of St. Francis, originally from La Espada, is now located at the Old Spanish Missions Center.

The original sculpture of St. John Capistran is located in the main altar of the Capistrano church in an eighteenth-century gilded altarpiece with Solomonic columns. The sculpture of the patron saint is flanked by two gilded sculptures also of eighteenth-century manufacture. The altarpiece, which is a recent acquisition from Mexico or Spain, has predella paintings of Our Lady of Guadalupe. Clothed sculptures of Jesus of Nazareth and Our Lady of Soli-tude with hinged arms and legs are placed on either side of the main altar area. There is a very fine painting of St. Francis in the Capistrano museum. Its original location may have been in the main altar of the Valero church.

In the main altar of the Espada church is a sculpture of St. Francis, which was originally gilded and later painted by Fr. Bouchu. It is flanked by clothed sculptures of Jesus of Nazareth and Our Lady of Sorrows.

The extant sculptures and paintings of the Espíritu Santo church are located in an altarpiece of modern construction. Some of the noteworthy sacred images are the relief sculpture of the Holy Trinity and the painting of Our Lady of Refuge. A clothed Jesus of Nazareth stands on a pedestal at the entrance of the nave, and further down in a wall niche are a sculpture of the Crucified Christ and a clothed sculpture of Our Lady of Sorrows. There is a polychromed sculpture of St. Joseph on a wall bracket on the other side of the nave.

Conclusions

The Texas missions have suffered from too much exposure or too little. Both have obscured our view of the missions. This study is intended to provide a clearer examination of them as art and architecture in terms of form, function, content, and meaning. Their relation to sources and antecedents in central New Spain has also been considered in efforts to place them within a broader historical context. All these points of reference have made it possible to gain a greater appreciation of their intrinsic qualities as art and architecture.

The missions have had an incalculable impact on the development of Texas in general and San Antonio in particular. Without them the settlement and later development of San Antonio and Texas would have been different. What remains is an important reminder of this colonizing enterprise, which provided the spiritual, historical, cultural, social, political, and economic foundations for a civilized society. Their presence as art and architecture has been just as important and should be appreciated for its own intrinsic value. This study is intended to serve as an important step in that direction.

EPILOGUE

1. John Tedesco, "Blaze Strikes Espada," *San Antonio Express-News,* January 27, 1998, p. 1A. See also Susana Hayward, "Espada Blaze Blamed on Short," *San Antonio Express-News,* January 28, 1998, p. 1A.

2. I first learned from Fr. Herb Jones, OFM, pastor of Mission San José, that the sculpture of St. Francis was back in its original location (personal communication, December 14, 1999). Information about the fire and restoration work was obtained from Rosalind Rock, park historian, San Antonio Missions National Historical Park, and J. Michael Parker, *San Antonio Express-News* religion writer (personal communications, May 8, 2001).

3. Habig, *The Alamo Chain of Missions,* p. 226.

4. J. Michael Parker, "Stolen Statues Leave Christian Leaders Stunned: Missing Pieces Considered Priceless," *San Antonio Express-News,* August 3, 2000, p. 1A. See also San Antonio Police Department, "Stolen Antique Statues," http://www.ci.sat.tx.us/sapd/statues.htm, pp. 1–2.

5. Personal communication from Jon Thompson, fall 2000.

On January 27, 1998, the roof of the Espada church was destroyed by a fire caused by an electrical short.[1] The sculptures in the main altar of the church suffered smoke damage. They were cleaned, repaired, and restored by Esther Siegfried Schmidt. The most spectacular result of the work was the restoration of the habit worn by St. Francis to its original gilded surface (Figs. 7.7, 7.8).[2] It is generally assumed that the habit was painted dark brown by Fr. Francis Bouchu sometime between 1858 and 1907 when he was in charge of the church. Fr. Habig, however, reported that Fr. Bouchu found "some old statues . . . of St. Francis, the Blessed Virgin, and Christ Crucified. These he regilded and put on the altar of the sanctuary."[3] Evidently, the habit was painted by someone else in the twentieth century. Regardless of who painted the habit and why the restoration work was done, the result is that the sculpture is closer to its original state than it was before.

The recent robberies of religious images at the mission churches of Concepción and Capistrano have not had the same positive results. Sometime in late June 2000 a sculpture of the Virgin Mary was stolen from the Concepción church. Over a month later, on the night of July 31 or the early morning of August 1, 2000, the sculptures of St. John Capistran, St. Joseph, and St. Francis and four paintings of Our Lady of Guadalupe were stolen from the Capistrano church (Fig. 6.10). Although the works date from the eighteenth century, only the titular saint of the Capistrano church is original and is among those listed in the eighteenth-century inventories. The four paintings of Our Lady of Guadalupe and the sculpture of the Virgin Mary were recovered in March 2001.[4] There is no trace yet of the other missing sculptures.

Other matters relating to the study of the mission churches merit a brief mention. Jon Thompson, associate professor in the Department of Architecture at the University of Texas, has recently used the golden section rectangle to analyze the proportions of the facades, portals, and doorways of the Valero, San José, Concepción, and Espada churches (Figs. 3.11, 4.17, 5.10, and 7.4).[5]

According to Thompson, the first stage of the Valero church portal or the "triumphal arch" coincides with a golden mean rectangle, as does the facade of the San José church. The doorways of the Valero, San José, and Concepción churches are also based on a golden mean rectangle. The edges of the Valero doorway within the "triumphal arch" and the height of the pillars of the

Valero and San José doorways are determined by the square of a golden mean rectangle.

Thompson was unable to determine the overall geometry of the Valero and Concepción church facades. He noted, however, that the intended tower bases up to the first story of the Valero church or "the outer limits of the facade" may be the result of two golden mean rectangles. He also projected several possible solutions for the Concepción church facade by using a square defined by the central axis of the towers and the ground line. In one projection, he found that the shape of the pediment over the doorway "points to the intersection of the central axis" of the basic square.

Thompson used geometry and comparative analysis to deal with the "misplaced" voussoirs of the Espada arch (Fig. 7.4). He suggested "repositioning the lower arch stones" and rotating and switching them to produce "a Renaissance circle and square proportion." That would extend the width of the doorway to coincide with its height. The inner profile of the mixtilinear arch would then reflect the outlines of three smaller circles within it. Two other proposed solutions would change the height of the doorway. In the first, the doorway up to the impost level is inscribed within a square and a half-circle above it for the outer profile of the arch. In the second, the doorway is inscribed within a golden section rectangle. He also compared the "proposed" Espada arch to other mixtilinear arches found at San José and Concepción to strengthen his argument (Figs. 4.19, 4.27, and 5.17). Its proposed configuration is the same as the examples cited above.

Schuetz was primarily interested in determining how the ancient and Spanish master builders arrived at the size and proportions of the plans, doorways, facades, and portals of the missions.[6] She found that they used geometric ratios based on ancient geometry that "concerned itself with the relation between a circle and its circumscribed . . . square, or more specifically the areas within the circumference of the circle." Comparative measurements were then used to find the areas of the circle and its circumscribed square. (In modern geometry, the area of a circle is calculated mathematically.) Using ancient geometry in her work, Schuetz began her analysis by looking for the basic square in a given building. Once this was done, she found that the method known as "the doubling of the square" was used to establish the size of an area or group of buildings. Another method was to impose an eight-pointed star on the basic square of the building to determine the size of the various parts of a plan and elevation (Fig. 3.12).

George was interested in finding the original design of the Espada church doorway (Fig. 7.6). He followed the approach used by Humberto Rodríguez Camilloni in his study of the church of San Francisco de Lima, Peru.[7] According to George, Rodríguez Camilloni found that the regulating lines governing the design of the San Francisco church "comprised a square that enclosed a circle . . . that itself encompassed a second, diagonally oriented square." The diameter of the circle "was subdivided by three smaller circles, arranged along the vertical axis." In his analysis of the facade and doorway of the Espada church, George used a module of a small circle with a diameter equal to a vara (32.909 inches) and a circle three varas in diameter. His suggested reconstruction includes rearranging the voussoirs to create "an unbroken extrados [outer profile of the arch] of three varas in diameter" and adding

6. Schuetz, "Proportional Systems and Ancient Geometry," pp. 2–7.

7. George, "Espada Doorway: A Lesson in Harmony," pp. 15–18; Humberto Rodríguez Camilloni, "Architectural Principles of the Age of Humanism Applied: The Church of San Francisco, Lima," *Society of Architectural Historians Journal* 28 (December 1969): 245–250.

8. Will N. Noonan, "The Espada Doorway: Yesterday and Today," *San Antonio Express,* February 5, 1933, p. 5C: newspaper clipping without a date or page number, courtesy of Jon Thompson, who obtained a copy of it from Lewis Fisher, author of *Spanish Missions of San Antonio* (San Antonio: Maverick Publications, 1998). Fisher provided me with the date and page number of the article. Jo Myler, librarian at the San Antonio Public Library, also provided me with the date of the article and information on Will N. Noonan. Personal communications, May 8, 2001.

the "missing lower voussoirs" at the base or springer of the mixtilinear arch to complete its intended design in accord with the governing geometry of the facade.

Finally, it is interesting to note that Will N. Noonan long ago suggested a solution to the problem of the "misplaced" voussoirs of the Espada church in an article published in the *San Antonio Express.*[8] It is essentially the same as the one proposed by Thompson. Noonan's solution was based primarily on an analysis of the two "misplaced" voussoirs above the pillars.

Due to the angles in the arch stones, when they are reversed and reset, the Moorish lines [mixtilinear arch] on the inside of the arch are entirely lost, and the width of the doorway is increased approximately two feet. It is with satisfaction, however, that we notice that the outer line of the arch is now semicircular, and that the new design taken on is in keeping with the rest of the structure.

A CENSUS OF MISSIONS FOUNDED, 1680–1793

The missions founded in Texas from 1680 to 1793 are the most visible evidence of the efforts to convert the Indians. Only a few of the more than thirty missions founded survived the many problems the missionaries encountered in this enterprise.

The missions are numbered and discussed chronologically and identified by the name of the city or town, river, or geographical area where they were located. The discussion includes the name of each mission, its primary founder, its location, and its suppression, abandonment, or secularization. The Indians for whom the missions were founded are listed under the missions not discussed in the main body of the book.

THE MISSIONS OF EL PASO DEL NORTE

1. CORPUS CHRISTI DE LA ISLETA

Corpus Christi de la Isleta was founded by Antonio de Otermín, the governor of Nuevo México (1677–1683), and Fr. Francisco Ayeta on the southern side of the Río Grande a few miles south of El Paso del Norte in 1680 or 1682. It was intended for the Tigua Indians of the Mission of Isleta in northern New Mexico. The first church was built of logs, and a second one of adobe was constructed in 1774. This mission and Nuestra Señora del Socorro ended up on the United States side of the border when the river changed course.[1] The church, rebuilt in 1748, burned in 1917. The old walls were used for the reconstruction of the present building.

2. NUESTRA SEÑORA DE LA CONCEPCIÓN DEL SOCORRO

Nuestra Señora de la Concepción del Socorro was founded in 1680 or 1682 by Governor Otermín and Fr. Ayeta for the Piros Indians from Socorro, New Mexico. It was located on the southern side of the Río Grande a few miles south of the Isleta mission. It is now on the United States side of the border. The original church no longer exists. There is now a modern structure at the site.

THE MISSIONS OF LA JUNTA DE LOS RÍOS

3. LA NAVIDAD DE LAS CRUCES

4. EL APÓSTOL SANTIAGO

Fr. Nicolás López, the superior at Mission Guadalupe in El Paso del Norte, founded La Navidad de las Cruces on December 29, 1683, and El Apóstol Santiago

1. For the El Paso missions, see Burke, *Missions of Old Texas,* pp. 114, 116; G. B. Eckhart, "Spanish Missions of Texas," *Kiva* 32, no. 3 (1967): 80.

two days later.[2] Each site had a newly built mud and wattle church. La Navidad was located on Cíbolo Creek, south of present Shafter, Texas. Fr. Acevedo was left in charge of the mission, and Fr. Zavaleta joined him the following spring. The Santiago church, larger than La Navidad, was located on Alamitos Creek about eight miles below present Presidio, Texas. Fr. López left the area on January 1, 1684. The two missionaries abandoned the missions a short time later due to hostilities.

5. SAN CLEMENTE

San Clemente was founded and dedicated by Fr. López on March 16, 1684. The temporary mission was built while the Domínguez-López expedition was camped on the Conchos from March 15 until May 1, 1684. It was located at the junction of the Concho and Colorado Rivers, approximately fifteen miles southeast of present Ballinger, Texas. The two-story church/fortress was constructed of wood and reeds on a hill. According to Domínguez, Mass was celebrated every day for about six weeks, including Easter services, on the ground-floor room. The room above served as a lookout station.

6. EL SEÑOR SAN JOSÉ

7. SAN ANTONIO DE PADUA

8. SAN CRISTÓBAL

El Señor San José was founded for the Púlique Indians in 1715 by the Trasviñas y Retis expedition below La Junta de los Ríos.[3] Fr. Gregorio Osorio was left in charge and was later joined by other missionaries. San Antonio de Padua, located downriver from La Junta de los Ríos a short distance southeast of Señor San José, was founded for the Concho Indians by Fr. Joseph de Arránegui, adjutant general of the Custodia of New Mexico. It is likely that a simple chapel was built at this time. San Cristóbal, founded for the Poxsalme (Posalme) Indians, was located south of San Antonio de Padua. All three missions remained in operation with resident missionaries until 1726, when Indian hostility forced them to leave. Missionaries may have worked at the three missions intermittently after that year. The church of San Cristóbal was found without a missionary by an expedition of 1747. It continued until at least 1760, when a presidio was built there.

9. SAN ANTONIO DE LOS PÚLIQUES

The founding date of this mission and its exact location at La Junta de los Ríos are not known. An entrada led by Captain Joseph Idoyaga in 1747, however, found the mission of a church they identified as one used by the Púlique Indians.

10. LOS CÍBOLOS

Although the exact name of this mission is not known, it was founded in 1715 on Cíbola Creek about 24 miles northwest of Presidio near Shafter, Texas. The mission, sometimes identified with Santa María la Redonda de los Cíbolos, was served by Fr. Osorio. Two expeditions of 1747 found the ruins of a church at the site.

11. NAME UNKNOWN (THE MISSION AT REDFORD)

This mission was located 18 miles downriver from La Junta de los Ríos. Expeditions of 1747 found the ruins of a church at the site.

2. For the west Texas missions, see "Itinerary of Juan Domínguez de Mendoza, 1684," in *Spanish Exploration in the Southwest, 1542–1706,* ed. Bolton, pp. 325–326, 338.

3. For the missions at La Junta de los Ríos, see Reindorp, "The Founding of Missions at La Junta de los Ríos," pp. 118, 120; Eckhart, "Some Little-Known Missions in Texas," *Masterkey* 37, no. 1 (1963): 13.

THE EAST TEXAS MISSIONS I

12. SAN FRANCISCO DE LOS TEJAS

San Francisco de los Tejas was founded in May 1690. On May 24 a temporary church was built, and all the official events took place on the following day. On May 26 De León and the missionaries looked for a permanent site. Fr. Massanet described the search for a permanent site for the church in his letter to Don Carlos de Sigüenza.

> The next morning I went out with Captain Alonso de León a little way, and found a delightful spot close to the brook, fine woods, with plum trees like those of Spain. And soon afterwards, on the same day, they began to fell trees and cart the wood, and within three days we had a roomy dwelling and church wherein to say mass with all propriety. We set in front of the church a very high cross of carved wood.[4]

A reference to the construction of the church is found in De León's diary entry for Saturday, May 27, 1690:

> Saturday, the 27th; Sunday, the 28th; Monday, the 29th; Tuesday, the 30th; and Wednesday, the 31st, they labored to build the church and the dwelling of the apostolic fathers, in the midst of the principal settlement of the Texas.[5]

San Francisco de los Tejas was located on San Pedro Creek northwest of present Weches, Texas. After a series of problems, two of the four missionaries at the mission left to work elsewhere. News of a plot by the French and Indians to massacre the Spaniards was received in October 1693. On October 25 the missionaries and the soldiers buried their prized possessions, set fire to the buildings, and left the area.

13. EL SANTÍSIMO NOMBRE DE MARÍA

El Santísimo Nombre de María was founded in June 1690 by Fr. Francisco Casañas de Jesús María.[6] The mission was located five miles northwest of Weches, Texas, on the Neches River near the town of Alto in Houston County.

The missionaries had little success at the mission because of linguistic difficulties and because they were so few in number. The shamans blamed an epidemic of fever among the Indians on the missionaries' use of holy water. When the mission was destroyed by a flood in 1692, the missionaries went to Mission San Francisco de los Tejas.

THE EAST TEXAS MISSIONS II

On August 2, 1721, Aguayo sent small parties accompanied by Querétaran missionaries to the former missions (San Francisco de los Tejas and Nuestra Señora de la Purísima Concepción) to repair the buildings in preparation for their reestablishment.[7] A small party went to the former Zacatecan missions (Nuestra Señora de Guadalupe, Nuestra Señora de los Dolores de los Ais, and San Miguel de Linares de los Adáes) for the same purpose.

14. NUESTRO PADRE SAN FRANCISCO DE LOS TEJAS

San Francisco de los Tejas was refounded by the Querétaran missionaries on July 10, 1716, about six miles farther inland from the original site and renamed Nuestro Padre San Francisco de los Tejas.[8] Fr. Manuel Castellanos was placed in charge of the settlement. The presidio of Nuestra Señora de los Dolores de los Tejas was erected near the mission in the same year. Following the French attack on the

4. Fr. Massanet quoted in Bolton, *Spanish Exploration in the Southwest,* pp. 379–380.

5. Ibid., p. 417.

6. Burke, *Missions of Old Texas,* pp. 67–68.

7. Buckley, "The Aguayo Expedition, 1719–1722," pp. 45–49.

8. Fr. Espinosa, "Ramón Expedition," pp. 358–360, for the three Querétaran missions reestablished as planned from June 30 to July 10, 1716 (San Francisco de los Tejas, La Purísima Concepción, and San José de los Nazonis).

Presidio Los Adáes in 1719, the mission was abandoned (see below for the reestablishment of this mission with the new name of San Francisco de los Neches at a different location).

15. NUESTRA SEÑORA DE LA PURÍSIMA CONCEPCIÓN

Nuestra Señora de la Purísima Concepción, founded on July 7, 1716, was located six miles to the northeast of San Francisco de los Tejas, beyond the Angelina River. Following the French attack on the Presidio Los Adáes in 1719, the mission was abandoned.

Fr. Gabriel de Vergara and Fr. Benito Sánchez went to La Purísima Concepción with a small party on August 2, 1721. The mission was reestablished on August 6, 1721; Fr. Espinosa, president of the Querétaran missionaries, and Fr. Vergara remained at the mission. It was the least damaged of the missions attacked by the French in 1719. The mission was temporarily moved to the Colorado River in 1730 and was moved to its present location on the San Antonio River in 1731.[9] The name was changed to Nuestra Señora de la Purísima Concepción de Acuña to honor the viceroy Don Juan de Acuña Marqués de Casa Fuerte (see Chapter 5 for more information on this mission).

16. SAN JOSÉ DE LOS NAZONIS

San José de los Nazonis was founded on July 10, 1716. As president of the Querétaran missionaries, Fr. Espinosa established his headquarters at this mission and appointed Fr. Benito Sánchez as the first resident missionary. The mission was located on a branch of Shawnee Creek about two and one-half miles north of the present town of Cushing, Texas. The mission was abandoned in 1719 following the French attack on the Presidio Los Adáes.

San José de los Nazonis was refounded on August 13, 1721, and Fr. Sánchez was left in charge. The presidio of Nuestra Señora de los Dolores de los Tejas was reestablished on August 15, 1721. The mission was temporarily moved to the Colorado River in 1730 and was moved to its present location on the San Antonio River in 1731. Its name was changed to San Juan Capistrano because there was already a San José mission in San Antonio (see Chapter 6 for more information on this mission).

17. NUESTRA SEÑORA DE GUADALUPE DE LOS NACOGDOCHES

Nuestra Señora de Guadalupe de los Nacogdoches, founded on July 9, 1716, was located in present Nacogdoches, Texas.[10] Fr. Antonio Margil de Jesús, president of the Zacatecan missionaries, made his headquarters at this mission. Fr. Matías Sáenz de San Antonio served as the resident missionary. The church and house for the missionaries were built of logs. The mission was abandoned in 1719 following the French attack on the Presidio Los Adáes.

A small party reached Nuestra Señora de Guadalupe de los Nacogdoches on August 10, 1721, and found that nothing remained of the original church. On August 16 the Aguayo expedition reached the Zacatecan mission; on the following day the church was rebuilt and the house for the missionary was repaired. The mission was reestablished on August 18, 1721. Guadalupe de los Nacogdoches was suppressed in 1772, as recommended by the Marqués de Rubí, who inspected the mission in 1767.

18. SAN MIGUEL DE LINARES DE LOS ADÁES

Fr. Margil dedicated San Miguel de Linares de los Adáes for the College of Zacatecas in 1717. Fr. Mariano de Anda y Altamirano, a missionary from the College of

9. For the move of Nuestra Señora de la Purísima Concepción, San José de los Nazonis, and San Francisco de los Neches (formerly San Francisco de Los Tejas) to the Colorado River in 1730 and then to the San Antonio River in 1731, see Habig, *The Alamo Chain of Missions,* pp. 154, 191, 233.

10. Fr. Espinosa, "Ramón Expedition," p. 360.

Zacatecas, served at this mission and at the Bahía mission as well. The mission was located on the banks of Arroyo Hondo, about three miles from Spanish Lake; the site is identified with Robeline, Louisiana. The mission was abandoned in 1719 following the French attack on the Presidio Los Adáes (see below for the reestablishment of this mission with the new name of San Miguel de Cuéllar de los Adáes at a different location).

19. NUESTRA SEÑORA DE LOS DOLORES DE LOS AIS

Nuestra Señora de los Dolores de los Ais, founded in 1717 by the Ramón expedition, was located one-half mile south of present San Augustine, Texas, near the Louisiana border. It was midway between La Purísima Concepción and the new San Miguel mission. The mission was abandoned in 1719 following the French attack on the Presidio Los Adáes.

Nuestra Señora de los Dolores de los Ais was moved to another site (in present San Augustine), where a church was built on August 22, 1721; the mission was officially reestablished on the following day. Fr. José Albadadejo was left in charge of the mission. Shortly thereafter, the presidio Nuestra Señora del Pilar was erected. The church of the presidio was dedicated on October 12, 1721. Dolores de los Ais was suppressed in 1773, as recommended by the Marqués de Rubí, who inspected the mission in 1767.[11]

20. SAN FRANCISCO DE LOS NECHES

Fr. José Guerra went to San Francisco de los Tejas in 1721. The mission was renamed San Francisco de los Neches and founded at a new location on August 5. Fr. Guerra was left in charge of the mission. The mission was temporarily moved to the Colorado River in 1730 and was moved to its present location on the San Antonio River in 1731. Its name was changed to San Francisco de la Espada (see Chapter 7 for more information on this mission).

21. SAN MIGUEL DE CUÉLLAR DE LOS ADÁES

San Miguel de Linares de los Adáes was renamed San Miguel de Cuéllar de los Adáes and relocated on September 29, 1721, near the presidio Nuestra Señora del Pilar. The mission was abandoned in 1773.

THE SAN ANTONIO MISSIONS

22. SAN ANTONIO DE VALERO

See Chapter 3 for information on the founding of San Antonio de Valero.

23. SAN JOSÉ Y SAN MIGUEL DE AGUAYO

See Chapter 4 for information on the founding of San José y San Miguel de Aguayo.

24. SAN FRANCISCO XAVIER DE NÁXERA

San Francisco Xavier de Náxera was founded by the Marqués de Aguayo on the San Antonio River one league from San Antonio de Valero, on March 10, 1722.[12] In 1726 the Indians were moved to the Valero mission and the lands were added to Nuestra Señora de la Purísima Concepción.

25. NUESTRA SEÑORA DE LA PURÍSIMA CONCEPCIÓN DE ACUÑA

See Chapter 5 for information on the founding of La Purísima Concepción.

11. Ibid., p. 360, for the founding of San Miguel de los Adáes and Nuestra Señora de los Dolores de los Ais; see also Fr. Espinosa, *Crónica de los colegios de Propaganda Fide,* p. 724 (according to Cañedo, n. 2, Castañeda, who thought Espinosa gave the wrong date for these two missions, was wrong himself when he assigned the date of 1716). For the founding of the Zacatecan missions in east Texas in 1721, see Buckley, "The Aguayo Expedition, 1719–1722," pp. 49–53. For the Rubí recommendations, see L. Kinnaird, *The Frontiers of New Spain,* pp. 7, 29–32; see also Morfi, *History of Texas,* pp. 415–440.

12. Buckley, "The Aguayo Expedition," pp. 54–55.

26. SAN JUAN CAPISTRANO

See Chapter 6 for information on the founding of San Juan Capistrano.

27. SAN FRANCISCO DE LA ESPADA

See Chapter 7 for information on the founding of La Espada.

THE ESPÍRITU SANTO MISSION

28. NUESTRA SEÑORA DEL ESPÍRITU SANTO DE ZÚÑIGA

See Chapter 8 for information on the founding of Espíritu Santo.

THE SAN XAVIER MISSIONS

The Querétaran missionaries established three missions along the San Xavier (San Gabriel) River, near present Rockdale, Texas, in 1748 and 1749. The three missions were abandoned in 1755 and moved temporarily to the San Marcos River. They were abandoned again in 1757.

According to Fr. Ortiz (1756), the San Xavier missions were founded for the Maicies (Mayeyes), Herbipianes (Hierbipiames), Tancagues (Tancahues), Cocos, and other groups (Yohuanes and Deadosos).[13]

29. SAN XAVIER DE HORCASITAS

San Xavier de Horcasitas, founded on May 7, 1748, was intended to serve the Tonkawan Indians, which included the Mayeye, Hierbipiame, and Yohuane tribes. The mission was located two and one-half miles above the junction of Brushy Creek with the San Xavier (now the San Gabriel) River on present Kolb's Hill in the southwestern part of Milam County, near present Rockdale, Texas.

The missionaries had problems with the hostile tribes, and the Indians that congregated at the mission did not remain long. The mission was abandoned on August 23, 1755, following a lengthy process initiated by the soldiers of the presidio, who presented a petition to Captain Rábago y Terán on July 15, 1755. Eight days later Fr. Joseph López, Fr. Francisco Aparicio, and Fr. Sebastián Flores presented the captain with a similar proposal. The entire company was transported to the San Marcos River. The missionaries transferred the bells, ornaments, and other mission property to San Marcos. Many of the Indians went to the San Antonio de Valero Mission in San Antonio.

30. SAN ILDEFONSO

San Ildefonso, founded on February 25, 1749, was intended to serve the Atacapan Indians, which included the Bidae, Deadoso, and the Orcoquiza tribes. The mission was located six miles east of present San Gabriel in Milam County, near present Rockdale, Texas. The Indians abandoned the mission on February 25, 1752, when Fr. Juan José Ganzábal was murdered.

31. NUESTRA SEÑORA DE LA CANDELARIA

Nuestra Señora de la Candelaria, founded in April 1749, was intended for the Cocos and other Karankawan tribes from the coast region. The mission was located on the San Xavier (San Gabriel) River one and one-half miles from the present town of San Gabriel in Milam County.

13. For the San Xavier missions, see Bolton, "The Founding of the Missions on the San Gabriel River," pp. 365; Fr. Ortiz, *Razón,* vol. 1, p. 13.

THE ROSARIO MISSION

32. NUESTRA SEÑORA DEL ROSARIO

Nuestra Señora del Rosario was founded in November 1754 by the Zacatecan missionary Fr. Juan de Diós Camberres for the Coxanes (Cojanes), Guapites, Carancaguases (Karankawas), and Coopanes of Espíritu Santo (Matagorda Bay).

Fr. Solís arrived at El Rosario on February 26, 1768, and inspected the church, sacristy, and the rest of the mission from February 29 to March 4. He considered the property of the mission "good," the stockade made of wood stakes "very good," and the workshops and dwellings for the missionaries and the Indians "good and adequate." He was favorably impressed with the construction of the church and its furnishings:

> A very nice church made of logs lined with mud on the inside, whitewashed walls and roofed with good beams skillfully made, which seem like a carved panel very neat and clean.

In 1785 Fr. López reported that the church furnishings and ornaments were transferred to La Bahía, after it was "destroyed" and the Indians of the mission fled to the coast. Some of the ornaments were destroyed when the structure fell down.

The mission was located four miles west of present Goliad, Texas, and one mile south of the San Antonio River. Although the mission prospered initially, the Indians had deserted it by 1781. Nonetheless, the Indians returned, and the mission functioned until it was secularized in 1831.[14]

THE GUADALUPE MISSION

33. NUESTRA SEÑORA DE GUADALUPE

According to Captain Diego Ortiz Parrilla and other officials from San Antonio, by January 25, 1757, there were forty-one persons at the Guadalupe mission.[15] They found a settlement of several huts, four families of Spaniards, their servants, some Indians, and Fr. Francisco Aparicio and Fr. Miguel de Aranda.

Fr. Dolores attempted but failed to have the mission included in the San Sabá grant because Fr. Alonso Giraldo Terreros, who was in charge of the funds, ruled that they were meant to be used for the San Sabá project only.

When the Mission of San Sabá de la Santa Cruz was destroyed by the Comanches on March 16, 1758, Nuestra Señora de Guadalupe was abandoned for fear that it would suffer the same fate.

THE SAN SABÁ MISSION

34. SAN SABÁ DE LA SANTA CRUZ

The Mission of San Sabá de la Santa Cruz was founded on April 17, 1757, by Fr. Alfonso Giraldo de Terreros for the Lipan Apache Indians.[16] The Presidio of San Luis de las Amarillas was erected to protect the missionaries. The mission was located on the south bank of the San Saba River a short distance from the site of present Menard, Texas.

After repeated failures to get the Indians to congregate at the mission, some of the missionaries who had intended to work there were granted permission to leave the area. The mission was attacked by Comanches on March 16, 1758. Fr. Alonso Giraldo de Terreros and Fr. José Santiesteban were killed, and the mission was destroyed.

14. Castañeda, *Our Catholic Heritage,* vol. 3, p. 186; H. E. Bolton, "The Founding of Mission Rosario: A Chapter in the History of the Gulf Coast," *Quarterly of the Texas State Historical Association* 10, no. 2 (October 1906): 113–139; Fr. Solís, "Diary," p. 39; Fr. López, "Documents," p. 49.

15. Bolton, *Texas in the Middle Eighteenth Century,* pp. 273–278.

16. Fr. Morfi, *History of Texas,* pp. 371–372.

THE ORCOQUISAC MISSION

35. NUESTRA SEÑORA DE LA LUZ DEL ORCOQUISAC

Nuestra Señora de la Luz del Orcoquisac was founded in 1756 or 1757 by the Zacatecan missionaries in the northeastern part of the Texas Gulf Coast in conjunction with the Presidio San Agustín de Ahumada. The mission was located near the mouth of the Trinity River six miles northwest of present Anahuac, across the bay from Houston in Chambers County.[17]

In August 1756 Governor Barrios y Jáuregui and the missionaries agreed upon a site at the arroyo of Santa Rosa del Alcazar; the viceroy gave his approval in January 1757 to set up the mission for the Orcoquiza and the Bidai Indians. A temporary structure, built in the summer of 1757, was made of wood, plastered with clay and moss. It was later replaced by a more substantial structure.

In February 1758 Fr. José Francisco Caro asked that the mission be moved or abandoned due to the unhealthy surroundings. He was recalled in 1758 and sent to Mission Nuestra Señora de los Dolores, where he died on October 19, 1761. He was replaced at Nuestra Señora de la Luz in 1759 by Fr. José Abad de Jesús María, who described the location of the mission and the structure of the church in a letter written to the viceroy on November 27, 1759:

> It is made of wood, all hewn (*labrada*), and beaten clay mixed with moss, and has four arched portals (*portales en círculo*). This building, because of its strength and arrangement, is the most pleasing in all those lands of the Spaniards and the French—or it would be if your Excellency should be pleased to have completed its construction, which for the present has been suspended.[18]

According to Fr. Marenti's inventory of 1766, the church was covered with shingles and plastered mortar and whitewashed. The sacristy was built in the same way.[19]

The mission was abandoned in 1771, a year before it was scheduled to be suppressed, as recommended by the Marqués de Rubí, who inspected the mission in 1767.

THE EL CAÑÓN MISSIONS

36. SAN LORENZO DE LA SANTA CRUZ DEL CAÑÓN

37. NUESTRA SEÑORA DE LA PURÍSIMA CONCEPCIÓN CANDELARIA DEL CAÑÓN

The San Lorenzo and Candelaria missions were founded by Captain Felipe Rábago y Terán and Fr. Diego Jiménez from the Río Grande missions.[20] San Lorenzo was located on the east bank of an upper branch of the Nueces River in the Valley of San José. It was near the present town of Barksdale in Edwards County. The Candelaria mission was located ten miles south of present Barksdale in Edwards County on the banks of the Nueces River near Montel, Texas.

Since there was no presidio to protect the missions, the missionaries were vulnerable to attack from hostile Indians. Without viceregal authorization and financial support, the missions were suppressed in 1766.

THE REFUGIO MISSION

38. NUESTRA SEÑORA DEL REFUGIO

Nuestra Señora del Refugio was founded in 1793 by Fr. Mariano de la Garza and Fr. Mariano Velasco. It was moved in 1794 to a site near Refugio, Texas (El

17. Eckhart, "Spanish Missions of Texas, 1680–1800," pp. 89–90.

18. Bolton, *Texas in the Middle Eighteenth Century,* p. 349. The name of the viceroy was Francisco Cajigal de la Vega (1758–1760).

19. Fr. Marenti, "Inventory of [Melchor Afán de] Rivera," in Clay, Tunnell, and Ambler, *Archaeological Excavations at Presidio San Agustín de Ahumada,* p. 15.

20. Bolton, *Texas in the Middle Eighteenth Century,* p. 94.

21. Dunn, "The Founding of Nuestra Señora del Refugio," pp. 178–182; Fr. Bernardino Vallejo, "Report on the Texas Missions, February 11, 1815," in *The San José Papers, Part III,* trans. B. Leutenegger, p. 25; "A Very Brief Resume [Summary of the Inventory of the Mission of Our Lady of Refuge in the Province of Texas]," by Fr. Manuel de Silva, September 8, 1796, in Oberste, "Texas Missions of the Coastal Bend, Part II," Appendix, pp. 8-IV–9-IV.

Rosario, El Espíritu Santo, and El Refugio are relatively close together along or near the lower San Antonio River, known as the Gulf Coast Bend). The mission was intended for several Indian groups from the other Gulf Coast missions. Fr. Vallejo listed the Papalaches, Pampopas, Borrados, Pacahues, Cujanes, Taxanames, and Carancahuas (Karankawas).

According to Fr. Silva, the foundations of the planned church were built only at the corners. The plan called for a nave and a transept, a belfry, and a baptistry. The church was located inside a stockade. Pending the completion of the new church, the first two of three rooms served as a church and the third as a sacristy. They were made of stone and lime (mortar), finished with brick and plaster, with "strong beams," and paved with bricks.[21]

Thirteen *jacales* were used as living quarters, offices, and workshops (carpentry). One of the missionaries lived in one of the huts that had adobe walls and a grass roof, a door with lock and key, and a small window. The other huts were used as living quarters by the Indians, the soldiers, and the servants.

The mission was secularized in 1828 or 1829.

APPENDIX 2

THE COLONIAL DOCUMENTS, 1740–1824

The letters, reports, and inventories prepared by the missionaries provide information on the Indians and the efforts to convert them and on the condition of the missions. Reports dealt with the status of the missionary effort, inventories with the physical plant needed to carry it out.

The primary focus of most of the reports was on the status of the conversion effort, broken down into spiritual and temporal matters. First and foremost was the teaching of Christian doctrine and anything that would help the missionaries achieve this goal. Economic matters also figure prominently in some of the reports, such as the unsuccessful efforts to build an irrigation system at Espíritu Santo and the decimation of the cattle herds. The loss of the herds caused a severe economic strain on the missionary effort in the region of the Espíritu Santo missions. The reports also include information on the many Indian tribes of Texas: names, classification as friendly or hostile, their nature, languages, social customs, superstition, diseases and health, and population.

The documents are discussed in chronological order under two broad categories: the letters/reports and the inventories. The review includes information on the individual or individuals who prepared the document, to whom it was addressed, who ordered it, and when it was prepared. A summary is provided on the content of the inventories, with a focus on the physical plant needed to carry out the conversion effort. The letters/reports on the status of the missionary effort are discussed in Chapter 2.

LETTERS/REPORTS

THE FR. FERNÁNDEZ REPORT, 1740

Fr. President Benito Fernández de Santa Ana wrote the report on the Querétaran missions in Texas in the form of a letter addressed to Fr. Guardián Pedro del Barco of the Querétaro College on February 20, 1740.[1] The report is the best known of the many letters and memorials Fr. Fernández wrote during the sixteen years he worked in San Antonio (1733–1749).

THE FR. CIPRIÁN REPORT, 1749

The first report on the Zacatecan missions in Texas was written by Fr. Ignacio Antonio Ciprián in 1749.[2] It is one of three reports on the missions prepared as the result of a number of charges made against the College of Zacatecas at the Council of the Indies in Madrid in late 1748. In efforts to respond to these

1. Fr. Benito Fernández de Santa Ana, "Descripción de las misiones del colegio de la Santa Cruz en el río de San Antonio," in *The San José Papers, Part I,* trans. B. Leutenegger, pp. 51–73.

2. "Report of Fr. Ciprián," in *San José Papers, Part I,* trans. B. Leutenegger, pp. 95–101.

charges, Fr. Mathías Velasco, the Franciscan commissary general in Madrid, ordered that a detailed report on the activities of the college be sent to him. His request to Fr. Juan Antonio Abasolo, commissary general of New Spain, was forwarded to Fr. Francisco Vallejo, guardian of the college (1747–1750). Fr. Ciprián was commissioned to visit the missions to gather information for the report. He wrote the report at the College of San Fernando, Mexico City, on October 27, 1749, and presented it to Fr. Abasolo.

The Fr. Ciprián report is an eyewitness account of the five Zacatecan missions in Texas. The other two reports, actually memorials, were prepared at the College of Zacatecas and signed by Fr. Guardian Vallejo and five other fathers on January 15, 1750. One of the memorials was addressed to King Ferdinand VI of Spain (1746–1759) and the other to Fr. Velasco, the Franciscan commissary general in Madrid.

THE FR. DOLORES Y VIANA REPORT, 1762

On October 16, 1761, Fr. Manuel de Náxera, commissary general of the Franciscan missions in New Spain, issued an order for a report on all the missions there.[3] On October 28 Fr. Francisco Xavier Ortiz, the guardian of the College of Querétaro, transmitted it to the San Antonio missionaries.

The report on the Querétaran missions in Texas was prepared by Fr. Dolores y Viana, president of the Texas missions and in charge of San Antonio de Valero. He was assisted by the eight missionaries who worked at all four missions in San Antonio. The report was sent to Fr. Ortiz on March 6, 1762.

THE FR. HIERRO REPORT, 1762

Fr. Simón Hierro (Yerro or Fierro) prepared a report on the seven Zacatecan missions in Texas on January 8, 1762.[4] This was in response to the request for a report on the Franciscan missions in New Spain made by Fr. Commissary General Manuel de Náxera on October 16, 1761.

The Zacatecan missionaries had three missions on the upper and lower San Antonio River (San José de Aguayo, El Espíritu Santo, and El Rosario), one on the lower Trinity (La Luz del Orcoquisac), and three in northeastern Texas beyond the Angelina River (Guadalupe de los Nacogdoches, Dolores de los Ais, and San Miguel de los Adáes).

THE FR. SOLÍS DIARY, 1767–1768

Fr. Guardian Gaspar José de Solís made a tour of the six Zacatecan missions in Texas by order of the Council of the College and Fr. Guardian Tomás Cortéz.[5] He inspected El Rosario and Espíritu Santo in La Bahía, San José de Aguayo in San Antonio, and San Miguel de los Adáes, Dolores de los Ays, and Guadalupe de los Nacogdoches in east Texas.

THE FR. MORFI DIARY, 1777–1778, AND *History of Texas, 1673–1779*

Fr. Morfi wrote several texts on the Texas missions. He kept a diary during the entire expedition covering the dates from August 4, 1777, to June 1, 1781, and wrote a more formal text, titled *Memorias,* which was meant to be a report submitted to the authorities on the findings of the expedition. *Memorias* was written in Arizpe, Sonora, in early 1780, and covers only the first part of the expedition from August 4, 1777, to February 24, 1778, the day they arrived at the border between Coahuila and Nueva Vizcaya.

Fr. Morfi also wrote a *History of Texas,* which was intended to correct the biased history of the province by Antonio Bonilla (*Breve compendio,* 1772), who faulted the missionaries for the failure of the missions.[6] Fr. Morfi used his own

3. Fr. Dolores, "Inventories, 1759." See also Fr. Mariano Francisco de los Dolores y Viana, "Relación del estado en que se hallan todas y cada una de las misiones en el año de 1762," in *Documentos para la historia eclesiástica y civil de la provincia de Texas o Nuevas Philipinas, 1720–1779.*

4. Simón Hierro, "The Fr. Guardian Simón Hierro Report," in Bolton, *Texas in the Middle Eighteenth Century,* pp. 99–101.

5. Fr. Solís, "Diary," pp. 28–76.

6. Fr. Morfi, *History of Texas;* idem, *Diario y derrotero;* idem, *Excerpts from the Memorias for the Historia of the Province of Texas,* ed. and trans. Frederick Charles Chabot and jointly trans. Carlos Eduardo Castañeda (San Antonio: privately published; printed by the Naylor Printing Co., 1932); Don Antonio Bonilla, *Breve compendio de los sucesos ocurridos en la provincia de Texas desde su conquista o redacción hasta la fecha, por el teniente de infantería Don Antonio Bonilla, México, 10 de noviembre de 1772.*

notes, the research he conducted during his visit of the northern provinces, and the many documents he gathered at the College of Zacatecas to write the text. He died in 1783 before he could complete the *History of Texas,* which provides information on the San Antonio missions, the missionaries, and the Indians.

THE FR. LÓPEZ REPORT, 1785

Fr. José Francisco López, father president of the Texas missions, prepared a report on the Zacatecan missions in Texas in accordance with a royal order issued on January 31, 1784.[7] He signed the report at San Antonio de Valero on May 5, 1786. The order was sent to the Most Reverend Rafael José Verger, bishop of Nuevo León, on August 4, 1785, by Viceroy Bernardo de Gálvez. The report focuses on the spiritual progress and economic status of the missions inspected by Fr. López: San Antonio de Valero, La Purísima Concepción, San José de Aguayo, San Juan Capistrano, and San Francisco de la Espada in San Antonio and El Espíritu Santo and El Rosario in La Bahía.

THE FR. LÓPEZ REPORT OF 1792

The report on the San Antonio missions by Fr. José Francisco López was addressed to the Superiors of the College of Zacatecas on September 7, 1792.[8] He recommended the secularization of San Antonio de Valero and the merging of the remaining four missions into two missions with resident missionaries. The other missions would be converted to submissions or *visitas.*

THE FR. VALLEJO REPORT, 1815

This report on the Texas missions was prepared by Fr. Bernardino Vallejo for the governor of Texas.[9] Fr. Vallejo resided at San José and served as father president of the Texas missions. He began to prepare the report toward the end of 1814 but did not complete it until February 11, 1815, because he had to wait for information from Fr. José Manuel Gaitán and Fr. Juan María Sepúlveda, the two missionaries at El Refugio. The missions included in the report are San José de Aguayo, La Purísima Concepción, San Francisco de la Espada, San Juan Capistrano, Espíritu Santo, and El Refugio.

THE PADILLA REPORT, 1820

Juan Antonio Padilla prepared a report on the Indians of Texas and the province and signed it at Villa de Mier on December 27, 1819.[10] The only Spanish settlements at this time were San Antonio de Béxar and the Presidio of Bahía del Espíritu Santo.

INVENTORIES

INVENTORIES, 1745–1824

7. Jack Jackson, *Los Mesteños: Spanish Ranching in Texas, 1721–1821,* pp. 290, n.16.

8. Fr. López, "Report on the San Antonio Missions in 1792," pp. 488–498.

9. Fr. Bernardino Vallejo. "Report on the Texas Missions, February 11, 1815," in *The San José Papers, Part III,* trans. B. Leutenegger, pp. 20–27.

10. Padilla, "Texas in 1820," pp. 47–60.

Inventories were ordered to determine whether the physical plant of the mission was adequate to carry out its assigned spiritual and temporal functions. The ordering of inventories also had to do with the completion of the missionary work, as in the case of San Antonio de Valero and its secularization of 1793, or as the result of major changes in the political situation in Spain and its colonies, such as the expulsion of the Jesuits from the Americas in 1767 and the independence of Mexico from Spain in 1821.

Many of the documents contain a census of the Indian population at the time the texts were written as well as the number of baptisms, marriages, and burials.

The physical plant needed to carry out the aims of the missionaries can be subsumed under the spiritual or religious function and economic function of the missions. The first includes the art and architecture needed to carry out the religious purpose of the missions: churches, sacristies, *conventos* or friaries, houses for the Indians, and other related buildings, sacred images (sculptures and paintings), pulpits, confessionals, fonts, and other furnishings, as well as liturgical vestments, sacred vessels, and other sacred items. The second includes all the units needed to carry out the economic function of the missions: the workshops (textile, masonry, carpentry, and blacksmith), kilns, forges, storerooms, and related structures, farms and orchards, *acequias* for irrigation, pasturelands, and livestock.

THE FR. ORTIZ REPORT, 1745

Fr. Francisco Xavier Ortiz traveled from the Querétaro college to San Antonio in the middle of 1745 to inspect the four Querétaran missions established along the San Antonio River.[11] He began his inspection at San Antonio de Valero and continued it at San Juan Capistrano, La Espada, and La Purísima Concepción. Fr. Ortiz inspected the missions and wrote the report on his findings during a period of a little over a month that he spent in San Antonio.

Although the document is identified as a report, it is actually an inventory. It is therefore listed as an inventory/report in this text to distinguish it from the others included in this section.

Fr. Ortiz inspected the books of administration of each mission and listed the number of baptisms and deaths since its founding. He also took a census at each mission and described its buildings and its holdings, including a description of the church, its altars and sacred images, vessels and other ornaments, the sacristy, the Indian houses, the friars' quarters (*convento*), the textile workshop and other workshops (carpentry, masonry, and blacksmith), the pasturelands and cultivated fields, irrigation canals, the granary, and the stock (cattle, sheep, goats, and horses).

THE FR. MARMOLEJO REPORT, 1755

Fr. Ildefonso José Marmolejo prepared a report on San José de Aguayo soon after his arrival at the mission in 1755.[12] The report includes a copy of the inventory prepared by Fr. Miguel Núñez de Haro in December 1753 and a progress report from that date to Fr. Marmolejo's arrival on October 4, 1755.

Fr. Marmolejo provided information on the number of baptisms in the Book of Administration, the church, the sacristy, the *convento,* the Indian houses, implements for work, the granary, the farm, the carpenter's shop, the forge, the textile workshop, the stock (horses, sheep, and cattle), the *corral* (fenced-in area), the sugarcane hut, the orchard, and the accounts of the mission.

THE FR. NÚÑEZ INVENTORY, 1753

Fr. Núñez noted the number of persons baptized up to the time the inventory was prepared (from the Book of Administration).[13] He described the church, the sacred images in the altars, the sacristy and all the items stored in it, the *convento* (offices or workrooms, kitchen, and upper cell) and its furnishings, the Indian houses, tools, the granary, the farm, the other workshops (carpenter, masonry, and textile), the forge, and the stock.

THE FR. ORTIZ INVENTORY, 1756

Fr. Francisco Xavier Ortiz made a second trip to Texas in May and June 1756 to inspect the Querétaran missions on the San Xavier and San Antonio rivers.[14] He received the commission to carry out the inspection (visitation) from Fr. José

11. Fr. Ortiz, *Visita de las missiones,* pp. 7–41.

12. Fr. Ildefonso Marmolejo, "Inventory and Report of San José," October 4, 1755, in *San José Papers, Part I,* trans. B. Leutenegger, pp. 110–111.

13. Fr. Miguel Núñez de Haro, "Inventory of San José Mission, December 1753," in *San José Papers, Part I,* trans. B. Leutenegger, pp. 108–110.

14. Fr. Ortiz, *Razón* (vols. 1–3).

Antonio de Oliva, the commissary general (1755–1761) of all the missions of New Spain. The visitation secretary was Fr. Joachin (Joaquín) Baños, who had earlier served at San Sabá.

The primary purpose of Fr. Ortiz's visit was to determine the status of each mission and to relate its history from the time it was founded to the time of his inspection.

Fr. Ortiz inspected the San Xavier missions on May 13, 1756. He also visited the presidio San Francisco Xavier de Gigedo. The San Xavier missions, founded by decree of the viceroy Juan Francisco de Güemes y Orcasitas (Horcasitas) on February 14, 1747, were San Francisco Xavier de Horcasitas, San Ildefonso, and Nuestra Señora de la Candelaria. Ortiz inspected the San Antonio missions— San Francisco de la Espada, San Juan Capistrano, Nuestra Señora de la Purísima Concepción, and San Antonio de Valero—from May 29 to June 9, 1756.

The final report/inventory was divided into three parts: Part I on the San Xavier missions and La Espada in San Antonio; Part II on San Juan Capistrano and La Purísima Concepción; and Part III on San Antonio de Valero. It provides information on the presidio and the Querétaran missions of San Xavier and San Antonio. Fr. Ortiz inspected the physical plant of each mission (the church and its ornaments, sacred vessels, and other ecclesiastic items), the administrative books, and the other items needed to carry out its religious and economic functions. He also discussed the environmental conditions at San Xavier and the state of affairs of the missionaries, soldiers, civilians, and Indians.

Fr. Ortiz had been instrumental in having the San Xavier missions founded during his earlier visit to Texas in 1745. In May 1754, when Captain Pedro Rábago y Terán arrived to take command of the presidio, San Ildefonso had been abandoned, and there were seventy Indians at San Xavier and none at La Candelaria. By the time Fr. Ortiz arrived at San Xavier in 1756, the missions had been abandoned and relocated on the San Marcos River. The mission ornaments and sacred vessels had been set aside for the new mission planned for the San Saba River area.

Following the inspection of the San Antonio missions, Fr. Ortiz noted the date each mission was founded, the number of baptisms and deaths listed in the books of administration since its founding, the number of marriages listed in the books of marriages, and the number of Indians at each mission. He also described each church, its furnishings and sacred images, the ornaments and sacred vessels stored in the sacristy, the *convento,* the Indian houses, the workshops, the granary, the farms, the orchards, the irrigation canal, and the livestock.

THE FR. DOLORES Y VIANA REPORT, 1759

Fr. Mariano Dolores y Viana received a commission from Fr. José Antonio de Oliva, commissary general (1755–1761), to inspect the four Querétaran missions along the San Antonio River and submit a status report on his findings.[15] He carried out the inspections of the missions during the month of April in 1759. He began his inspection at La Espada on April 7 and traveled north to San Juan Capistrano on April 9, La Concepción on April 19, and San Antonio de Valero on April 25, 1759. His instructions were to report on each mission and its holdings: the church, sacred vessels and other items pertaining to divine worship, the sacristy, the books of administration, the census lists, the workshops, the inventories, and the account books.

Fr. Dolores y Viana provided information on the Indian population at the time of his visit, the number of baptisms and deaths since the founding of each mission, a description of the church, the sacred images and furnishings, the vestments, sacred vessels and other items in the sacristy, the Indian houses, the *convento,* the

15. Fr. Dolores, "Inventories, 1759."

library, the textile workshop and other workshops (carpentry, masonry), tools, the forge, the sugarcane mill, the farms and orchards, and the stock (cattle, sheep, horses, burros, mules, goats).

Fr. Dolores y Viana did not provide information on the number of baptisms and deaths at San Antonio de Valero or a census of the mission population at the time of his visit.

THE FR. SILVA INVENTORY, 1766

The inventory of the goods of Nuestra Señora de la Luz del Orcoquisac was drawn up on September 12, 1766, by Fr. Bernardo de Silva and Melchor Afán de Rivera, the temporary captain of the Presidio San Agustín de Ahumada.[16] The inventory was based on the one drawn up by Fr. Luis Salvino, the missionary in charge of the mission from 1764 to 1766. The new inventory was signed by Fr. Silva and Captain Rivera because the goods of the mission were stored in the presidio following a hurricane that completely destroyed the church on September 4, 1766. Captain Rivera signed a copy of the original text with some notes on May 25, 1768.

Following the introductory text, Fr. Silva simply noted that "there [was] no church." The inventory includes the paintings of sacred images, other sacred items, and church furnishings (the altar table, a lectern, and a confessional).

THE FR. MARENTI INVENTORY, 1766

The inventory of La Luz del Orcoquisac was prepared by Fr. José Marenti (Marentes).[17] It seems unlikely that the date given for the Marenti inventory is correct. A number of sources list a Fr. Manuel Mariano Marentes at the mission in 1767, a year after the devastating hurricane of September 1766 which destroyed the church. Since the church was rebuilt on the same spot it had previously occupied, it is likely that references to it in the inventory were made in 1767 and not 1766 because of the time needed to carry out that construction.

The inventory provides information on the church, the choir, the sacristy, and the furnishings.

THE FR. SÁENZ INVENTORIES, 1772

The expulsion of the Jesuits in 1767 from all the colonies of Spain led to the change in administration of the Texas missions.[18] When the Franciscans were asked to take over the missions founded by the Jesuits in Sonora and Arizona, the Querétaran missionaries requested permission to leave Texas so they could serve at the newly assigned missions. They were not ready to turn the Texas missions over to the secular authorities. Their request to have the missions turned over to the Zacatecan missionaries was granted, and the order was given by Viceroy Antonio Bucareli y Ursua on July 28, 1772.

The 1772 inventories were used to transfer all the mission holdings to the Zacatecan missionaries.[19] The transfer was carried out with the assistance of Juan María Barón de Ripperdá, governor and general commander of Texas; Fr. Ramírez, president of the Zacatecan missions; and Fr. Juan José Sáenz de Gumiel, president of the Querétaran missions. The inventories were turned over to Governor Ripperdá and Fr. Ramírez in December 1772. Fr. Ramírez received the inventories from Fr. Sáenz and approved them on December 14, 15, 16, and 17, 1772, for San Antonio de Valero, La Espada, La Purísima Concepción, and San Juan Capistrano, respectively. Fr. Buenaventura Antonio Ruiz de Esparza, guardian of the College of Zacatecas, accepted them in March 1773.

The inventories provide information on the holdings of each mission: the

16. Fr. Bernardo de Silva, "[Inventory of the Goods of Nuestra Señora de la Luz de] Orcoquiza, September 12, 1766," p. 1.

17. Fr. Marenti, "Inventory to [Melchor Afán de] Rivera," in Clay, Tunnell, and Ambler, *Archaeological Excavations at Presidio San Agustín de Ahumada*, p. 15.

18. Fr. Sáenz, *Inventory of the Mission San Antonio de Valero;* idem, "Inventory of Espada Mission"; idem, "Testimony and Inventory of Mission Purísima Concepción"; idem, "Inventory [of Mission San Juan Capistrano]."

19. Castañeda, *Our Catholic Heritage*, vol. 4, pp. 259–272.

church and its furnishings, the altars and holy images, the books of administration, the sacristy, the Indian houses, the living quarters of the friars (the main entrance, cells, offices), the cemetery, the forge, the workshop, the infirmary, the kitchen, the refectory, the granary, and the fields.

THE VASCONCELOS INVENTORY, 1783

The inventory of El Rosario prepared by Fr. Mariano Antonio de Vasconcelos was submitted to Fr. José Mariano de Cárdenas, the missionary of El Espíritu Santo, in 1783. (The exact date is unknown. Fr. Vasconcelos was at El Rosario in 1783 and left Texas in 1787.)

The inventory of the goods of El Rosario includes a listing of the precious objects and sacred images in the altarpieces, the furnishings of the church and related buildings, books in the library, a book of entries, and tools and supplies in the workshops (carpentry, blacksmith), the kitchen, the farm, and the ranch (branding irons). Fr. Vasconcelos noted that "only a few cows remained on a farm."[20] The other farm animals (oxen and horses) were taken by the Espíritu Santo Mission.

THE FR. CÁRDENAS INVENTORY, 1783

Fr. Joseph Mariano Cárdenas prepared the inventory of Espíritu Santo on November 27, 1783.[21] He and Fr. Mariano Antonio de Vasconcelos of El Rosario received instructions from Fr. Manuel Julio de Silva, the father guardian of the Apostolic College of Zacatecas, to prepare inventories of their respective missions.

THE FR. SALAS INVENTORY, 1785

Fr. José María Salas de Santa Gertrudis prepared the inventory of San José de Aguayo for Fr. José Agustín Falcón, father president of the Texas missions, who made an official visitation of the missions in 1785.[22] Fr. Falcón served as father president of the Texas missions from 1784 and 1785.

Fr. Salas prepared a detailed account of everything that belonged to San José de Aguayo in 1785. His description includes the location, size, and function of all the buildings and their furnishings as well as other items needed to carry out the economic and religious functions of the mission. He began the inventory with a description of the walled-in area and continued with the granary, the workshops, the church (the facade and the altar with its sacred images), the sacristy (storage units, vestments and other sacred items), and the *convento* (cells, offices, workroom, furnishings, books in the library, account books, and documents).

Fr. Salas listed the information pertaining to the economic side of the mission: the fenced-in pasture, *acequia,* orchard, sugarcane field, crop yield (corn, beans, cotton, and chile), and livestock (cattle, horses, sheep and goats). He also listed the amount of money the missionaries owed.

THE FR. LÓPEZ INVENTORY, 1793

San Antonio de Valero was secularized on January 9, 1793, by order of the viceroy at the request of the superiors of the College of Zacatecas.[23] Upon receiving the viceregal order, Manuel Muñoz, the governor of Texas (1790–1798), issued a proclamation to that effect on February 23. Fr. López delivered the inventory to Governor Muñoz on April 23 in the presence of Fr. José Mariano de la Garza, the representative of the College of Zacatecas, who was asked to supervise the delivery and the secularization of the mission.

Fr. López divided the inventory of the San Antonio de Valero mission and its holdings into two parts, the first devoted to a description of the buildings of the

20. Fr. Mariano Antonio Vasconcelos, "Inventory of Mission Rosario" (probably 1783), in Oberste, "Texas Missions of the Coastal Bend, Part I," Appendix, p. 7.

21. Fr. Joseph Mariano Cárdenas, "Inventory [of Mission Espíritu Santo]—1783," in Oberste, "Texas Missions of the Coastal Bend, Part I," Appendix, pp. 1–31.

22. "Inventory of Fr. Salas," in *The San José Papers, Part I,* trans. B. Leutenegger, pp. 214–245.

23. Fr. López, "Inventory of San Antonio de Valero, April 23, 1793," p. 2.

mission and their furnishings and the second to the farmlands, *acequias,* and live-stock.

Fr. López provided information on the stage of construction of the unfinished church and its facade with sculptures already in place in the first-stage niches, which he considered "beautiful," the sacristy used as a temporary church "in good condition," the church furnishings, which included the religious images in the altars, the condition of the missionary quarters, the number and condition of the Indian houses, the granary in a temporary structure (because the granary was damaged), a kiln, and the condition of the mission wall and the materials used in its construction.

Fr. López also included the seeds for corn and beans and the salt in storage. He described the farmlands and the *acequias* used for irrigation of the fields and listed the number of horses and cattle, most of which were turned over to the Indians; the rest were sent to El Refugio mission.

THE FR. SILVA INVENTORY, 1796

Fr. Manuel de Silva, the cofounder of Nuestra Señora del Refugio with Fr. José (listed as Joséf) Francisco Mariano de la Garza, prepared the inventory of its holdings and turned it over to Fr. José Antonio de Jesús Garavito and his assistant, Fr. José María Sáenz, on September 8, 1796.[24]

The inventory includes a description of the planned church located inside a stockade. A foundation for the church had already been laid. It was to have a transept, a tower, and a baptistry. In the meantime a temporary chapel was housed in two rooms with masonry walls, wooden beams, and brick floors. A third room served as a sacristy.

A good part of the inventory is devoted to a detailed description of all the religious images (sculptures and paintings) in the altarpieces of the church.

The inventory also includes information on the *jacales* (huts used for living quarters by the soldiers, Indians, and servants) with walls made of adobe mixed with grass, the *convento* made of timber, the workshops (carpentry, blacksmith), and the books in the library. Documents relating to the establishment of the mission were stored in a large chest. The inventory also includes the number of Indians living at the mission and the number of cattle, oxen, horses and breeding mares, mules, and hogs.

THE FR. DÍAZ INVENTORIES, 1824

The complete secularization of the San Antonio missions was ordered by the Mexican government on September 15, 1823.[25] The superiors of the College of Zacatecas accepted the order on December 13, 1823. Fr. José Antonio Díaz de León prepared the inventories of the four San Antonio missions, signed them on February 29, 1824, and turned the missions over to the Rev. Francisco Maynes, the representative of the bishop of Monterrey as well as the military chaplain in San Antonio and pastor of San Fernando.

The missions listed by Fr. Díaz are San José de Aguayo, La Purísima Concepción, San Juan Capistrano, and San Francisco de la Espada.

The inventories include detailed information on each mission: the church, the sacristy, the religious images, the vestments, sacred vessels and other furnishings, and items used for divine worship.

24. "A Very Brief Resume [Summary of the Inventory of Our Lady of Refuge in the Province of Texas, by Fr. Manuel de Silva, September 8, 1796]," in Oberste, "Texas Missions of the Coastal Bend, Part II," pp. 8-IV–9-IV; "Inventory of Mission Refugio [September 8, 1796]."

25. Fr. Díaz de León, "1824 Secularization Inventory: San José, Concepción, San Juan, and Espada."

GLOSSARY

Acequia (Spanish): Irrigation ditch.

Altar: Table for celebration of the Mass. *Altar* is used in a special sense by writers of the later viceregal period in New Spain to refer to a *retablo*.

Alto relievo (also *alto rilievo,* Italian for high relief, almost detached from its background): Terms erroneously used by Kingsbury ("Notes from My Knapsack," p. 176) to describe the San José portal sculptures, which are completely detached from the wall, or free-standing sculptures.

Apse: The rectilinear, polygonal, or semicircular enlargement of the main altar end (traditionally the eastern end) of a church to provide more space and emphasis for the altar.

Arcade: A row of arches on columns, usually carrying a roof, wall, or some other superstructure. American travelers referred to "arcaded cloisters," an "arcaded gallery," an "arched gallery," and "cloistered arches" in their descriptions of the friary that had arcaded corridors (singular *portal* in Spanish, to be distinguished from the English *portal* or *door*).

Architrave: Lowest horizontal division of an entablature (q.v.). Decorated characteristically for each of the religious orders and their variations.

Archivolt: An architrave or wide molding carried around an arch.

Azulejo (Spanish): Glazed (colored) tile.

Baldachin: A canopy of fabric carried in church processions or placed over an altar; an ornamental canopy standing over an altar.

Balustrade: A row of balusters or vase-shaped uprights, surmounted by a rail.

Baptistry: The place where the baptismal font stands.

Baroque: Style of art and architecture common in Spain and New Spain and the rest of the Western world in the seventeenth and eighteenth centuries A.D. Divided into Early Baroque (1650 to 1750) in New Spain, characterized by the use of the Solomonic column on facades and altarpieces, and Late Baroque (1750 to 1790), characterized by the use of the *estípite* column; Toussaint (*Colonial Art in Mexico*) used Ultra-Baroque to describe the style (1770 to 1790) characterized by the use of the Ornamental niche-pilaster.

Barrel vault: A tunnel-like vault.

Basket arch: An arch whose curve resembles that of a basket handle.

Bay: Compartmental division of a nave, aisle, or other long space; also used to describe the divisions of a portal.

Belfry: A tower in which one or more bells are hung.

Bracket: A small supporting piece of stone, often formed of scrolls or volutes, to carry a projecting weight.

Buttress: A strong, projecting vertical support for a wall. May be a pier buttress
(solid pier attached to wall) or flying buttress (arches brought from upper parts
of building to piers at some remove from the wall).

Campanario (Spanish): A wall with openings in which bells are hung; a bell wall.

Camposanto (Spanish): Cemetery, graveyard.

Capital: The carved top of a column or pilaster.

Chapel: A chamber or recess for meditation, prayer, or subordinate services, usually with a separately dedicated altar.

Cherub (plural cherubim): An angelic cherub, portrayed as a winged child with a
chubby, rosy face.

Choir loft (*coro alto* in Spanish): Choir on an upper level in churches where the
choir is placed over the entrance at the end opposite the altar; the area under
the upper-level choir is called the *coro bajo* in Spanish.

Christ in the Sepulchre: A sculpture sometimes displayed in the church and used
in processions during religious holy days; the fourteenth Station of the Cross.

Cloister: Open court, usually with planting, surrounded by covered passages, in
the residential part of a friary (Spanish *claustro*).

Column: An architectural support of definite proportions, usually cylindrical in
shape with a shaft and capital (and sometimes a base). May be free-standing or
attached to a wall ("engaged") as a half or three-quarter column (cut vertically
into halves or into three-quarters).

Confessional: The place in the church where a priest hears confessions.

Convento (Spanish): Sixteenth-century conventual architecture of viceregal
Mexico; included a church, an open chapel, an open space in front called an
atrio (Spanish for atrium), a friary, a cloister, a refectory, and other buildings.

Cornice: Topmost horizontal division of an entablature (q.v.). Sometimes isolated
and used separately as a strong molding.

Credence table: The table upon which the wine and water, candlesticks, humeral
veil, burse, and chalice are kept until needed during a solemn Mass.

Cross: One of the principal Christian symbols; architecturally, of the Latin type
(with one arm longer than the others) or the Greek type (with all arms of
equal length).

Crossing: Area where the nave and transept intersect.

Cross-vault: Also called a "groin vault"; a tunnel vault intersected at right angles
by another tunnel vault of the same size; a series of such vaults along the nave
at a high or cornice level can provide lighting for the nave.

Cruciform plan: A floor or ground plan laid out in the shape of a cross.

Cupola (Spanish *cúpula*): A rounded roof; a dome, but usually on a smaller scale; a
lantern.

Curb-stone: A stone or row of stones that constitutes a curb.

Descent from the Cross: Sculptures representing the thirteenth Station of the
Cross used in ceremonies during religious holy days.

Diadem: A crown worn by sculptures of saints and other holy persons.

Dome: A cupola; a convex roof, usually circular at the base and semicircular or
paraboloid in elevation.

Drum: A vertical wall, usually cylindrical (or polygonal) in plan, used to support
a dome. The drum often has openings or windows for lighting the interior
below.

Entablature: The horizontal section above columns or pilasters. In classical architecture and its derivatives, the entablature is divided into three horizontal parts
from bottom to top: the architrave, the frieze, and the cornice. Each of the
orders had a characteristic entablature, with special decorative enrichment of
the parts.

Epistle side: Right side of the altar as one faces it.

Espadaña (Spanish): An extension of a facade with openings in which bells are hung.

Estípite (Spanish): Special pillar or pilaster made up of a base, inverted obelisk, and various blocks and moldings (sometimes medallions as well), crowned with a Corinthianesque capital. First used in a developed form in the later seventeenth century. Became a type of "order" in mid- and later-eighteenth-century viceregal Mexico.

Estofado (Spanish): Figural and ornamental sculptural technique, involving the coating of carved wood with layers of fine gesso as a foundation for gilding and polychromy. A special variant relating to faces and hands is called *encarnación*.

Evangelical side (also Gospel side): Left side of the altar as one faces it.

Facade: The front or frontispiece of a building.

Feast of Corpus Christi: The feast commemorating the institution of the Eucharist; a solemn public procession of the Blessed Sacrament is prescribed for the feast.

Flagellation of Christ: Scene of Jesus being scourged and crucified by Pilate's soldiers; sometimes included in depictions of the Stations of the Cross.

Fluting: Vertical channeling (usually concave) of a columnar or pilaster shaft. Used to describe the painted "fluted pilasters" on the Concepción belfries.

Frieze: Middle horizontal division of an entablature (q.v.). Decorated characteristically for each religious order and its variations.

Frontispiece: The main facade of a building or its principal entrance.

Good Friday: The Friday of Holy Week, the day on which Christ died on the cross, commemorated by the church with liturgical services.

Greek cross: An equilateral cross.

Grisaille: A painting executed entirely in monochrome, in a series of grays.

Half column. See "Column."

Holy Thursday: The Thursday of Holy Week; commemoration of Christ's institution of the Holy Eucharist at the Last Supper.

Jacal or *xacal* (Spanish): Hut; crude dwelling.

Jambs: The sides of a doorway or a window.

Jerusalem cross: A cross with four arms, each terminating in a crossbar.

Keystone: The central stone of an arch; sometimes carved.

Latin cross: A cross with a longitudinal member and shorter transverse members; the type of cross used in the Crucifixion of Christ.

Lintel: The horizontal beam framing the top of a door or other opening.

Lunette: Any semicircular opening or surface, as on the wall of a vaulted room.

Memorial (Spanish): Advisement, usually written, of some event or events that have already taken place.

Merlon: A raised portion on a parapet or at the base of a dome.

Missal stand: The stand used for the missal or liturgical book with which the priest says Mass.

Mitote (from Náhuatl *mitotl*): A dance performed by the Aztecs. The Franciscan friars used the word to describe any Indian dance; generally refers to noise, excitement, noisy fun.

Mixtilinear (*mixtilíneo* in Spanish): Usually applied to the upper edge of an opening that has a broken line when seen from the front. An "arch" of a more complex shape than a semicircle or point, reflecting late medieval, Islamic, and Baroque interest in unusual broken, curved, and stepped rims of openings.

Nave: From the Latin word for ship. The central longitudinal space or aisle of a church. Traditionally (in medieval Europe) oriented west (the entrance) to east (the altar); in Mexico churches had many orientations.

Niche: A recess in a wall for holding a sculpture or other ornament.

Obraje (Spanish): Work or workshop in the mission where Indians worked.

Ochavado arch (Spanish for octagonal): An arch in the shape of a half-octagon.

Oficina (Spanish): A workplace where something is manufactured.

Ogee window: A shape comprised of a double-curved line made up of a convex and a concave part.

Ogival: Arches of ogee or double curved shape.

Orders: (1) In architecture, the basic columnar types of the classical-oriented architectural world; the Doric, Ionic, and Corinthian of the Greeks and the Doric, Tuscan, Ionic, Corinthian, and Composite of the Roman, Renaissance, and later eras. (2) In religion, the divisions of monks and nuns into special administrative units, such as the Franciscan Order.

Oriel: A projecting bay window on an upper floor, supported from below with corbels or brackets.

Ornamental niche-pilaster: A figure niche, with massing of ornament above and below, made into a quasi pilaster; especially common in New Spain between 1770 and 1790.

Palanquin: A covered litter on poles carried on the shoulders of two or four people.

Pedestal: In classical architecture, the base supporting a column or colonnade; also the base for a sculpture.

Pediment: A low-pitched gable or triangular area, formed by the two slopes of a temple in classical architecture; framed by horizontal and raking cornices; sometimes used for sculptures.

Pendentive: A spherical triangle used as the transition from a squared space to a drum or dome.

Pilaster: A flattened columnar form, rectilinear in shape, always attached to a wall.

Pillar: A slender architectural support, usually rather tall; sometimes squared or rounded.

Plateresque: A style of architecture and ornament combining late Gothic and Renaissance elements.

Portal: A doorway or entrance; especially one that is large and imposing.

Portería (Spanish): The entrance to the friary in sixteenth-century conventual architecture in viceregal Mexico.

Predella: The base of a large altarpiece (*retablo*), frequently decorated with painted "predella panels" or sculpture expanding the theme of the major panel or panels above.

Presbytery: The section of the church reserved for the higher clergy.

Quatrefoil frames: Shapes comprised of four lobes or foils.

Raking cornice. See "Pediment."

Refectory: A room where meals are served.

Renaissance: A style of art and architecture of the fifteenth and sixteenth centuries A.D. Characterized by harmony of parts, (symmetrical) balance, and clarity, strongly influenced by classical sources.

Repoussé: Metalworking; a design hammered into relief from the reverse side.

Reredos (Spanish): An ornamental screen behind an altar. Some writers use this word in place of retable or *retablo,* both of which are used in this text.

Retablo (Spanish): From the low Latin *retaulus* (retro-tabula), something "behind the table" or altar. Usually in Spain and viceregal Mexico a large screen to enhance an altar. (The Spanish word *altar* [q.v.] was more commonly used than *retablo* in the literature of the viceregal period.)

Roman arch: A round "true arch" made of voussoirs.

Rose window: A round window, usually with tracery.

Sacristy (*sacristía* in Spanish): A room for robing the clergy.

Salomónica (Spanish): A Solomonic column, that is, one with a twisted shaft, usually with a Corinthianesque capital, and a base. So called from the presumed use of such columns in Solomon's temple.

Sanctuary: The part of the church where the altar is placed.

Segmental pediment: The upper cornice of a pediment that takes the curve of a segment of a circle.

Shaft: Section of a column or pilaster between the capital and base.

Sounding board: A structure suspended behind or over a pulpit to reflect the speaker's voice to the audience.

Spandrel: The space, usually decorated, between the exterior curve of an arch and the right angle that frames it.

Springer: The lowest part or spring of an arch; the first stone of an arch placed on the impost (cap of the supporting pier or pillar).

Stations of the Cross: Christ's journey to Calvary, usually divided into fourteen scenes or stations; a series of devotions initiated by the Franciscans in the fourteenth century focusing on this event includes each picture in sequence, with specific prayers and devotions.

Tabernacle: A receptacle for the consecrated Host and wine of the Eucharist.

Tequitqui: A term used in Mexico to describe viceregal art, usually low-relief stone carving, that reflects an indigenous sensibility.

Tower: A high squared or rounded structure; generally squared in New Spain and used singly or in a pair to frame a church facade.

Transept: The interior space of a church at right angles to the nave; where the transept intersects the nave is the crossing, which often has a dome-shaped covering higher than the nave or transept. The transept has many orientations in Mexico.

Tuscan style (Tuscan order): One of the classical orders resembling the Doric but of greater simplicity.

Ultra-Baroque. See "Baroque."

Vault: A masonry arched roof.

Vecinos agregados (Spanish): *Vecino,* a citizen of good standing; usually a property owner. *Agregado,* someone who occupies a rural property with a house for free or as a rental. The two words together refer to people without property.

Via Sacra (also Via Dolorosa, Road of Sorrows; Via Crucis, Stations of the Cross): Sacred Way; a reference to the Stations of the Cross.

Viaticum: Holy Communion given to a person in danger of death.

Voussoir: One of the parts of an arch; the apex voussoir is the keystone.

SELECTED BIBLIOGRAPHY

ABBREVIATIONS

OLLU   Our Lady of the Lake University
OSMHRL   Old Spanish Missions Historical Research Library
SBCAP   State Building Commission Archaeological Program
SHQ   *Southwestern Historical Quarterly*
THC   Texas Historical Commission
UTSA   University of Texas at San Antonio

UNPUBLISHED SOURCES

Díaz de León, Fr. José Antonio. "1824 Secularization Inventory: San José, Concepción, San Juan, and Espada." Texts prepared by Donna Pierce for "The Decorative and Applied Arts at the Missions: Final Report, August 10, 1982," Jacinto Quirarte, project director, UTSA, Research Center for the Arts (unpublished).

———. "Inventory [of the Church of Mission de S. Francisco de la Espada, February 29, 1824]." San Antonio: OSMHRL, OLLU (unpublished), Roll 10.4188.

———. "Inventory [of the Church of San José y San Miguel de Aguayo, February 29, 1824]." San Antonio: OSMHRL, OLLU (unpublished), Roll 4.5569.

Dolores y Viana, Fr. Mariano Francisco de los. "Inventories of the San Antonio Missions, 1759." San Antonio: OSMHRL, OLLU, Roll 9, 1469–1504.

Gentilz, Theodore. "Notes." San Antonio: Daughters of the Republic of Texas Library.

"Inventory of Mission Refugio." [Incomplete; author unknown.] San Antonio: OSMHRL, OLLU. Rolls 3.3860, 1.0030, and 2.1339.

Ivey, J. E., and M. B. Thurber. "The Missions of San Antonio: A Historic Structures Report and Administrative History: Part 1, The Spanish Colonial Missions." National Park Service, Southwest Cultural Resources Center. Draft report on file at Center for Archaeological Research, UTSA.

López, Fr. José Francisco. "Inventory of San Antonio de Valero, April 23, 1793." San Antonio: OSMHRL, OLLU, Roll 4.5808.

Oberste, William H. "Texas Missions of the Coastal Bend, Espíritu Santo, El Rosario, El Refugio." Typescript, 1980.

Ortiz, Fr. Francisco Xavier. *Visita de las missiones.* Archivo del Colegio de Querétaro. W. E. Dunn Transcripts, 1729–1758. University of Texas Library.

Quirarte, Jacinto. "The Decorative and Applied Arts at the Missions, Final Report, August 10, 1982." San Antonio: UTSA, Research Center for the Arts (unpublished).

Sáenz Gumiel, Fr. Juan Joseph de. "Inventory of Espada Mission." San Antonio: OSMHRL, OLLU (unpublished), Roll 10.4191–4229.

———. "Inventory [of Mission San Juan Capistrano]." San Antonio: OSMHRL, OLLU (unpublished), Roll 10.4268.

———. "Testimony and Inventory of Mission Purísima Concepción/Ynbentario de la misión de la Purísima Concepción." San Antonio: OSMHRL, OLLU (unpublished), Roll 10.4235.

Silva, Fr. Bernardo de. "Inventory of the Goods of Nuestra Señora de la Luz de Orcoquiza, September 12, 1766." San Antonio: OSMHRL, OLLU.

PUBLISHED SOURCES

Alarcón, M. de. *Diary of the Alarcón Expedition into Texas, 1718–1719.* Translated by F. Celiz and edited by F. L. Hoffman. Los Angeles: Quivira Society, 1935; republished by Arno Press, 1967.

Alcocer, Fr. J. A. *Bosquejo de la historia del Colegio de Nuestra Señora de Guadalupe y sus missiones, año de 1788.* Edited by Fr. R. Cervantes. Mexico City: Editorial Porrúa, S.A., 1958.

Almaráz, F. D., trans. and ed. *Inventory of the Rio Grande Missions: 1772, San Juan Bautista and San Bernardo.* Report 2. San Antonio: UTSA Center for Archaeological Research, 1980.

Ashford, G. "Old Spanish Paintings May Return Home." *San Antonio Express-News.* Sunday, December 21, 1965.

Baer, K. *Architecture of the California Missions.* Berkeley: University of California Press, 1958.

Baird, J. A. *The Churches of Mexico: 1530–1810.* Berkeley: University of California Press, 1962.

Barnes, T. C., T. H. Naylor, and C. W. Polzer. *Northern New Spain: A Research Guide.* Tucson: University of Arizona Press, 1981.

Bartlett, J. R. *Personal Narrative of Explorations and Incidents in Texas, New Mexico, California, Sonora, and Chihuahua.* 2 vols. New York and London: D. Appleton & Co., 1854.

Benedictine Monks of St. Augustine's Abbey, Ramsgate. *The Book of Saints.* New York: Macmillan Company, 1932.

Bollaert, W. *William Bollaert's Texas.* Edited by W. E. Hollon and R. L. Butler. Norman: University of Oklahoma Press, 1956.

Bolton, H. E. *Coronado: Knight of Pueblos and Plains.* New York: Whittlesey House, 1949.

———. "The Founding of Mission Rosario: A Chapter in the History of the Gulf Coast." *Quarterly of the Texas State Historical Association* 10, no. 2 (October 1906): 113–139.

———. "The Founding of the Missions on the San Gabriel River, 1745–1749." *SHQ* 17, no. 4 (April 1914): 323–378.

———. *Spanish Exploration in the Southwest, 1542–1706.* New York: Charles Scribner's Sons, 1908. Rpt. New York: Barnes & Noble, 1959.

———. "The Spanish Occupation of Texas, 1519–1690." *SHQ* 16, no. 1 (July 1912): 1–26.

———. *Texas in the Middle Eighteenth Century* (1915). Austin: University of Texas Press, 1970.

Bonilla, Don A. *Breve compendio de los sucesos ocurridos en la provincia de Texas desde su conquista o redacción hasta la fecha, por el teniente de infantería, Don Antonio Bonilla, México, 10 de noviembre de 1772. Anales del Museo,* 2d series (1904).

———. "A Brief Compendium of the History of Texas, 1772." Annotated translation by Elizabeth H. West. *SHQ* 8, no. 1 (July 1904): 3–78.

Brooks, C. M. *Texas Missions, Their Romance and Architecture.* Dallas: Dealey & Lowe, 1936.

Buckley, E. C. "The Aguayo Expedition, 1719–1722." *Quarterly of the Texas State Historical Association* 15 (July 1911): 45–49.

Burke, J. W. *Missions of Old Texas.* South Brunswick and New York: A. S. Barnes & Co., 1971.

Castañeda, C. E. *Our Catholic Heritage in Texas, 1519–1936.* 7 vols. and supplement. Austin: Von Boeckmann–Jones Co., 1936–1958. Rpt. New York: Arno Press, 1976–.

Chabot, F. C. *The Alamo: Mission, Fortress and Shrine.* San Antonio: privately published, 1941.

Ciprián, Fr. I. A. "Report of Fr. Ignacio Antonio Ciprián, 1749." In *The Texas Missions of the College of Zacatecas in 1749–1759.* Translated by Fr. B. Leutenegger; introduction and notes by Fr. M. A. Habig, pp. 18–32. San Antonio: OSMHRL at San José Mission, 1979.

Clark, J. W., Jr. *Mission San José y San Miguel de Aguayo: Archaeological Investigations, December 1974.* Archaeological Report 29. Austin: Texas Historical Commission, 1978.

Clark, R. C. "Louis Juchereau de Saint-Denis and the Re-establishment of the Texas Missions." *Quarterly of the Texas State Historical Association* 6, no. 1 (July 1902): 1–26.

Clay, J. V., C. D. Tunnell, and J. R. Ambler. *Archaeological Excavations at Presidio San Agustín de Ahumada.* Report No. 6. Austin: State Historical Building Commission Archaeological Program, March 1967.

Corner, W. *San Antonio de Béxar: A Guide and History.* San Antonio: Bainbridge & Corner, 1890.

Cox, I. W. *Archaeological Monitoring of the San José Acequia, Wastewater Facilities Improvement Program, San Antonio, Texas.* Archaeological Survey Report No. 175. San Antonio: UTSA, Center for Archaeological Research, 1988.

Day, J., J. B. Frantz, B. Proctor, J. Schmitz, L. Tinkle, and D. H. Winfrey, *Six Missions of Texas.* Waco: Texian Press, 1965.

Díaz del Castillo, B. *The Discovery and Conquest of Mexico, 1517–1521.* Translation, introduction, and notes by A. P. Maudslay. New York: Grove Press, 1958.

———. *Historia verdadera de la conquista de la Nueva España.* Prologue by C. Pereyra. Mexico City: Espasa-Calpe, 1955.

Díaz de León, Fr. José Antonio. "Inventory of the Church of Mission San José." In *The San José Papers: Edited Primary Manuscript Sources for the History of Mission San José y San Miguel de Aguayo, Part III: July 1810–February 1824,* trans. B. Leutenegger, ed. Sister C. Casso, pp. 149–159. San Antonio: OSMHRL, OLLU, 1990.

Documentos para la historia eclesiástica y civil de la provincia de Texas o Nuevas Philipinas, 1720–1779. Madrid: Ediciones J. Porrúa Turanzas, 1961.

Dolores y Viana, Fr. Mariano de los. "A Report about the Status of the Texas Missions in 1762." In *Letters and Memorials of Fray Mariano de los Dolores y Viana, 1737–1762,* pp. 327–363. Translated by Fr. B. Leutenegger; intro. and notes by Fr. M. A. Habig. San Antonio: OSMHRL, OLLU, 1985.

Duell, P. *Mission Architecture as Exemplified in San Xavier del Bac.* Tucson: Arizona Archaeological and Historical Society, 1919.

Dunn, W. E. "The Founding of Nuestra Señora del Refugio, the Last Spanish Mission in Texas." *SHQ* 25 (1921–1922): 178–182.

Eastman, S. *A Seth Eastman Sketchbook, 1848–1849.* Introduction by L. Burkhalter. Austin: University of Texas Press, 1961.

Eaton, J. D. *Excavations at the Alamo Shrine (Mission San Antonio de Valero).* Archaeological Survey Report No. 10. San Antonio: UTSA, Center for Archaeological Research, 1980.

Espinosa, Fr. I. F. de. *Crónica de los colegios de Propaganda Fide de la Nueva España, 1746.* Notes and intro. by L. Cañedo. Washington, D.C.: Academy of American Franciscan History, 1967.

———. "Ramón Expedition: Espinosa's Diary of 1716." Translated by G. Tous. *Mid-America* 12 (April 1930): 339–361.

Ferguson, M. G. *Signs and Symbols in Christian Art.* New York: Oxford University Press, 1961.

Fox, A. A. *Archaeological Investigations at Mission Concepción, Fall of 1986.* Archaeological Survey Report No. 172. San Antonio: UTSA, Center for Archaeological Research, 1988.

———. *Archaeological Investigations in Alamo Plaza, 1988 and 1989.* Archaeological Survey Report No. 205. San Antonio: UTSA Center for Archaeological Research, 1992.

———. *Archaeological Investigations to Locate the Northwest Corner of Mission Concepción, San Antonio, Bexar County, Texas.* Archaeological Survey Report No. 212. San Antonio: UTSA Center for Archaeological Research, 1992.

———. *Monitoring of Utility Trenches at Mission Concepción, San Antonio, Texas.* Archaeological Survey Report No. 180. San Antonio: UTSA Center for Archaeological Research, 1989.

———. *Test Excavations at Mission San Francisco de la Espada.* Archaeological Survey Report No. 108. San Antonio: UTSA Center for Archaeological Research, 1981.

———. *Testing for the Location of the Alamo Acequia at Hemisfair Plaza, San Antonio, Texas.* Archaeological Survey Report No. 142. San Antonio: UTSA Center for Archaeological Research, 1985.

Fox, A. A., F. A. Bass, and T. R. Hester. *The Archaeology and History of Alamo Plaza.* Archaeological Survey Report No. 16. San Antonio: UTSA Center for Archaeological Research, 1976.

Fox, A. A., and I. W. Cox. *Testing of the San José Mission Acequia, San Antonio Missions National Historical Park, Bexar County, Texas.* Archaeological Survey Report No. 207. San Antonio: UTSA Center for Archaeological Research, 1991.

Fox, A. A., and T. R. Hester. *Archaeological Test Excavations at Mission San Francisco de la Espada.* Archaeological Survey Report No. 22. San Antonio: UTSA Center for Archaeological Research, 1976.

Gilmore, K. K. *Mission Rosario: Archaeological Investigations, 1973.* Archaeological Report 14, Part 1. Austin: Texas Parks and Wildlife Department, Parks Branch, 1974.

———. *Mission Rosario: Archaeological Investigations, 1974.* Archaeological Report 14, Part 2. Austin: Texas Parks and Wildlife Department, Parks Division, Historical Sites and Restoration Branch, 1975.

———. *The San Xavier Missions: A Study in Historical Identification.* Report 16. Austin: SBCAP, 1969.

Gregg, Josiah. *Diary and Letters of Josiah Gregg.* Vol. 1, *Southwestern Enterprises, 1840–1847.* Edited by M. G. Fulton. Norman: University of Oklahoma Press, 1941.

Habig, M. A. *The Alamo Chain of Missions: A History of San Antonio's Five Old Missions.* Chicago: Franciscan Herald Press, 1968.

———. *San Antonio's Mission San José.* Chicago: Franciscan Herald Press, 1968.

Hallenbeck, C. *Spanish Missions of the Old Southwest.* New York: Doubleday, 1926.

Hard, R. J., A. A. Fox, I. W. Cox, K. J. Gross, B. A. Meissner, G. Mendez, C. L. Tennis, and J. Zapata. *Excavations at Mission San José y San Miguel de Aguayo, San Antonio, Texas.* Archaeological Survey Report No. 218. San Antonio: UTSA Center for Archaeological Research, 1995.

Hargreaves-Mawdsley, W. N. *Eighteenth-Century Spain, 1700–1788.* Totowa, N.J.: Rowman & Littlefield, 1979.

Harris, E. W. *San José, Queen of the Missions.* San Antonio: n.p., 1942.

Hatch, J. A. *Anonymous Traveller 1837: An Anonymous Contemporary Narrative.* Austin: University of Texas Press, 1958.

Huddleston, L. E. *Origins of the American Indians: European Concepts, 1492–1729.* Austin: University of Texas Press, 1967.

Hughes, A. E. "The Beginnings of Spanish Settlement in the El Paso District." *University of California Publications in History* 1, no. 3 (1914): 295–392. Rpt. Millwood, N.Y.: Kraus Reprint Co., 1974.

Hughes, George W. *A Memoir Descriptive of the March of a Division of the United States Army, under the Command of Brigadier General John E. Wool, from San Antonio de Bexar, in Texas, to Saltillo, in Mexico.* Washington, D.C.: printed by W. M. Belt, 1850.

Jackson, Jack. *Los mesteños: Spanish Ranching in Texas, 1721–1821.* College Station: Texas A&M University Press, 1986.

Kendall, D. S., and C. Perry. *Gentilz.* Austin: University of Texas Press, 1974.

Kendall, G. W. *Narrative of the Texan Santa Fe Expedition.* 2 vols. New York: Harper & Brothers, 1844.

Kessell, J. L. *The Missions of New Mexico since 1776.* Albuquerque: University of New Mexico Press, 1980.

Kingsbury, C. P. "Notes from My Knapsack: Number I." *Putnam's Monthly* 3, no. 14 (February 1854): 170–180.

Kinnaird, L. *The Frontiers of New Spain: Nicolas de Lafora's Description, 1766–1768.* Berkeley: Quivira Society, 1958; republished by Arno Press, 1967.

Kubler, G. *Mexican Architecture of the Sixteenth Century.* New Haven: Yale University Press, 1948.

———. *The Religious Architecture of New Mexico.* Colorado Springs: Taylor Museum, 1940.

Kubler, G., and M. Soria. *Art and Architecture in Spain and Portugal and Their American Dominions, 1500–1800.* Baltimore: Penguin Books, 1959; rpt. 1969.

Leutenegger, B., trans. *The San José Papers: Edited Primary Manuscript Sources for the History of Mission San José y San Miguel de Aguayo, Part I: 1719–1791.* Compiled and annotated by M. A. Habig. San Antonio: OSMHRL, San José Mission, 1978.

———, trans. *The San José Papers: Edited Primary Manuscript Sources for the History of Mission San José y San Miguel de Aguayo, Part III: July 1810–February 1824.* Edited by Sister C. Casso. San Antonio: OSMHRL, OLLU, 1990.

López, Fr. José Francisco. "Documents: The Texas Missions in 1785." Translated by J. A. Dabbs. *Mid-America* 22 (January 1940): 38–58.

———. "Report on the San Antonio Missions in 1792, by Fr. José Francisco López." Translated by Fr. B. Leutenegger. Introduction and notes by M. A. Habig. *SHQ* 77, no. 4 (April 1974): 487–498.

Madlem, W. *San Jose Mission: Its Legends, Lore, and History.* San Antonio: Naylor Co., 1934.

Martínez Reyes, A. "Los Cinco Señores: Una pintura del siglo XVI en la Catedral de México." In *Estudios acerca del arte novohispano: Homenaje a Elisa Vargas Lugo,* pp. 77–82. Mexico City: Universidad Nacional Autónoma de México, 1983.

Mason, H. M. *Missions of Texas.* Birmingham, Ala.: Southern Living Books, 1974.

McAndrew, J. *The Open-Air Churches of Sixteenth-Century Mexico.* Cambridge, Mass.: Harvard University Press, 1965.

McCaleb, W. F. *The Spanish Missions of Texas.* San Antonio: Naylor Co., 1954.

McClintock, W. A. "Journal of a Trip through Texas and Northern Mexico in 1846–1847." *SHQ* 2, 34, no. 2 (October 1930): 144–145.

McCloskey, M. B. *The Formative Years of the Missionary College of Santa Cruz of Queretaro, 1683–1733.* Washington, D.C.: Academy of American Franciscan History, 1955.

Meissner, B. A. *The Alamo Restoration and Conservation Project: Excavations at the*

South Transept. Archaeological Survey Report No. 245. San Antonio: UTSA Center for Archaeological Research, 1996.

Meskill, F. K. *Archaeological Testing within the Southeast Corner of the Plaza at Mission Espada San Antonio, Bexar County, Texas.* Archaeological Survey Report No. 208. San Antonio: UTSA Center for Archaeological Research, 1992.

Minge, W. A. *Acoma: Pueblo in the Sky.* Albuquerque: University of New Mexico Press, 1976.

Morfi, Fr. J. A. *Diario y derrotero (1777–1778).* Ed. E. del Hoyo and M. D. McLean. Monterrey, Mexico: Instituto Tecnológico y de Estudios Superiores de Monterrey, 1967.

———. *History of Texas, 1673–1779.* Translated by C. E. Castañeda. 2 vols. Albuquerque: Quivira Society, 1935; republished New York: Arno Press, 1967.

Neuerburg, N. *Santos para el Pueblo, Saints for the People.* Los Angeles: Loyola Marymount University Art Gallery, 1982.

Newcomb, R. *The Old Mission Churches and Historical Houses of California: Their History, Architecture, Art, and Lore.* Philadelphia and London: J. B. Lippincott Co., 1925.

Olmsted, F. L. *A Journey through Texas or a Saddle-Trip on the Southwestern Frontier.* New York: Dix, Edwards & Co., 1857; republished Austin: University of Texas Press, 1978.

Ortiz, Fr. F. X. *Razón de la visita a las misiones de la provincia de Texas, 1756.* 3 vols. Mexico City: Vargas Rea, 1955.

Oviedo y Valdez, G. F. "The Expedition of Pánfilo de Narváez." From Oviedo's *Historia general y natural de las Indias,* Book 35. 3d ed. Salamanca, 1547. Edited by H. Davenport. *SHQ* 27 (October 1923): 120–139 (Chapter 1) and 27 (January 1924): 217–241 (Chapter 2).

Padilla, J. A. "Report on the Barbarous Indians of the Province of Texas." Translated by M. A. Hatcher as "Texas in 1820." *SHQ* 23 (1919–1920): 47–60.

Pelikan, J. *Mary through the Centuries.* New Haven: Yale University Press, 1996.

Reindorp, R. C. "The Founding of Missions at La Junta de los Ríos." *Mid-America* 20 (April 1938): 107–131.

The Restored San Jose Mission Church. San Antonio: n.p., April 18, 1937.

Sáenz de Gumiel, Fr. J. J. *Inventory of the Mission San Antonio de Valero: 1772.* Translated and edited by B. Leutenegger. Austin: THC, 1977.

"San Antonio Lives Again." *San Antonio Express Magazine* (April 16, 1950): 25.

Scarborough, W. F. "Old Spanish Mission in Texas II: San Francisco de la Espada." *Southwest Review* 13, no. 3 (1928): 367–397.

———. "Old Spanish Mission in Texas III: San José de [*sic*] San Miguel de Aguayo de Buena Vista." *Southwest Review* 13, no. 4 (1928): 491–504.

Schmitz, J. W. *Mission Concepción.* Waco: Texian Press, 1965.

Scholes, F. V. "Documents for the History of the New Mexico Historical Review." *New Mexico Historical Review* 4 (Santa Fe, 1929): 45–58.

Schuetz, M. K. *Historical Background of the Mission San Antonio de Valero.* Report 1. Austin: SBCAP, 1966.

———. *The History and Archaeology of Mission San Juan Capistrano, San Antonio, Texas.* Vol. 1: *Historical Documentation and Description of the Structures.* Report 10. Austin: SBCAP, 1968.

———. *The History and Archaeology of Mission San Juan Capistrano, San Antonio, Texas.* Vol. 2: *Description of the Artifacts and Ethnohistory of the Coahuiltecan Indians.* Report 11. Austin: SBCAP, 1969.

———. "Professional Artisans in the Hispanic Southwest." *Americas* 40, no. 1 (July 1983): 17–71.

———. "Proportional Systems and Ancient Geometry." *Southwestern Mission Research Center* (insert in *SMRC Newsletter,* 1980): 2–7.

Schuetz, M. K., and R. K. Winn. "The Art of the Era." In *San Antonio in the Eighteenth Century,* pp. 118–128. San Antonio: Clark Printing Company, 1976.

Scurlock, D., and D. E. Fox. *An Archaeological Investigation of Mission Concepción, San Antonio, Texas.* Office of the State Archaeologist Report 28. Austin: THC, 1977.

Solís, Fr. G. J. de. "Diary of a Visit of Inspection of the Texas Missions Made by Fray Gaspar José de Solís in the Year 1767–68." Translated by M. Kennedy Kress; intro. by M. A. Hatcher. *SHQ* 35, no. 1 (July 1931): 28–76.

Sturmberg, R. *History of San Antonio and the Early Days in Texas.* San Antonio: Press of the Standard Printing Co., 1920.

Toussaint, M. *Arte colonial en México.* Mexico City: Universidad Nacional Autónoma de México, 1948.

———. *Colonial Art in Mexico.* Translated by E. Weismann. Austin: University of Texas Press, 1967.

Trens, M. *María: Iconografía de la Virgen en el arte español.* Madrid: Editorial Plus-Ultra, 1946.

Tunnell, C. D., and J. R. Ambler. *Archaeological Investigations at Presidio San Agustín de Ahumada.* Report 6. Austin: SBCAP, 1967.

Turner, D. A. *Excavations at San Juan Capistrano, 41 Bx 5, Bexar County, Texas.* Archaeological Survey Report No. 171. San Antonio: UTSA Center for Archaeological Research, 1988.

Wakefield, J. W. *Missions of Old Texas.* New York: A. S. Barnes & Co., 1971.

Weddle, R. S. *San Juan Bautista: Gateway to Spanish Texas.* Austin: University of Texas Press, 1968.

———. "San Juan Bautista: Mother of Texas Missions." *SHQ* 71 (April 1968): 542–563.

———. *The San Sabá Mission: Spanish Pivot in Texas.* Austin: University of Texas Press, 1964.

Weismann, E. W. *Mexico in Sculpture: 1521–1821.* Cambridge, Mass.: Harvard University Press, 1950.

The Zacatecan Missionaries in Texas, 1716–1834. Excerpts from the *Libros de los Decretos of the Missionary College of Zacatecas, 1707–1808.* Translated by Fr. B. Leutenegger. Office of the State Archaeologist Report, no. 23. Austin: Texas Historical Survey Committee, August 1973.

Index

Abasolo, Fr. Juan Antonio, Commissary General of New Spain, 208

Acevedo, Fr. Agustín (Antonio): journey of, to Junta de los Ríos, 13; El Apóstol Santiago administered by, 198

Acuña, Viceroy Juan de, Marqués de Casa Fuerte: request to move East Texas missions sent to, 19; name of, added to Concepción mission, 20, 200

Aguayo, Marqués de San Miguel de, Governor of Texas (1719–1722): 1721 expedition to reoccupy Texas Province by, 19; Espíritu Santo mission founded by, 20, 163; east Texas missions repaired by order of, 199; Los Nacogdoches mission reached by expedition of, 200; San Xavier de Náxera founded by, 201

Ainais Indians, 32, 33

Alamo. *See* San Antonio de Valero

Alarcón, Don Martín de, interim of governor of Coahuila and governor of Texas, 19, 20

Albadadejo, Fr. José: at Dolores de los Ais mission, 201

Ambler, J. Richard, 7

Anda y Altamirano, Fr. Mariano de, 200

Andrés, Fr. Juan, of College of San Fernando de México, 22

Angelina River, 31, 200, 208

Apache Indians, 20; raids by, 21–22; enemies of the Comanches, 22; missions for, 23; Urrutia campaign against, 29; Gulf Coast mission cattle taken by, 36; raids against Espada mission by, 149

Apalache, 29

Aparicio, Fr. Francisco, 21, 202, 203

Apostolic College of Our Lady of Guadalupe at Zacatecas: inspection teams from, 5; founding of, 5n.9; missionary training center at, 18; El Rosario mission established following conflict between missionaries from, and Querétaro, 21; monitoring function of, 27; Fr. Solís left from and returned to, 31; Fr. Guardian Ruiz de Esparza of, 34; Fr. Garza of, and secularization of Valero mission, 36; east Texas missionaries return to, 37; San José mission founded by Fr. Margil of, 65; relationship of Our Lady of Guadalupe and, 92; San José portal used to instruct Indians about, 93; selection of titular saints by, 179; painting of Our Lady of Refuge at, 183; missions administered by, 185, 186; titular saints from, 187; Linares de los Adáes dedicated for, 200, 201; charges made against, 207; Fr. Ciprián report prepared at, 208; Fr. López 1792 report addressed to superiors at, 209; Fr. Sáenz 1772 inventories accepted by Fr. Guardian Esparza of, 212; Fr. Manuel Julio de Silva of, 213; secularization of San Antonio de Valero requested by superiors of, 213; 1823 order to secularize missions accepted by superiors of, 214

Apostolic College of San Fernando, 22, 208

Apostolic College of the Holy Cross at Querétaro: inspection teams from, 5; founding of, 5n.9; Fr. Massanet from, 17; Fr. Hidalgo at, 18; Fr. Espinosa from, 18; San Xavier missions established by missionaries from, 20; El Rosario mission established following conflict between missionaries from, and Zacatecas, 21; missions administered by, turned over to Zacatecan control in 1772, 25; monitoring function of, 27; sculptures ordered from, 71; selection of titular saints by, 179; Texas missions administered by, 185; sacred images brought from, 187; Fr. Guardian Barco from, 207; Fr. Guardian Ortiz from, 208

Aquatalla Indians: at San José mission, 65

Aranda, Fr. Miguel de: at Guadalupe mission, 21, 203

Arizona: study of missions in, 6; formerly part of Pimería Alta, 25; Jesuit missions in, 34; missions in, taken over by Franciscans, 212

Arránegui, Fr. José (Joseph) de: on Trasviña y Retis expedition, 16; San Antonio de Padua founded by, 198

Arroyo del Cíbolo: presidio and garrison at, 24

Asinai (Hasinai) or Texas Indians: confederacy of, 17; Fr. Fernández report reference to, 29

Atacapan Indians: San Ildefonso mission founded for, 202

Austin, Tex.: missions temporarily founded on Colorado River near present site of, 19, 28

Ayeta, Fr. Francisco: Isleta and Socorro missions founded by, 197

Ays (Ainais) Indians: references to, by Fr. Solís and Fr. Ciprián, 32, 33

Aztec Indians: language of, 3; conquest of, 12, 12n.3

Babbitt, Major E., 52

Baer, Kurt: book on California missions by, 6

Baird, Joseph Armstrong, Jr.: book on colonial art of Mexico by, 6

Baños, Fr. Joachin (Joaquín): with Ortiz tour of Texas missions, 211

Barco, Fr. Pedro del, guardian of Querétaro College, 207

Barrios y Jáuregui, Jacinto, Governor (1751–1759): presidio, mission, and settlement for Orcoquiza and Bidae Indians recommended by, 23; La Luz mission founded by, 23, 204

Bartlett, John Russell: on sad state of mission buildings, 5; on San José mission, 75–76, 77, 80–81, 82; on Concepción mission, 117, 118, 119–120; on Capistrano mission, 139; on Espíritu Santo mission, 165–166; on Judge Lea's living quarters, 166; on other buildings, 167

Bay of Espíritu Santo (La Bahía): search for the French at, 17; settlement of, 19

Bedia Indians: attack on San Sabá mission by, 22

Bidae (Bidai, Vidays) Indians: La Luz mission for, 23, 204; damage to crops of Guadalupe mission by, 33

Blancpain, Joseph, French trader: arrested by Spanish soldiers, 23

Bollaert, William: assessment of mission art and architecture by, 5; on the Alamo, 52; on San José mission, 75, 76, 80, 81, 82; on Concepción mission, 117; on Capistrano mission, 139, 141; Espada mission compared to Capistrano mission by, 156

Bolton, Herbert Eugene: on expulsion of Jesuits, 25nn.27,28; on Fr. Hierro Report, 31

Bonilla, Antonio: book on history of Texas province by, 208

Borrados Indians: and Refugio mission, 205

Bouchu, Fr. Francis: visited Capistrano, 139; restoration of Espada church by, 156, 157; restoration of St. Francis sculpture by, 193

Brazos de Diós: Fr. López (1792) reference to, 38

Brazos River: Fr. Solís reference to, 31

Brooks, Charles Matoon, Jr.: book on missions of Texas, 6

Brushy Creek, Tex.: Presidio Xavier de Gigedo located by, 21; Horcasitas mission located by, 202

Buboes: Gulf Coast Indians affected by, 36

Bucareli y Ursúa, Antonio, viceroy (1771–1779): order given by, to turn over Querétaran missions to Zacatecan missionaries, 202

Burke, James W.: book on missions of Texas by, 6

Cabeza de Vaca, Alvar Núñez, 12

Cacame Indians: at San José mission, 65

Cadó Indians: language of, 39

Calahorra y Sáenz, Fr. José de: at Guadalupe mission, 33

Calhoun County, Tex.: Refugio mission located in, 25

California: study of missions in, 6

Camargo, Diego de: and effort to establish colony at Río de las Palmas, 12

Camberos, Fr. Juan Diós María: at El Rosario mission, 21

Campeche: missions of, 6

Cano Indians: at San José mission, 65

Capistrano mission. *See* San Juan Capistrano

Carancaguase (Karankawa) Indians: El Rosario mission for, 203

Cárdenas, Fr. José Mariano: 1783 inventory of Espíritu Santo mission by, 34, 35, 36, 167, 213; on sacred images, 164, 172, 188; Vasconcelos 1783 inventory of El Rosario submitted to, 213

Casañas de Jesús María, Fr. Francisco: mission founded by, 199

Casas, Captain Bernabé: offer by, to expel English from "La Florida," 16

Castañeda, Carlos, 147

Castellanos, Fr. Manuel: at San Francisco de los Tejas mission, 199

Central Texas missions, 11

Chabot, Frederick C.: monograph on Alamo by, 6

Chihuahua, modern Mexican state of: formerly part of Reino de Nueva Vizcaya, 13

Cíbola, search for, 11; tales of, 12

Ciprián, Fr. Ignacio Antonio: 1749 report by, 30, 31, 32, 33, 207, 208

Clark, John W., Jr.: archaeological report on San José mission by, 7

Coahuila: 1747 expeditions mounted from, 16; settlement of, 17, 185; east Texas missions founded by missionaries from, 17; expeditions mounted from, 17, 19, 185; in 1762 Fr. Dolores y Viana report, 29; Fr. Morfi arrived at, in 1778, 208

Coco Indians: Valero mission for, 43; San Xavier mission for, 202

Cojane (Coxane, Cujane) Indians, 21n.22, 203, 205

Colleges. See Apostolic College of Our Lady of Guadalupe at Zacatecas; Apostolic College of San Fernando; Apostolic College of the Holy Cross at Querétaro

Colonia de Santander (Tamaulipas, México), 21

Colorado River, 16; east Texas missions refounded on banks of, 19; Fr. Solís reference to, 31; Padilla reference to, 38; Concepción mission moved from, 103, 200; Capistrano mission moved from, 131; San Clemente mission located by, 198; Los Nazonis mission (renamed Capistrano) moved to, 200; Los Neches mission (renamed Espada) moved to, 201

Comanche Indians: San Sabá mission attacked by, 22, 203; punitive campaign against, 22; description of, 39

Concepción church, Mexico City: facade sculpture of, 124

Concepción mission. See Nuestra Señora de la Purísima Concepción de Acuña

Concho Indians: San Cristóbal mission founded for, 198

Concho River, 198

Coopanes Indians: El Rosario mission for, 201

Corner, William: book by, 6, 189; on the Alamo, 54, 55, 57; on San José, 78, 79,

82, 89; on Concepción church portal inscription and facade polychromy, 118; on Capistrano church nave polychromy, 139, 141; on Espada restoration and belfry bells, 157

Coronado, Francisco Vázquez de: exploration of New Mexico by, 12

Corpus Christi de la Isleta mission, 11n.1, 12, 197

Cortés, Hernán: joined by Garay, 12

Cortez, Fr. Tomás, guardian of Zacatecas college, 208

Coxane (Cojane, Cujane) Indians, 21n.22, 203, 205

Croix, Teodoro de la, Commander General, 36

Cujane (Cojane, Cuxane) Indians, 21n.22, 203, 205

Culiacán: Cabeza de Vaca and three survivors arrived at, 12

Deadoso Indians: San Ildefonso mission founded for, 202

De León, Alonso, governor of Coahuila province and captain of presidio: led expedition to find French settlement, 17; search for Los Tejas mission site by, 199

Díaz de León, Fr. José Antonio: on San José, 69, 72, 73, 99, 100; on Concepción, 107, 112, 114; on Capistrano, 137, 144, 145, 146; on Espada, 145, 146, 150, 153, 154, 161–162, 188; 1824 inventories by, 214

Dolores de los Ays [Ais] mission: founded, 31; inspected by Fr. Solís, 208

Dolores y Viana, Fr. Mariano, president of Texas Missions: 1762 report by, 208; 1759 report by, 211–212

Domínguez, Fr. Francisco Atanasio: description of missions of New Mexico by, 6

Domínguez Mendoza, Juan: expedition of, 12, 13; San Clemente mission founded by, 198

Drossaerts, Archbishop Arthur J., 82, 120

Duell, Prentice: monograph on San Xavier del Bac mission by, 6

Durango, Mexico, modern state of: formerly part of Reino de Nueva Vizcaya, 13

Eastman, Seth: depictions of former churches by, 52; drawings of San José mission church by, 77; drawing of San José church portal by, 78; San José mission attributed to Jesuits by, 82

East Texas missions, 11

Eaton, Jack D.: work on the Alamo by, 7; Alamo facade projected by, 62

El Apóstol Santiago (mission), 13
El Cañón (southeast of San Antonio): missions of, 11, 23, 24, 204
El Orcoquisac: archaeological work by Gilmore on presidio at, 7; missions founded in geographical area of, 11; mission of, 22; settlement at, abandoned, 24; surplus food sent to, from San José mission, 65. *See also* Nuestra Señora de la Luz del Orcoquisac
El Paso del Norte (now El Paso, Tex.): missions of, 11, 11n.1, 12
El Refugio mission. *See* Nuestra Señora del Refugio
El Rosario mission. *See* Nuestra Señora del Rosario
El Santísimo Nombre de María (mission), 17, 199
El Señor San José (mission), 198
Espada mission. *See* San Francisco de la Espada
Esparza, Fr. Buenaventura Antonio Ruiz de, 34, 212
Espinosa, Fr. Isidro Félix de: Ramón expedition accompanied by, 18; Aguayo expedition accompanied by, 19; at Concepción mission in East Texas, 200; at Los Nazonis mission, 200; and founding dates for Los Adáes and Dolores de los Ais missions, 201n.11
Espíritu Santo mission. *See* Nuestra Señora del Espíritu Santo de Zúñiga
Everett, Edward: depictions of the Alamo by, 52; drawing of San José mission church by, 76; drawing of Concepción church by, 118, 119

Falcón Mariano, Fr. José Agustín, president of Texas Missions, 213
Ferdinand VI, King of Spain (1747–1759), 208
Fernández de Santa Ana, Fr. Benito, president of the San Antonio missions: 1743 petition by, 22; 1740 report by, 28, 29, 30, 207
Florida: Spaniards sailing out of, 11
Fox, Daniel E., 7

Gaitán, Fr. José Manuel, El Refugio missionary, 209
Galván, Lt. Juan: and founding of San Xavier missions, 20
Gálvez, Bernardo de, Viceroy, 209
Ganzábal, Fr. Juan José: murder of, 21
Garavito, Fr. José Antonio de Jesús, 214
Garay, Francisco de: Pineda expedition authorized by, 11; expeditions led by, 12
Garza, Fr. José Mariano de la, representative of College of Zacatecas: El Refugio founded by Fr. Silva and, 25, 204; and secularization of San Antonio de Valero, 36, 213
Garza, Fr. Refugio de la, 1n.2
Gentilz, Theodore: drawing of sculpture at San José by, 79
"Gentleman from New York," 167
George, Eugene: study of proportions of Espada mission church portal by, 194
Gilmore, Kathleen K.: archaeological work by, 7
Goliad, Tex.: Espíritu Santo mission in, 1, 3; altarpiece at Espíritu Santo in, 4; presidio and mission moved to location near, 20, 28, 163; El Rosario mission located west of, 203
Gregg, Josiah: on art and architecture, 5; on the Alamo, 55, 57; on San José mission, 75, 76, 78, 79, 82; on Concepción, 117, 118, 119; on Capistrano mission, 139, 141; on Espada church, 156; on vandalism in 1840s, 189
Guadalupe mission. *See* Nuestra Señora de Guadalupe; Nuestra Señora de Guadalupe de los Nacogdoches
Guadalupe River: 1726 move of Espíritu Santo mission and presidio to, 20, 163; proposed mission on, 21; Fr. Solís reference to, 31
Guapite Indians: El Rosario founded for, 203
Güemes y Orcasitas (Horcasitas), Juan Francisco de, viceroy (1746–1755): Espíritu Santo mission moved by order of, 32; San Xavier missions founded by decree of, 211
Guerra, Fr. José: at Los Neches mission, 201
Gulf Bayou, Calhoun County, Tex.: El Refugio mission located by, 25
Gulf Coast: discovery of, 2; geographical area of, 11; and exploration of Texas, 11, 12; French settlement of, 17; fear of French presence along, 23; settlement of (1762–1794), 24
—missions: secularization of, 3, 186; conflict of, with San Antonio missionaries, 21n.22; Espíritu Santo, 19, 30; Querétaran, 28; in early settlement of, 185; La Luz, 204, 205
Gulf Coast Bend, missions of, 205
Gulf of Mexico: area of Nuevo León extended to, 16; reference to, in Fr. Fernández (1740) report, 29

Habig, Marion A.: books by, 6; on disappearance of San José church doors, 93
Hallenbeck, Cleve: book of missions of southwest by, 6
Harris, Ethel Wilson: booklet on San José mission by, 6

Hatch, Joseph Addison, 54
Hidalgo, Fr. Francisco: letter to French authorities by, 18
Hierbipiame (Herbipiane) Indians: San Xavier missions founded for, 202
Hierro (Yerro or Fierro), Fr. Simón: 1762 report by, 31, 208; on conversion efforts at El Rosario and La Luz missions, 33; on Sacra Via at San José mission cemetery, 74; on Espíritu Santo mission, 163, 165

Idoyaga, Captain Joseph: expedition led by, 16, 198
Indian Revolt of 1680, 12
Insurrectionists in New Mexico, 30
Inventories (1745–1824), 209–214

Jamestown, 16
Jesuits: expulsion of, 25, 25n.27, 34, 209, 212; and change in administration of missions in Texas, 34; San José mission attributed to, 82; Concepción mission attributed to, 117; painting of Our Lady of Refuge brought to Mexico by, 183
Jiménez, Fr. Diego, 23, 204
Jironza Pétriz de Cruzate, Domingo, Governor (1683–1686, 1689–1691), 13
Jones, Fr. Herb, 193n.2
Joyuane (Yohuane) Indians, 29, 202
Junta de los Ríos (Presidio, Tex.): missions at, 11, 12, 15, 197–198

Kendall, George Wilkins: on the Alamo, 52, 55; on San José, 75, 76, 78, 79, 80, 82; on Concepción church, 117, 119; on Capistrano, 139, 141; visit to Espada by, 156
Kessell, John L.: book on New Mexico missions by, 6
Kingsbury, Charles: on Alamo, 52, 55, 57; on San José, 76, 77, 78, 79, 80, 82; on Concepción, 117, 119
Kubler, George: books by, 6; on San José church portal, 88n.23; on polygonal arches in Mexico City and Querétaro, 124, 124n.24

"La Florida," 16
La Junta de los Ríos. See Junta de los Ríos
La Luz mission. See Nuestra Señora de la Luz del Orcoquisac
La Navidad de las Cruces (mission), 13, 197–198
Lanier, Sidney, 76, 118
La Purísima Concepción. See Nuestra Señora de la Purísima Concepción de Acuña
La Salle, Robert Cavalier, Sieur de, 17, 163
Lea, Judge, 166, 167

León, General Alonso de, Governor of Coahuila: expedition led by, 17
Lipan Indians: Gulf Coast cattle decimated by, 36; San Sabá mission founded for Apache and, 203
López, Fr. José Francisco, president of the Texas Missions: 1755 petition to leave San Xavier missions sent to, 202
—1785 report by, 35, 36, 209; on Concepción, 36, 105, 114, 115, 116, 117; on San José, 67, 69; on Capistrano, 131, 138; on Espada, 150, 155; on Espíritu Santo, 163, 165; on El Rosario mission church ornaments and furnishings transferred to La Bahía, 203
—1792 report by, 36, 37, 38, 209
—1793 inventory of Valero mission by, 36, 213–214; on Valero church, 43; on facade, 44; on altarpiece, 47; on sacristy, 48; on convento, 50; on Indian houses, workshops, granary, and wall, 51
López, Fr. Nicolás, superior of El Paso del Norte Guadalupe: Navidad de las Cruces and El Apóstol Santiago missions founded by, 197; San Clemente mission founded by, 198
Los Adáes presidio. See Nuestra Señora del Pilar de los Adáes
Los Cíbolos mission, 16, 198
Louisiana: missions in, 17–18; Hidalgo letter to French governor of, 18; in Fr. Fernández (1740) report, 29

Maicies (Mayeye) Indians: San Xavier missions founded, 202
Manos de Perro, 163
Marenti (Marentes), Fr. José, 204, 212
Margil de Jesús, Fr. Antonio: Aguayo expedition accompanied by, 19; San José mission founded by, 65; headquarters established at Nacogdoches mission by, 200; Linares de los Adáes mission dedicated by, 200
Marmolejo, Fr. Ildefonso José: 1755 inventory of San José by, 71, 73, 74, 210
Mason, Herbert M.: book on missions of Texas by, 6
Masoni, Colonel Juan Joseph, 16
Massanet, Fr. Damián: De León expedition accompanied by, 17; Fr. Hidalgo accompanied by, 18; search for Los Tejas mission site described by, 199
Mayeye (Maicies) Indians, 202
Maynes, Rev. Francisco, representative of bishop of Monterrey, 214
McAndrew, John: book on sixteenth-century open chapels of Mexico by, 6
McCaleb, Walter F.: book of missions of Texas by, 6

McClintock, William A., 52, 165

Medina River: reached by Fr. Morfi, 34

Mesquite Indians: San José mission for, 65

Mexican American war, 14

Mexican Independence: missions secularized following, 25

Mexico City: move to reoccupy Texas began after 1714 in, 18; concern in, over conflict between missionaries in Texas, 21n.22; Fr. Morfi left, in 1777, 34; cathedral in, source of architectural tradition, 88; Basilica of Guadalupe in, 89, 124; San José de los Naturalies in, 92; Concepción church in, 124; Our Lady of Guadalupe appearance to Juan Diego north of, 183; cult of Valvanera instituted in, 184; painting of Los Cinco Señores in Cathedral of Mexico in, 184; Acolman northeast of, 187; College of San Fernando in, 208

Minge, Ward Alan: book on Acoma mission by, 6

Mission at Redford, Tex., 198

Monterrey, 16, 214

Morfi, Fr. Agustín: texts written by, 3, 5, 34, 208–209; visit to Concepción mission by, 105

—diary: on Morfi expedition, 34; on San José, 65, 67, 68, 72, 74; on Espada, 149; information on, 208

—History of Texas: part of, based on Fr. Solís report, 34; on Indians and Fr. Ramírez, 34; on Indians at San José and Valero, 35; on Valero, 43, 48, 50, 51; on San José, 72, 73, 74, 188; on Concepción, 105, 115, 116, 117; on Capistrano, 131, 138; on Espada, 155; information on, 208–209

Muñoz, Manuel, Governor of Texas (1790–1798): proclamation by, on secularization of Valero mission, 36, 213

Muro, Fr. Miguel, 1n.2

Nabedache Indians, westernmost division of Tejas or Asinais (Hasinai), 17

Narváez, Pánfilo de: expedition led by, 12

Natchitoches, Fort of, 18

Navasoto/a River, 31

Náxera, Fr. Manuel de, Commissary General of Franciscan Missions in New Spain, 208

Neches River: missions located near, 17, 199; Fr. Solís reference to, 31

Neraz, Bishop John C., 79, 119

New Braunfels, Tex.: Guadalupe mission near present, 21

Newcomb, Rexford: book on California missions by, 6

New Mexico: studies of missions in, 6; explorations into, 12; Indians in, 39; Piros Indians from Socorro, 197

New Orleans, 29

"New Regulation of Presidios," 24

New Spain: sources for missions found in central and northern, 1; studies of art and architecture of, 5, 6; links between provinces of, in proposals to conquer and Christianize Indians, 16; San Sabá project funded by mine owner from Pachuca in central, 22; missions and presidios built to extend northern borders of, 23; "New Regulation of Presidios" and the frontiers of, 24; missions established in northern frontiers of, 27; retable facades in, 59; Ultra-Baroque in, 59, 187; shell arches in, 59; Franciscans and Dominicans in, 62; Late Baroque in, 88; estípite in north-central, 88; Los Cinco Señores in, 91, 184; Our Lady of Guadalupe and people of, 93, 98, 179; St. Joseph and Indians of, 92; San José sacristy window frame and others like it in, 96; Plateresque architecture of, 97; Baroque style of, 124, 187; polychromed exterior surfaces in central, 177; settlements moved northward from central, 185; sixteenth-century conventos of, 186, 187; trained craftsmen from northern, 186; Latin Cross plans in, 187; sacred images found in Texas and those of central, 190; sources and antecedents for Texas missions found in central, 190–191; report on Franciscan missions in, 208; Fr. Oliva, Commissary General of all missions of, 210–211

Nicolás, Fr.: journey of, to La Junta de los Ríos, 13

Niza, Fr. Marcos de: exploration in New Mexico by, 12

Noonan, Will, 195

Nueces River, 31

Nuestra Señora de Guadalupe (mission, in El Paso del Norte), 11n.1

Nuestra Señora de Guadalupe (mission, on Guadalupe River): plan to found, 21; abandoned, 28; information on, 203

Nuestra Señora de Guadalupe de los Nacogdoches (mission): founding of, 18; refounding of, 19; suppression of, 24; number and social customs of Indians at, 33; information on, 200

Nuestra Señora de la Candelaria (mission): founding of, 20; abandonment of, 28; information on, 204; inspection of, by Fr. Ortiz, 211

Nuestra Señora de la Concepción del Socorro (mission), 11n.1, 12, 197

Nuestra Señora de la Luz del Orcoquisac (mission): founding of, 23, 30; abandonment of, 24; Fr. Fernández (1740) report on, 31, 208; "little progress" at, 33; painting of titular saint at, 179; Our Lady of Light at, 180; information on, 204; inventories of, 212

Nuestra Señora de la Purísima Concepción (mission, east Texas): founding of, 18, 200; refounding of, 19, 200; moved to banks of Colorado River, 19; Acuña added to name of, 20; abandoned Indians of, served by mission Guadalupe missionary, 33; moved to San Antonio, 103, 200; buildings at, repaired, 199; location in east Texas of, 202

Nuestra Señora de la Purísima Concepción Candelaria del Cañón (mission), 23, 204

Nuestra Señora de la Purísima Concepción de Acuña (mission): architectural features of, 1; church pendentive paintings of, 2, 180; construction of, 3, 4; neglect and vandalism at, 4; monograph on, 6; archaeological work on, 7; shortened name of, used in this book, 11; Náxera mission lands added to, 20, 202; partial secularization of, 25; Concepción mission of east Texas refounded in 1731 as, 28; Fr. Morfi's *History of Texas* on, 34; Fr. López 1785 report on, 35, 210; Spanish language ability of Indians of, 35; reduction in population at, in 1788, 35; decline in Indian population at, 36; 1815 Fr. Vallejo report on, 37, 209; 1820 Padilla report on, 37; Fr. López 1792 recommendations for, 37; status of, following recommendation by Fr. López 1792 report, 38; Corner's comparison of, to Valero church, 54, 55; Fr. Solís visit to, 68; Morfi reference to quarry near, 71; Corner comparison of, to San José, 76; polychromed facade of, 86; shell-shaped arches at, 98; compared to Capistrano church, 131; Indian houses of, compared to those at Capistrano, 138; Espíritu Santo church portal compared to church portal of, 171; dedication of, to Virgin Mary, 178; Franciscan emblem in spandrels of church portal of, 179; titular saint at, 180; four of eight principal Franciscan saints depicted in pendentive paintings of, 180; sculpture of Crucified Christ at, 180; sculptures of sacred images at, 181; two paintings of Crucifixion at, 182; paintings of Divine Shepherdess, Divine Pilgrim at, 183; painting of Immaculate Conception at, 184; location of mission buildings within wall at, 186; sources in New Spain for church plan and elevation of, 187; church elevation of, as model for Valero church, 187; cross on top of church facade of, 187; polychromy of church facade of, 187; sacred images at, described by Fr. Sáenz, 188; disappearance of gilded altarpieces and pendentive paintings at, 188; condition of church of, 189; Fr. Ortiz (1745) report on, 210; Fr. Ortiz (1756) on, 211; Fr. Dolores y Viana (1759) on, 211; Fr. Sáenz (1772) inventory on, 212; Fr. Díaz (1824) on, 213

Nuestra Señora del Espíritu Santo de Zúñiga (mission): art and architecture of, 1; plan and elevation of church of, 3; neglect of, following secularization, 4; analysis of art and architecture of, 7; founding and change of location of, 20, 28, 30; secularization of, 25; reports on, by Fr. Ciprián (1749) and Fr. Hierro (1762), 31; Fr. Solís diary on, 31; nature of Indians at, 32; Fr. Morfi's *History of Texas* on, 34; Fr. López (1785) report on, 35; Indians fleeing from, 35; Fr. Vallejo (1815) report on, 38; sculpture of Jesus of Nazareth at, 181; two sculptures and painting of Our Lady of Guadalupe at, 182; painting of Our Lady of Refuge at, 183; painting of Our Lady of Valvanera at, 184; information on architecture of, 186, 187

Nuestra Señora de Loreto, presidio (La Bahía), 20, 163

Nuestra Señora de los Dolores de los Ais (mission): founding of, 18; refounding of, 19; suppression of, 24; fear of baptism at, 33; information on, 199, 201

Nuestra Señora del Pilar de los Adáes, presidio (Los Adáes): San Xavier mission founded with soldiers from, 20; El Orcoquisac presidio erected with soldier recruits from, 23; suppression of, 24; San Miguel mission close to, 33; French attack on, 200, 201

Nuestra Señora del Refugio (mission): founding of, 25, 30; secularization of, 25; Fr. Vallejo (1815) on, 37, 209; Fr. López (1792) on, 38; titular saint for, 180; sacred images at, 182; temporary church of, 188; information on, 204–

205; Valero mission livestock sent to, 214; Fr. Silva (1796) inventory of, 214

Nuestra Señora del Rosario (mission): archaeological work at, by Gilmore, 7; founding of, 21, 21n.22, 203; secularization of, 25; founding of, 30; Fr. Hierro (1762) report on, 31, 208; inspection of, by Fr. Solís in 1768, 31; Fr. Solís on Indians of, 32; Fr. Hierro and Fr. Solís on conversion status of, 33; Fr. Morfi's *History of Texas* on, 34; Fr. López (1785) report on, 35, 209; livestock from, decimated by Indians, 36; Fr. López (1792) recommendations for, 37; Espíritu Santo church compared to church of, 163; Our Lady of the Rosary for, 180; information on, 203; location of, 204–205; Fr. Solís diary on, 208; Vasconcelos (1783) inventory on, 213

Nuestra Señora del Socorro. *See* Nuestra Señora de la Concepción del Socorro

Nuestro Padre San Francisco de los Tejas (mission), 18, 199

Nueva Extremadura, 17, 185

Nueva Galicia (present state of Jalisco, Mexico), 12

Nueva Vizcaya (present states of Chihuahua and Durango, Mexico): establishment of, 12; expedition mounted from Reino de, 13; Nuevo León created from eastern limits of, 16; Peñalosa scheme to take over silver mines in, 17; expeditions from, into Texas, 185; information on, 208

Nuevo León: establishment of, 16; settlement of Texas and, 17; Fr. Fernández (1740) report on, 29; settlement of Texas from, 185; Rev. Verger, bishop of, 209; Fr. López (1785) report on, 209

Nuevo México: oldest Texas mission in, 11; El Paso del Norte missions in, 12, 197; expeditions into Texas from, 13; Diego de Peñalosa, former governor of, 17; Juan de Oñate in, 17; geographical area of, in Fr. Fernández (1740) report, 29; explorations of Texas from, 185; construction of mission churches in, 186

Núñez Cabeza de Vaca, Alvar, 12

Núñez de Haro, Fr. Miguel: sculpture of St. Michael listed by, 72; inventory by, 210

Núñez del Prado, Juan Francisco: sculpture of St. Joseph donated by, 111

Oliva, Fr. Joseph Antonio de, Commissary General (1755–1761) of all the mission of New Spain, 210–211

Olivares, Fr. Antonio de San Buenaventura: Alarcón accompanied by, 19

Oñate, Juan de, 17

Orcoquiza Indians: recommended settlement on Gulf Coast for, 23; Fr. López (1792) report on, 38; San Ildefonso mission for, 202

Ortiz, Fr. Francisco Xavier, guardian of the College of Querétaro: proposal to establish mission on Guadalupe River received by, 21; on Valero altarpiece table, 44; on Valero granary, 51; on Concepción mission church, 103; on Concepción *convento,* 115; on Espada church, 149; on San Xavier missions, 202; order received from Fr. Náxera transmitted to San Antonio missionaries by, 208; 1762 Dolores y Viana report received by, 208; 1745 report by, 210

—1756 report by: on Concepción, 107, 112, 113, 114, 115, 117; on Capistrano, 133, 136, 137, 148; on Espada, 155; information on, 210–211

Ortiz Parrilla, Diego, commander of the San Xavier presidio: new presidio at San Sabá served by, as commander, 22; number of people at Guadalupe mission reported by, 203

Osorio, Fr. Gregorio: statements by, 16n.10; at El Señor San José, 198

Otermín, Fr. Antonio de: La Isleta mission founded by, 197

Pacahue Indians: El Refugio mission founded for, 205

Pachuca (central New Spain), 22

Padilla, Juan Antonio, 1820 report by, 209

Pampoa Indians: San José mission for, 65

Pampopa Indians: El Refugio mission founded for, 205

Pansacola (Panzacola, Pensacola), geographical area of: Fr. Fernández (1740) report on, 29

Pánuco (Tampico, Mexico), 21

Papalache Indians: El Refugio mission founded for, 205

Pastia Indians: San José mission for, 65

Paya Indians: Valero mission for, 35

Peñalosa, Diego de, former governor of Nuevo México (1661–1664): scheme of, to seize Nueva Vizcaya silver mines, 17

Pimería Alta (Mexican state of Sonora and southern Arizona), 25

Pineda, Alonso Alvarez de: expedition of, 11

Piro Indians: Socorro mission founded for, 197

Posalme Indians: San Cristóbal mission founded for, 198

Presidio, Tex., 11, 198

Presidio del Norte: survival of, after missions abandoned, 11

Púlique Indians: San Antonio de los Púliques founded for, 16, 198; El Señor San José founded for, 198

Querétaro: Phelipa (Felipa) Villa Nueva y Terreros of, 109; Congregación church in, 124. *See also* Apostolic College of the Holy Cross at Querétaro

Quivira: geographical area of, in Fr. Fernández (1740) report, 29

Rábago y Terán, Felipe, captain of the presidio (San Xavier and San Sabá): murder of Fr. Ganzábal blamed on, 21; abandonment of presidio by, 22; and establishment of El Cañón missions, 23; petition presented to, by soldiers, 202; command of San Xavier presidio taken by, 211

Rábago y Terán, Pedro, governor of Coahuila: expedition led by, 16

Ramírez, Fr. Andrés: accompanied Trasviña y Retis expeditions, 16

Ramírez de Arellano, Fr. Andrés, president of the Zacatecan missions (in charge of San José mission): and transfer of Querétaran missions in Texas to Zacatecan control, 34, 212; high praise by Fr. Morfi for, 34

Ramón, Captain Domingo: expedition of, 18, 19, 20; Dolores de los Ais mission founded by, 201

Real de San Francisco de Cuéllar de Mina, 16

Red River: fort built on, 18; Toavaya villages on, 22

Refugio, Tex.: El Refugio mission moved in 1794 near present, 25, 204

Refugio mission. *See* Nuestra Señora del Refugio

Reino de Nueva Vizcaya (Chihuahua and Durango): expedition mounted from, 13. *See also* Nueva Vizcaya

Río de las Palmas (Río Grande): attempt to establish colony at, 12

Río Grande (Río Grande del Norte): El Paso del Norte missions established on southern side of, 12, 197; expeditions from settlements below, 13; missions founded on northern side of, at La Junta de los Ríos, 16; expedition to explore Texas mounted from settlements south of, 17; San Juan Bautista established on southern side of, 18; St. Denis trek for, 18; El Cañón missions established near, 23, 204; removal of San Sabá presidio to, 24; Fr. Fernández (1740) report on, 29; Fr. Solís arrival at banks of, 31; Fr. Ciprián reference to supplies from San Antonio and, 32; Fr. Morfi on presidio del, 34

Ripperdá, Juan María Barón de, governor (1770–1778) and general commander of Texas, 24, 34, 212

Rivera, Melchor Afán de, temporary captain of Presidio San Agustín de Ahumada, 212

Rock, Rosalind: information on Espada church sculpture of St. Francis provided by, 194n.1

Rodríguez Camilloni, Humberto: on proportions of San Francisco de Lima, 194

Romero, Fr. Anastasio de Jesús: La Luz mission founded by, 23

Rose, N. H.: photograph of San José church portal by, 79

Rubí, Marqués de (Cayetano María Pignatelli Rubí Clement): expedition led by, 24; Nacogdoches suppressed as recommended by, 200; La Luz abandoned before it could be suppressed as recommended by, 204

Ruiz, Marcos, Lieutenant (La Bahía presidio): arrest of Blancpain by, 23

Sáenz, Fr. José María: as assistant to Fr. Garavito, 214

Sáenz de Gumiel, Fr. Juan José, president of the Querétaran missions: inventories by, 3, 4, 212–213; and transfer of missions, 34, 212; on Valero mission, 43, 44, 47, 50, 51; on San José mission, 100; on Concepción mission, 103, 107, 108, 112, 113, 114, 115, 117, 127; on Capistrano mission, 131, 133, 134, 136, 137, 138, 145, 146, 147; on Espada mission, 148, 152, 154, 155, 161, 188

Sáenz de San Antonio, Fr. Matías: at Nacogdoches mission, 200

St. Denis, Louis Juchereau de, 18

Salado River: Fr. Solís reference to, 31

Salas de Santa Gertrudis, Fr. José María: text by, 3; 1785 inventory by, 4, 213; on San José mission, 69, 71, 73, 74, 95, 96, 99, 100

Saltillo: conquest of north-central region as far north as, 13; Fr. López (1785) reference to San José church and sacristy as "most beautiful . . . this side of," 69

Salvino, Fr. Luis: at La Luz mission, 212

Sama Indians: Valero mission founded for, 38

San Agustín de Ahumada, presidio (Orcoquisac): archaeological work by Gilmore at, 7; abandonment of, 24; surplus food sent to, 65; founding of, 204; Afán de Rivera temporary captain of, 212

San Antonio de Béxar, presidio (San Antonio): establishment of, 19; 1739 raid against Apaches by Captain Urrutia of, 29

San Antonio de Béxar settlement, 209

San Antonio de los Púliques (mission): founding of, 16; information on, 198

San Antonio de Padua (mission): founding of, 16, 16n.10; location of, 198

San Antonio de Valero (mission): art and architecture of, 1; original plans and elevations evident in church of, 3; optimum conditions of, in 1772, 3; secularization of, 3; change of, to military fortress in 1802, 4; monograph on, by Chabot, 6; archaeological work on, by Schuetz and Eaton, 7; name of, used in this book, 11; founding of, 19; Indians moved to, following suppression of Náxera, 20; secularization of, 25, 36, 38; Fr. Dolores y Viana (1762) report on, 28; Fr. Fernández (1740) report on, 29; Fr. Morfi's *History of Texas* on, 34; Fr. López (1785) report on, 35; Fr. López (1792) report on, 37; San José mission wall compared to wall of, 85; painting of St. Francis found at Concepción by Castañeda may be originally from, 146; Fr. Ortiz (1756) report on paintings at, 147; focus on Immaculate Conception of church portal of, 177; sculptures of Franciscan saints in church portal niches of, 178; sculpture of titular saint of, 179–180; sculptures in church portal and church choir altar of, 181; sacred images in main altar of, 182; location of church of, 186; church plan and elevation of, compared to Concepción church, 186; planned belfry towers and cruciform plan of church of, 187; church portal sculpture of, 187; evaluation of sacred images at, by Fr. Sáenz (1772), 188; unfinished church of, used for military purposes, 188; essential components of church facade of, 189; disappearance of church portal sculptures of, 189

San Antonio River: missions moved to, 19, 20; Rosario mission on, 21; Refugio mission near junction of Guadalupe River and, 25; reference to five missions along, in Fr. Fernández (1740) report, 28; location of presidio, Villa de San Fernando, and missions in relation to, 29; San José mission moved several times along, 30; Espíritu Santo mission along lower, 30, 31, 163; San José mission founded on, 31, 65; El Rosario and Espíritu Santo missions and presidio along, 34; Valero mission founded on west bank of, 43; Concepción mission on, 200; Los Nazonis mission (changed to Capistrano) moved to its present location on, 200; Los Neches mission (changed to Espada) moved to its present location on, 201; Náxera mission founded on, 201; El Rosario mission located one mile south of, 203; El Rosario, Espíritu Santo, and El Refugio missions located on, 206; Zacatecan missions founded on, 208; Fr. Ortiz (1745) inspection of five missions along, and Fr. Ortiz (1756) report on missions on San Xavier River and, 210; Fr. Dolores y Viana (1759) report on four Querétaran mission along, 211

San Bernardo (La Bahía), coast of, 38

Sánchez, Fr. Benito: at Concepción mission in east Texas, 200; at Los Nazonis mission, 200

San Clemente (mission): founding of, 13; information on, 198

San Cristóbal (mission): founding of, 16; information on, 198

San Fernando de Austria: San Sabá garrison moved to, 24

San Francisco de la Espada (mission): art and architecture of, 1, 3; neglect of, following secularization, 4; analysis of art and architecture of, 7; east Texas Neches mission renamed, 20, 28; secularization of, 25; Dolores y Viana report (1762) on, 28; Fr. Fernández (1740) report on, 29; Fr. Morfi's *History of Texas* on, 34, 131; Fr. López (1785) report on, 35; Fr. Vallejo (1815) report on, 37, 38; Padilla (1820) report on, 37; Fr. López (1792) recommendations for, 37; Capistrano as submission of, 38; language ability of Indians at, 38; Fr. Solís visit to, 68; Capistrano as visita of, 131; Fr. Bouchu of, and his visit to Capistrano, 139; image of Our Lady of Solitude originally at, 146; St. Francis at Capistrano, thought to be originally at, 146; sculpture of titular saint of, 180; painting of Crucifixion at, 180; Jesus of Nazareth at, 181; Our Lady of Sorrows at, 182; Our Lady of the Rosary at, 182; painting of Our Lady of Refuge at, 183; church by west wall of, 186; *espadaña* of, 187; extant sculpture at, 190

San Francisco de los Neches (mission): name of Nuestro Padre San Francisco de los Tejas changed to, 19, 200; temporary relocation of, on Colorado River, 19; name of, changed to Espada, 20; abandoned Indians of, served by Guadalupe missionary, 33; relocation of, on San Antonio River, 201; information on, 201

San Francisco de los Tejas (mission): founding of, 17; relocated and name changed to Nuestro Padre San Francisco de los Tejas, 18; information on, 199

San Francisco Xavier de Gigedo presidio: establishment of, 21; Fr. Ortiz visit to, 211

San Francisco Xavier de Horcasitas (San Xavier de Horcasitas) (mission): founding of, 20, 28; information on, 202; Fr. Ortiz visit to, 211

San Francisco Xavier de Náxera (mission): founding of, 19; Indians of, moved to Valero mission, 20; information on, 201

San Ildefonso (mission): founding of, 20; abandonment of, 28, 211; painting of titular saint for, 180; information on, 202

San José de Aguayo. *See* San José y San Miguel de Aguayo

San José de los Nazonis (mission): founding of, 18; temporary location of, on Colorado River, 19; relocated and name changed to Espada, 20; abandoned Indians of, served by Guadalupe missionary, 33; information on, 200

San José y San Miguel de Aguayo (mission): art and architecture of, 1, 2, 3, 4; monographs on, 6; archaeological work on, 7; location of, changed twice, 19; partial secularization of, 25; Fr. Fernández (1740) report on, 29; founded in 1720, 30, 31; Fr. Ciprián (1749) on, 31; Fr. Hierro (1762) on, 31; Fr. Solís (1767–1768) diary on, 31; Indians of, in Fr. Ciprián report, 32; Fr. Morfi's *History of Texas* on, 35; Fr. López (1785) report on, 35; Fr. Vallejo (1815) report on, 37; Padilla (1820) report on, 37; Fr. López (1792) report on, 37; Concepción a submission of, 38; Spanish language ability of Indians at, 38; Eastman drawings of, 52; sculptures of St. Dominic and St. Francis on

church facade of, 62; Indians who refused to join enemies at Valero sent to, 65; Fr. Solís at, 68; wall of, compared to Valero wall, 85; Concepción sacred images sent to, 112; texts by visitors to, 117; Capistrano church compared to church of, 131; Capistrano Indian houses compared to those at, 138; Bartlett on, 139; church of, 178, 186, 187, 188, 189; sculpture or painting of titular saint at, 180; Jesus of Nazareth at, 181; Our Lady of Sorrows at, 182; Our Lady of the Rosary at, 182; sculpture of St. Francis at, originally from Espada, 190

San Juan Bautista (mission): founding of, 18

San Juan Capistrano (mission): art and architecture of, 1, 3, 4; analysis of art and architecture of, 7; east Texas Nazonis mission renamed, 20, 28; partial secularization of, 25; Dolores y Viana report (1762) on, 28; Fr. Fernández (1740) report on, 29; Fr. Morfi's *History of Texas* on, 34, 131, 138; Fr. López (1785) report on, 35; languages spoken by Indians at, 35, 38; Fr. Vallejo (1815) report on, 37; Padilla (1820) report on, 37; Fr. López (1792) recommendations for, 37; as submission of Espada, 38; Fr. Vallejo (1815) report on, 38; Fr. Solís visit to, 68; Fr. Bouchu's visit to, 139; sculpture of Our Lady of Solitude at, 146; painting of St. Francis at, 148

San Lorenzo de la Santa Cruz del Cañón (mission): founding of, 23; information on, 204

San Luis de las Amarillas, presidio: establishment of, 22, 203

San Marcos River: San Xavier missions moved to, 21; information on, 202, 211

San Miguel de Cuéllar de los Adáes: name of San Miguel de Linares de los Adáes changed to, 19, 30; abandonment of, 24; information on, 201

San Miguel de Linares de los Adáes (San Miguel de los Adáes), 200–201

San Sabá de la Santa Cruz (mission): properties of San Xavier missions turned over for, 21; founding of, 22, 28; destruction of, 203; information on, 203

San Saba River, 21, 22, 23, 28, 203, 211

Santa Cruz fort at Arroyo del Cíbolo, 24

Santa María la Redonda de los Cíbolos (mission), 211

Santiesteban, Fr.: murder of, and destruction of San Sabá mission, 203

San Xavier de Horcasitas. *See* San Francisco Xavier de Horcasitas

San Xavier del Bac (mission): study of, 6

San Xavier missions: archaeological report on, 7; Felipe Rábago y Terán and, 23; abandonment of, 27; titular saints at, 179; information on, 202

San Xavier River, 20, 21, 30

Scarborough, Willard F.: article on Espada by, 6

Schmidt, Esther Siegfried: restoration of Espada church St. Francis sculpture by, 193

Schmitz, J. W.: monograph on Concepción by, 6

Schuetz, Mardith K.: archaeological work on Alamo, 6–7; conjectural drawing of Valero mission church facade, 59, 62; on keystone of Valero church portal, 63; on architectural sculpture of Valero church portal, 64; San José mission sacristy window attributed to Antonio Salazar by, 96; sacristy window iron grilled attributed to Francisco Poredano by, 97; information on extant sculpture at San José mission by, 102; San José mission church dome attributed to Cayetano Guerrero or Juan Banul by, 122; proportions of Concepción church portal by, 124; font sculpture attributed to indigenous artisan by, 125; Capistrano mission church belfry cross attributed to Cayetano del Valle or José Antonio Conde by, 141; Espada mission church belfry cross attributed to Cayetano del Valle or José Antonio Conde by, 158

Scurlock, Dan: archaeological report by, 7

Sepúlveda, Fr. Juan María: missionary of El Refugio mission, 209

Seven Years War (1756–1763), 24

Shaw, Bishop John Williams, 120

Sigüenza, Don Carlos, 199

Silva, Fr. Bernardo de: inventory by, 212

Silva, Fr. Manuel Julio, guardian of College of Zacatecas: El Refugio founded by, 25; 1796 inventory by, 188, 205, 214; inventories of El Rosario and Espíritu Santo missions based on instructions by, 213

Smallpox, 36

Solís, Fr. Gaspar José de, guardian of College of Zacatecas: diary (1767–1768) by, on Texas rivers, Indians, 31, 32; on failure of conversion effort, 33; San José commended by, 33; on lack of Indians at Nacogdoches mission, 33; diary of, used by Fr. Morfi's *History of Texas,* 34,

67; on San José, 65, 68, 74; on Espíritu Santo, 163, 165; on El Rosario, 203; information on diary by, 208

Soto, Hernando de: exploration of northern part of Gulf Coast by, 12

Strait of Anian: search for, by Pineda, 11

Strait to Cathay, mythical, 11

Tancames (Tancagues or Tankawan): Fr. Fernández (1740) report on, 29

Taxaname Indians: El Refugio mission founded for, 205

Tejas Indians: El Santísimo Nombre de María mission founded for, 17; Presidio Dolores de los Tejas named for, 18; Dolores presidio named for, 19; allies of the Comanches, 22; Fr. Salas described, 32; presidio named for, 199

Terreros, Don Pedro Romero de: San Sabá project funded by, 22

Terreros, Fr. Alonso Giraldo de: properties of San Xavier missions turned over to, 21; San Sabá mission founded by, 22; information on San Sabá mission and, 203

Thompson, Jon: study of proportional systems of San Antonio missions by, 193–194

Tigua Indians: La Isleta intended for, 197

Toavaya village: Spanish battle against, 22

Tonkawa (Tancague, Tancahue) Indians, 22

Toussaint, Manuel: book on Mexican colonial art and architecture by, 5; Baroque style described by, 124

Trasviña y Retis, Captain Don Juan Antonio de: expedition led by, 16; El Señor San José founded by, 198

Treviño, Captain José: offer by, to expel the English from "La Florida," 16

Trinity River, 23, 29, 204, 208

Tunnell, Curtis D., 7

Vallejo, Fr. Bernardino, president of the Texas Missions: report by, 209

Vallejo, Fr. Francisco, guardian of Zacatecan College (1747–1750), 208

Vasconcelos, Fr. Mariano Antonio de: information on 1783 inventory of, 213

Velasco, Fr. Mariano: El Refugio mission founded by, with Fr. Garza, 204

Velasco, Fr. Matthías, Franciscan Commissary General in Madrid: report on the Zacatecas College ordered by, 208

Vergara, Fr. Gabriel de: travel to Concepción mission in east Texas by, with Fr. Sánchez, 200

Verger, Rafael José, Bishop of Nuevo León, 209

Vidaurre, Fernando: expedition to La Junta de los Ríos led by, with Pedro Rábago de Terán, 16

Vidays (Bidae, Bidai) Indians, 23, 33, 204

Villa de Mier, south of Río Grande: Padilla report signed at, 209

Villa de San Fernando: Fr. Fernández (1740) report on, 29

Villa de Santiago de la Monclova: De León expedition left, in 1690, 17

Villa Nueva y Terreros, Phelipa (Felipa): sculpture of Jesus of Nazareth donated by, for Concepción mission, 109

War between France and Spain (1719), 18; second abandonment of Texas missions in 1719 as result of, 185

Weismann, Elizabeth Wilder, 6

Western Louisiana: missions established in east Texas and, 17

West Texas (Nuevo México) missions, 11

Xaunae Indians: San José mission for, 65

Yohuane (Joyuane) Indians, 29, 202

Zacatecas: portal of San Agustín church in, 85; Guadalupe church in, 89; mixtilinear frames in, 96. *See also* Apostolic College of Our Lady of Guadalupe at Zacatecas

Zavaleta, Fr. Juan: travel without military escort to Junta de los Ríos by, with Fr. Acevedo, 13; assigned to El Apóstol Santiago mission, 198